CREATIVE VEGETABLE GARDENING

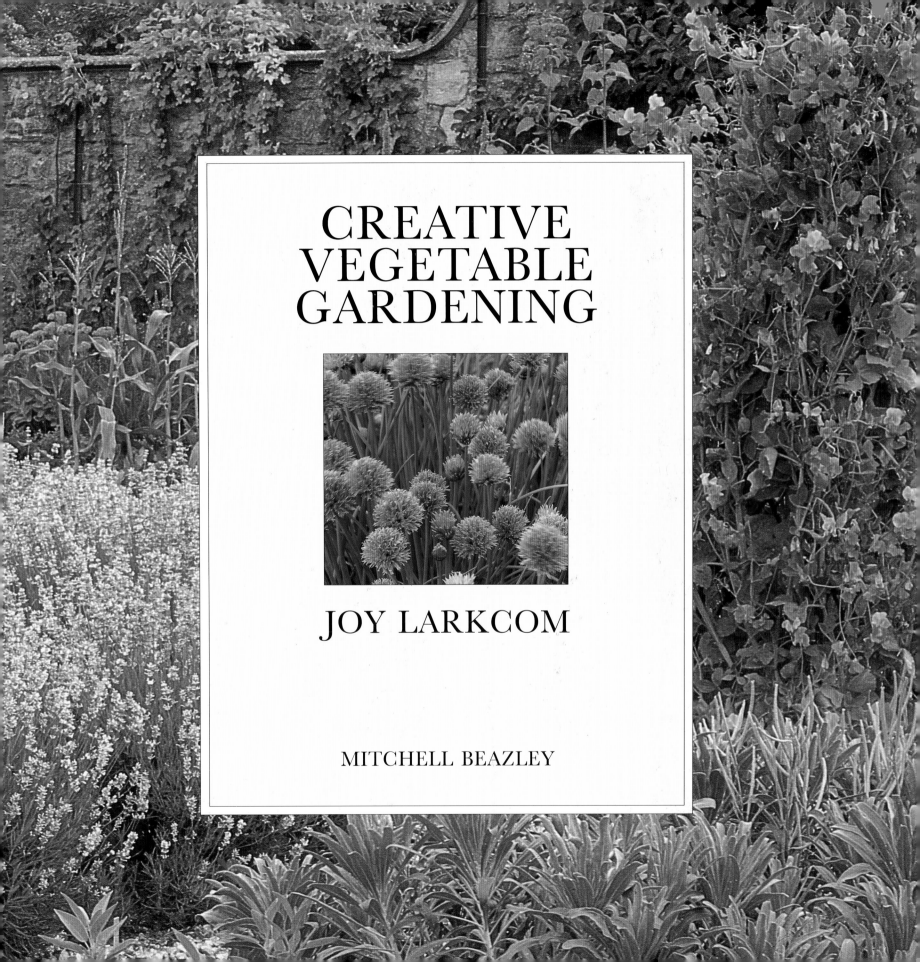

CREATIVE VEGETABLE GARDENING

JOY LARKCOM

MITCHELL BEAZLEY

To all the people who have shared their gardens with me
and in fond memory of my mother-in-law,
Mary Pollard, who died, aged 91, on the day I started writing this book.

First published in 1997 by Mitchell Beazley,
an imprint of Reed International Books Limited,
Michelin House, 81 Fulham Road, London SW3 6RB
and Auckland, Melbourne, Singapore and Toronto

A CIP catalogue for this book is available from the
British Library

ISBN 1 85732 805 1

Commissioned Photography: Stephen Robson

Publisher: Jane Aspden
Art Director: Gaye Allen
Executive Editor: Guy Croton
Executive Art Editor: Ruth Hope
Editors: Selina Higgins, Meg Sanders, Kirsty Brackenridge
Designers: Terry Hirst, David McCourt, Glen Wilkins
Production: Rachel Lynch
Picture Research: Jenny Faithfull
Illustrators: Gill Tomblin, James Robins

Half title: 'Lollo Rosso' lettuce and chives at The Old Rectory, Northamptonshire, central England
Title and title verso: The potager at Cranborne Manor, Dorset, south-west England

Produced in Singapore by Mandarin Offset
Printed in Singapore

CONTENTS

THE MAGIC IN VEGETABLE GARDENING

'Rien de plus simple, ni de plus beau, qu'un potager.'
Saint Ignatius 1491–1556
('There is nothing simpler, nor more beautiful,
than a kitchen garden.')

THIS BOOK IS FOR ALL VEGETABLE LOVERS who want the best of both worlds: a vegetable garden that is beautiful and productive. Above all it is for any would-be vegetable grower who ever dared voice the thought: 'My garden is not large enough to grow vegetables'. For lurking behind those simple words are all the old prejudices against vegetables: they are dull and ugly; aesthetics and vegetables don't mix; if you must grow vegetables, grow them tucked away out of sight. This book sets out to explode these myths and to show that a magical vegetable plot can be created in even the smallest of gardens.

LEFT: Self-sown *Verbena bonariensis* dominates the scene in Hadspen Gardens, Somerset, south-west England.

ABOVE: Lettuce seedlings nestle up to red cabbage, which can display an astonishing range of colours.

STARTING AT HOME

Our vegetable patch in Suffolk, east England is about 0.2ha (½ acre) of old farmland. For the last 20 years my husband Don Pollard and I have run it mainly as an experimental market garden. We've collected salad plants and oriental vegetables from around the world, tried them out here, and then encouraged seedsmen to list them so that they could be introduced to gardeners and chefs elsewhere. This has never left much time for the flower borders in the rest of the garden, so I have always tried to make the vegetable garden as pretty as possible.

The odds have been stacked against me. For sound practical reasons the vegetables have been grown in long narrow beds, broken up by greenhouses and inelegant polytunnels. The largest of these is a gaunt, 4m (13ft) high, steel-framed Nissen hut. The original corrugated iron has been stripped off and replaced with polythene film to make what has proved to be a superb cool greenhouse, where we have grown everything from oriental vegetables and exotic climbers to tomatoes and salad greens. But it is scarcely the perfect backdrop for an idyllic vegetable garden. And as the years have gone by, I have found myself dreaming more and more of that idyllic vegetable garden.

I took the first steps towards creating it about ten years ago. At that stage the entrance to our kitchen garden could only have been described, by even the kindliest of visitors, as a mess. The gate was concrete reinforcing mesh, the compost bins nearby were fabricated from

LEFT: **The woven willow fence around my Little Potager makes a lovely sheltered enclosure for plants and gardeners alike. Here is the summer scene with red orache, Chinese chives and runner beans in flower.**

the sort of bits and pieces that go with an old farm site and, given the mysterious magnetism by which mess attracts mess, bamboo canes and parts of cloches had accumulated nearby. Near the gate, however, was a smallish area, roughly 29 sq m (35 sq yd), and it occurred to me that I could make a little herb garden there. And then it hit me that a space of that size is all that many people have for a whole garden. Could I instead create a pretty miniature vegetable garden there, decorative enough to enliven the entrance, but suitable for any urban, suburban or even rural front garden, where the desire for 'something pretty in front' conflicts with the longing to grow vegetables? The idea of the 'Little Potager' was born.

Over the next two or three years the Little Potager evolved. It is an oval-shaped plot that is divided into four main sections by a central arch; these sections are subdivided by diagonal lines of herbs. Within a formal framework, the planting is relatively informal. At that stage I had three objectives: it had to be decorative; virtually everything in it had to be edible or have a practical use; and I wanted it to look good all year round.

Early on I realized that the third requirement was going to be the hardest to fulfil. The Little Potager tended to be at its best in mid-summer, but this is the key time here for planting winter vegetables such as curly kales and red 'Treviso' chicory. This would mean disturbing the summer vegetables, but to delay would mean sacrificing the quality of the winter vegetables. That was when the idea of the 'Winter Potager' was

conceived. I thought of all the bleak kitchen gardens I had seen in winter, with a patch of sprouts here, the browned remains of parsnips there, and leeks and celeriac somewhere else. Why not group together the vegetables that retain some colour or form in winter, and make a feature of them? And that is what I did.

I've had more pleasure and fun from those two 'Potagers' than from anything else in my gardening career. Time and again, when I've nipped out to the garden to pick herbs, dig up potatoes or for a breath of fresh air, I've been stopped in my tracks by the beauty of something in the potagers. It could be the evening light on dill seedheads, the brilliance of red orache among red cabbage, the crêpe texture of a kale leaf, or the blossoms on the 'Ballerina' apples. Who needs a herbaceous border, I've thought so often, when you have a potager?

ABOVE: **My Winter Potager is designed to be at its best in autumn and early winter. Here, in autumn, the Chinese chive flowers stand out clearly against the background of greens, blues and reds of the hardy winter brassicas.**

BELOW: **Much of my Little Potager's charm comes from allowing plants such as red orache and 'Pink Chiffon' poppies to self-seed, but there comes a time when they have to be pulled out to prevent overcrowding.**

WHAT IS A POTAGER?

This is the appropriate time to define the word 'potager'. The term, which some people find pretentious and others puzzling, has crept into usage since the eighties to describe a decorative vegetable garden. There is no straightforward answer to the question 'What is a potager?', because the term has come to embrace two styles of vegetable gardening – humble on the one hand and grand on the other – as well as various sorts of garden in between.

At the humble end, 'potager' is the French word for a kitchen garden, derived from its original role in providing the 'pot herbs' for soup or 'potage'. This evolved naturally into the garden where all the household vegetables were grown, and to many people, that's precisely what it still is: no less, no more than a plain kitchen garden. Then there's the world famous 'potager' at Château Villandry in the Loire Valley. This renaissance kitchen garden, which is laid out in patterned parterres outlined in box edging, is a glorious tapestry of texture and colour created by the skilful planting of vegetables and herbs. It has been so influential for thousands of gardeners all over the world that 'potager' has also come to mean a formal, designed, ornamental kitchen garden.

The story doesn't quite end there, for the blending of vegetables, flowers, fruits and herbs 'Villandry-style' has been adopted, adapted and modified in many much smaller gardens, which their owners also think of as 'potagers'. At the less formal end of the scale some are barely distinguishable from the traditional cottage garden. Of course, the old French 'potager' was itself a cottage garden, with fruit bushes and trees cultivated alongside vegetables which, in turn, mingled with both herbs and flowers, grown for medicinal and culinary use.

It seems to me appropriate to steal the word 'potager' and apply it today to any vegetable garden, of whatever size, which has been touched with the paintbrush of imagination. And at the risk of being pretentious, I feel it should be pronounced in the French way, 'pot-a-zhay', with equal stress on each syllable.

BELOW: **The famous gardens at Villandry epitomize the grand scale formal potager. Each of the nine squares has its own ornate pattern of box-edged beds.**

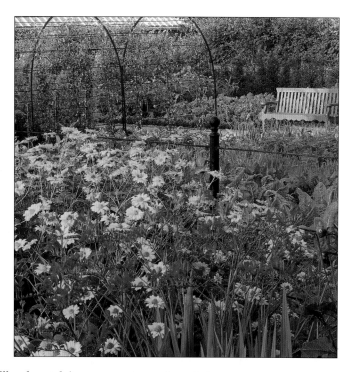

ABOVE: **Whereas the walled Victorian kitchen garden was laid out on a formal plan, wide borders of flowers introduced the colourful elements of cottage gardening.**

BELOW: **With the skilful mingling of vegetables with culinary and medicinal herbs, a garden can have the textures and tones of a decorative border while being essentially productive.**

THE THREADS OF INSPIRATION

Gardeners have always been influenced and inspired by other gardeners, either to keep abreast of fashion or as part of the enthusiastic exchange of plants, ideas and experience that characterizes the keen gardener. Indeed today, with so much gardening information dispensed via the media, it is very hard not to be affected by what other gardeners are doing. In far flung corners of the gardening world, from stately homes and châteaux to allotments and community plots, there will be vegetable lovers who will have forsaken orderly rows in rectangular beds and 'gone creative'. I have a hunch that for a great many of these gardeners, the original inspiration was the ornamental potager at Château Villandry, or Rosemary Verey's well-known potager at Barnsley House, Gloucestershire, west England. What intrigues me is how the makers of these gardens drew their inspiration from the past.

When the Spanish scientist Joachim Carvallo bought the 16th-century Villandry château in 1906 and set about its restoration, the gardens were laid out in what he considered to be an utterly inappropriate 'English

parkland style'. Almost all traces of the original garden had been obliterated: no plans were ever found. So where did he look for inspiration? Naturally enough, in the plans of other 16th-century château gardens. From these he retrieved the concepts of a formal layout around a broad central axis or alley, the intricately patterned beds with spindle-shaped pear trees at the corners, the carved fretwork of the fences and the cloister-like enclosing alleys of trellised grape vines and limes, trained overhead to form a vault.

Many of the features of Renaissance kitchen gardens had their origins in the monastic tradition, and it was to this source that Carvallo turned for further inspiration. He immersed himself in a study of abbey gardens (principally those of the Benedictine order) from the 17th century back to the abbey communities of the 10th and 11th centuries. Both their physical and spiritual dimensions moved him deeply. To him, the art of gardening was at its pinnacle as practised by the medieval monks who 'ennobled' a basic necessity of life. So monastic symbolism is woven into the fabric of the Château Villandry potager, and can be seen most obviously in the numerous cruciform-shaped beds, but also in the standard roses, which create eye-catching beacons of colour throughout the garden. (Thirty-six in each of the nine squares, to be precise.) According to tradition every monk would plant a rose, to symbolize himself at work, in the herb-edged bed for which he was responsible.

RIGHT: **The monastic tradition has been a source of inspiration to gardeners. In this drawing of a monastery in Turin, northern Italy, each hermit monk had his own garden alongside his house, while communal beds between were planted with herbs and vegetables.**

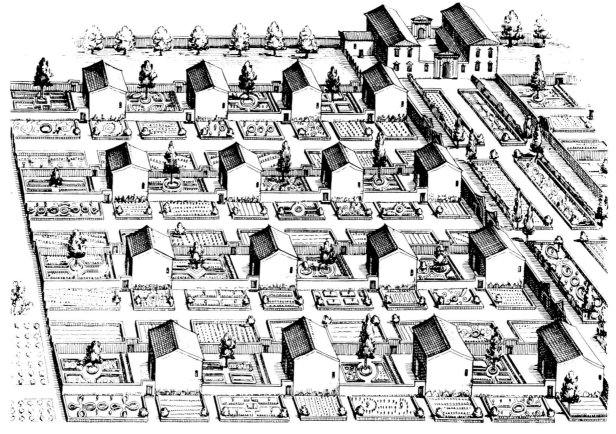

It may have been the 15th-century Spanish ecclesiastic, Saint Ignatius, who unknowingly bequeathed to Villandry its unique character. Expanding on the theme that God created everything for man he said, 'It is not enough to cultivate vegetables with care. You have the duty to arrange them according to their colours, and to frame them with flowers, so they appear like a well laid table.' In interpreting these words, Carvallo created the brilliant spectacle which is the ornamental kitchen garden at Château Villandry.

Villandry is a stunning demonstration of the visual qualities of vegetables, but it is a hectare (nearly 2½ acres) in extent, which is the standard size of the classical French château potager, and hardly the scale to strike a chord with the ordinary vegetable gardener. That

BELOW: **The drama at Villandry comes from the bold planting of decorative vegetables. The ornamental kales have tremendous impact when grown *en masse*.**

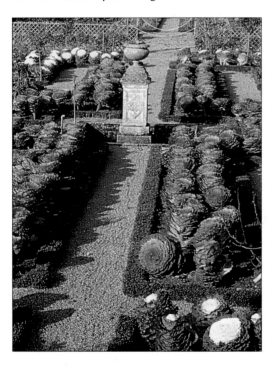

chord has, however, been struck by Rosemary Verey's potager at Barnsley House. In her own words, 'It's about the size of a tennis court and its surround.' This is a scale with which we can all identify. Since its creation in the late seventies, thousands have visited it, been captivated by it and returned home inspired, if not always to make a potager of their own, at least to incorporate some of its features into their vegetable gardens. It has that sort of magic.

What is it about Barnsley House kitchen garden that countless people find so beguiling? The short answer might be its colour, patterns, shapes and height. If you are visiting in summer, the first overwhelming impression is of the fragrant, bee-buzzed, blue-grey lavender borders overflowing on either side of the entrance path. Indeed, there is always some colour from flowers, be it the 'Little White Pet' roses, trained as standards in the centre, the hazel arches of old-fashioned sweet peas or the autumn planted tulips that push their way through the strawberry leaves in spring.

Follow the paths around the garden, with their changing patterns of bricks, and you become aware of the underlying symmetry of the potager. The four main squares are divided, in different ways, into box-edged beds of varying shapes and sizes. The corners may be marked with boxwood trained into balls or pyramids, or mopheads of golden privet. Interplanting within the beds makes more patterns; elsewhere equally dramatic effects are obtained by devoting a bed to one vegetable alone, such as globe artichokes.

But what I think distinguishes the garden at Barnsley House from any other is Rosemary Verey's imaginative touch with fruit, best seen in the quartets of apples and pears trained as elegant goblets in the beds by the entrance, and the screen of espaliered apples at the far end

of the potager where branches are grafted together to make enclosed, arching circles. Covered in pretty blossom in the spring, laden with fruit in summer and autumn, or bare-branched throughout the winter, they are not just beautiful features in themselves but play key parts in filling and framing the garden from one season to the next.

Many of the decorative features within Rosemary Verey's garden have been derived from her study of garden history. Where the potager is concerned, her Saint Ignatius was

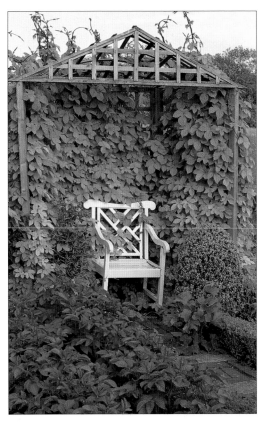

ABOVE: **A simple trellised arbour at Barnsley House potager, clad each year with a golden-leaved hop.**

LEFT: **The patterns at Barnsley are based on the designs of the 17th-century writer William Lawson, and have proved as practical now as they were then. The network of paths allows weeding without treading the soil.**

the 17th-century Yorkshire parson, William Lawson and his wonderfully practical books on gardening, *The Country Housewife's Garden* and *A New Orchard and Garden*. In her book, *Rosemary Verey's Making of a Garden*, she reveals that she still considers herself to be one of Lawson's 'country housewifes'.

From Lawson's books came the idea of a garden divided by a network of paths into patterns of small and narrow beds 'so the weeder women did not need to tread the soil'. The design of the Barnsley goblet squares is taken from a garden plan in his *A New Orchard and Garden*. It was Lawson's idea, too, to introduce flowers into the vegetable garden, for although he advocated that there should be separate gardens for flowers and vegetables he felt that 'the division need not be too severe', and a 'vegetable garden could include a comely border'. He also suggested devoting single beds to crops such as globe artichokes, cabbages or carrots.

Rosemary has gleaned other ideas from sources as far apart as a medieval illuminated manuscript and the famous 'King's Kitchen Garden' at Versailles, France. It was a visit to this key 17th-century garden, where the master gardener de la Quintinie perfected so many practical and beautiful methods of fruit training, that inspired most of her experiments with fruit at Barnsley House. Indeed it was in the King's Kitchen Garden that Rosemary first saw apples and pears trained in the elegant goblet shape, which has become one of the best known features of her garden. She worked with a local nurseryman to recapture the art of this skilful training.

CONTEMPORARY APPROACHES

In the last couple of years I have indulged myself in the ultimate luxury for any committed vegetable grower: taking time off in the middle of the main growing season to visit other people's gardens. I would have loved more time to wander at a slower pace and further afield to the north of England and Scotland, to more distant parts of Europe and to the southern hemisphere. There is no doubt, however, that the gardens I did see in the British Isles, France and in three weeks in North America, revealed a rich spectrum of creative vegetable gardening, from highly ordered, formal gardens to those where nature, in the name of ecology, had a free rein. I also saw many gardens where vegetables, herbs and fruits were weaved into the main garden. Asparagus in the herbaceous border, climbing beans over the front porch, squashes along the garden fence, alpine strawberries and mint as ground cover and flower beds edged with lettuce or rosette pak choi: these are the sort of things I love to find.

Where you choose to pitch your vegetable garden in the vast spectrum of possible styles is a personal matter. The size and location of the garden and the priority given to feeding the household are all factors to consider, but the key lies in the yearnings of whoever wears that 'head gardener' sweatshirt.

Of all styles of potagers, it is probably the classic formal potager that is the hardest to achieve. It demands an elegant setting, typically the dark green of a well-established yew, box or holly hedge, as a foil to colourful planting, or a mellow brick wall against which fruit and ornamental climbers can be trained into various shapes. On the whole (there will always be exceptions that prove the rule), it requires a fair amount of space, so that vistas, focal points and features, seats and arches can be accommodated gracefully and paths made wide enough to be seen. It will be a hard taskmaster in terms of skills and labour if you are aiming for the beautiful precision of box (*Buxus sempervirens*) or evergreen honeysuckle (*Lonicera nitida*) edges around patterned beds, or the drama of clipped topiary features. All these, of course, take up quite a lot of space. When a formal potager works, however, it is a wonderful place.

The majority of gardeners seeking to inject a colourful, creative note into their vegetable patch opt for the 'semi-formal' approach, which can take an infinite number of forms. The basic garden plan, for example, can be a symmetrical pattern of formal beds, but planted in an informal style. A single circular, rectangular or oval bed can be carved into segments defined by culinary herbs, then planted with bold blocks of coloured and textured vegetables. The semi-formal, but very simple device of surrounding vegetables with a border of colourful annual flowers spells instant cheerfulness. So 'semi-formal' is a chameleon

BELOW: **Interplanting keeps the beds full in Rosemary Verey's potager at Barnsley House. Here red cabbage are flanked with leeks and intercropped with spinach.**

category. Where the style is well-regulated and orderly it will claim kinship with the classic, aristocratic potager. If informality and a degree of *laissez-faire* win the day, it will come close to the popular concept of a 'cottage garden'. It can, of course, be any size.

To me, Hadspen in Somerset, south-west England, is a glorious example of a semi-formal kitchen garden. It is set within a 1ha (2.5 acre) walled garden. On the upper side of the garden a wide border follows the gently curving contours of the brick-faced wall, with flowering and climbing shrubs, perennials and annuals planted in a palette of colour graduating from yellows through oranges, reds, purples and pinks back to yellow. This is the backdrop for the 0.3ha (³⁄₄ acre) fruit and vegetable garden. Vegetables grow in ranks of rectangular beds (mainly 1.1m (3½ft) wide and 2.5m (8ft) long)

LEFT: **In Hadspen Garden, Somerset, wooden tepees of sweet peas, seeding spires of rhubarb and old terracotta blanching pots rise above broad-leaved artichokes and rhubarb.**

stretching down the sunny slope away from the wall. Not that I was aware of the beds when I was there in mid-summer, for this is the sort of exuberant, carefree garden where nasturtiums romp through the sweet corn, self-sown *Verbena bonariensis* strike a purple pose alongside red cabbage and pumpkin tendrils saucily embrace the runner beans. In a corner bed a dark spire of seeding rhubarb stood out starkly against the giant umbelliferous heads of angelica. The picture was completed by a mellowed rhubarb forcing pot and a hazel wood pyramid of brilliant bicoloured 'Yorkshire Ripple' sweet peas. That, I caught myself thinking, is landscaping with your kitchen garden plants.

Some of the prettiest vegetable gardens I know could be described as miniature cottage gardens. There is Susan Brooke's little garden in Buckinghamshire, central England, where maroon clematis and 'James Grieve' apple ramble on the arch over the greenhouse door, flanked by two trimmed balls of box. It's a crowded spot, where both vegetables and fruit have to compete for space among a profusion of geraniums, roses, sage and lavender. It makes the prettiest of pictures, though, it has to be said, is not the most productive method of growing fruit and vegetables (see the Plan of an Informal Potager, pp.30–1).

In the typical permaculture, organic, ecological or 'biologique' vegetable garden there's a lot of

ABOVE: **Only the steeliest of hearts can fail to be charmed by the cottage garden approach, though it may not be the most productive or the easiest to manage.**

the cottage-garden look. To judge from the large number of potagers run on organic lines – my own included – avoiding toxic chemicals and being creative with vegetables are practices that go together perfectly. The decorative elements also fulfil a purpose. Interplanting different vegetables helps to prevent the build up of pests and diseases, and creates appealing patterns. Planting flowers such as French marigolds (*Tagetes* sp.) and pot marigolds (*Calendula*) among vegetables introduces colour, as well as attracting beneficial insects and deterring harmful ones.

Allowing some vegetables and herbs to run to seed almost unfailingly adds a touch of beauty, and in so doing provides nectar for insects and food for birds. This is the reason why, in the demonstration 'suburban' garden at the Centre for Alternative Technology (CAT) in mid-Wales, something is left to seed in every

ABOVE: **The shrub rose *Rosa moyesii* is an example of a decorative plant with beautiful flowers and hips, which can also make a valuable contribution to the kitchen.**

bed. Members of the *Umbelliferae* family, such as parsnip, fennel and sweet cicely, are favourites: they supply nectar to myriads of small unseen insects and parasitic wasps. And to think that a lot of conventional gardeners have never even seen a parsnip bloom.

Before visiting CAT it had never occurred to me that growing vegetables in greenhouses and polytunnels could be anything other than prosaic. But seeing the results of 'designer beds' in greenhouses, with lots of flowers and herbs included for ecological reasons, opened my eyes to the opportunities for being creative 'under cover' (see Plant Protection, p.147).

The 'forest garden' is a unique type of ecological garden, pioneered by Robert Hart

RIGHT: **Pot marigolds, here mixing casually with violas and *Alchemilla*, have medicinal and culinary uses, but also attract beneficial insects and are colourful.**

FAR RIGHT: **Umbelliferous herbs, such as angelica, not only look dramatic when they run to seed, but also provide insects, such as aphid-eating hoverflies, with nectar.**

in his 0.05ha (⅛ acre) garden in Shropshire, western England. There's no pretending that the forest garden, with its emphasis on fruits and nuts, perennial vegetables and herbs, is likely to become the standard vegetable garden, but it is potentially such a beautiful, creative form of food garden, that it deserves a few words. Its sole purpose is to be as self-perpetuating and, in gardening terms, 'low-maintenance' as a multi-storeyed forest. Robert Hart's garden combines tall fruit trees as the 'upper canopy' with lower-growing nut bearers and fruit trees on dwarfing rootstocks. Carefully selected shade-tolerant varieties of fruit, including currants and raspberries, form the shrub layer beneath, and there's a place for trailing berries, wild and alpine strawberries, root crops and herbs as ground cover.

The annual vegetables are planted on mounds and in miniature clearings between the trees, and include leeks, onions, oriental mustards and self-seeders such as American land cress and salad rocket. The result is a calm, peaceful garden of extraordinary diversity. A 'Brandt' vine rambles up an old damson tree, forgotten salad plants such as bistort and alexanders nestle along the pathways elbowed by perennial sorrel and 'Good King Henry', and there are herbs everywhere.

Even the most decorative of the trees can, potentially, meet a need. Among the more glamorous denizens of this forest garden are the nut-producing shag bark hickory (*Carrya ovata*), the honey locust (*Gleditsia triacanthos*) with its long edible pods, the crimson-flowered rose *Rosa moyesii*, which produces edible hips in autumn, and beautiful natives such as whitebeam (*Sorbus aria*) and wild service tree (*Sorbus domestica*), which earn a place for their tasty berried fruits. (See Further Reading, p.201.)

THE HOME OF THE EDIBLE LANDSCAPE

And so to North America, where the barriers against growing 'edibles' in the front yard started to crumble in the early 80s. The phrase 'edible landscaping', which translates as consciously designing useful plants into the garden landscape, was coined by writer and environmentalist Robert Kourik. The garden designer Rosalind Creasy became the concept's most prominent practitioner, and in no time this Californian idea had been taken up enthusiastically all over North America, in both rural and urban areas.

In Europe, making a decorative feature of the vegetable garden is predominantly a country pastime and urban examples are rarer, so in New York and Boston I headed straight for the city community gardens. Instead of the rigid formality typical of most European allotments, you find imaginatively laid out gardens, plots of varying shapes and sizes, shaded nooks, ponds and pergolas, colourful communal areas and all of which, more often than not, are created on what had been a derelict lot.

There's colour everywhere. It seems that almost every plot growing vegetables has a few flowers and herbs mixed in, or a cheery stand of sunflowers, amaranths, *Tithonia* or *Cleome* in the background. The fact that plots are often tiny, some as small as 1.2 x 1.8m (4 x 6ft), has something to do with it. Why choose between food or frivolity when the answer could be to have both? I loved the ingenious recycling of whatever material is at hand, such as the paths

LEFT: **A typical scene in a New York Community Garden, where soil-starved urban dwellers use their creativity to turn the concrete jungle into a paradise of plants.**

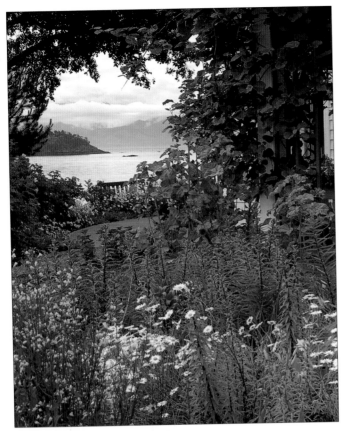

ABOVE: **Nothing is grown at Sooke Harbour House, Vancouver Island, unless it is edible. Even plants in the window boxes find their way to the kitchen.**

At Cook's Garden Seeds, south Vermont, I found a memorable example of 'vegetable art'. Shep Ogden had made a huge gateway at the entrance to the trial ground from a complex structure of giant bamboo poles. Lablab beans clambered upwards, intertwined with *Cobaea*, morning glory and canary creeper. 'Tromboncino' squashes 45cm (18in) long hung down dramatically, while skyscraper stands of coloured sweet corn took centre stage. There were even a couple of wooden garden seats nestled between angled bamboos and you had to brush aside a few pretty, white *Datura* flowers and encroaching bottle gourd leaves in order to sit there.

I must just mention the entrepreneurial creativity of the 'parking strip gardens', which I saw in Seattle and Portland. What an inspired idea to replace those boring strips of grass at the front of the house with productive grape vines, sweet corn, tomatoes, flowers and even shrubs and certain approved fruit trees. 'The mad pumpkin planters of Wallingford', I'm quoting a Seattle resident, went a step further one night and planted neighbourhood traffic islands with pumpkins. Now that's what I call creative vegetable gardening.

I saw countless examples of imaginative vegetable gardens, few larger than the size of a tennis court (without the surround) and many

much smaller. There were elegant designs, ingenious designs, supremely practical designs, all making an art out of supplying the kitchen, which brings me to Sooke Harbour House, Vancouver Island, which is renowned for its exquisite food. Beautifully situated overlooking the sea, at first sight it's just a conventional garden. Then it peels back its disguise. Everything here has a culinary role, from the kiwi over the front door to the dominating big leaf maple in the driveway and the giant firs on the perimeter. The colourful front borders are planted only with edible flowers, such as beebalm, tuberous-rooted begonias, borage and fuchsias. The window boxes are crammed with strawberries, herbs and nasturtiums. Corsican mint, which is used to flavour ice cream, innocently creeps on the stone steps and there are huckleberry hedges and banks of bearberries.

RIGHT: **Each New York Community Garden has its own character, often a reflection of its ethnic base. Recycled materials are ingeniously used in making beds and paths.**

pieced together from mosaic tile fragments, assortments of bricks and stonework reworked as edges, centrepieces and seats, and discarded timber used to contain raised beds. In short, these gardens were fun.

Wherever I went on my travels, people seemed to be getting enjoyment out of growing vegetables. Take the children's garden in the Brooklyn Botanic Garden. What joy to thread through the bamboo cane pathways of the squash maze, brushing aside the vines of watermelons, cucumbers and summer squash or to perch on a tree stump in the hayhouse, shaded by runner and lablab (hyacinth) beans.

ECSTASY OR ANGUISH?

Potagers, ornamental vegetable gardens, call them what you will, are seductive masters. Create one of your own, and it draws you to it like a magnet. There's a deep satisfaction in a beautiful, purposeful garden. Beware though, if you are serious about producing vegetables, of forfeiting productivity to the easy charms of herbs, self-seeding flowers and topiary shrubs. 'There's nowhere left to plant' is not an uncommon cry and, ironically, the larger the garden, the worse that problem can be.

There will be disappointments. The glorious visions that are conjured up when sowing or planting don't always materialize and the painful memories of my own failures lurk in my written records: 'Camomile path engulfed by chickweed; cat scratched up lettuce seedlings; first cabbage planting lost to pigeons; drought causing very slow pumpkin growth; 'Treviso' chicory disappeared. Rats again?'. There are bound to be highs and lows: no garden can be beautiful all the time.

Creating the effect that you want, whether immaculate tapestry or what I love to call 'sweet disorder', will be the most challenging of propects. No price can be put on the excitement of finding a combination that works, or a new, beautiful vegetable variety that proves perfect for your plot. Ecstasy, you can be sure, will far outweigh the anguish.

ABOVE: **Where annual flowers like cosmos are allowed to self-seed, glorious splashes of colour result. Here, they have chosen lavender and opium poppies as neighbours.**

BELOW: **At the Occidental Arts Center, California plants are left to seed with enchanting results. Here flower buds of the 'Roja' rocambole garlic create intriguing patterns.**

ELEMENTS OF DESIGN

ONE OF THE JOYS OF A DECORATIVE vegetable garden is that practicality and beauty go hand in hand. Take paths, the arteries of any kitchen garden. They must be serviceable, for they bear the traffic, enabling the work and harvesting to be done in even the poorest weather.

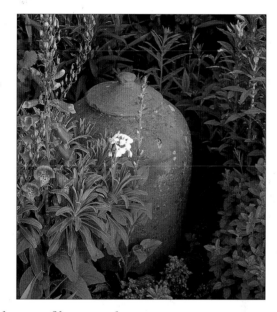

Yet the patterns they make, their colour, and the texture of their surface give the garden character in summer, and are a main source of delight in the bare winter months.

The same is true of fences, walls and trellises. They enclose and shelter a garden but good use can also be made of them for trained fruit and climbing vegetables. Arches, tunnels, and arbours are attractive in their own right and double as supports. Topiary herbs and strategically placed pots of bay can be key elements in a design and supply the kitchen. And what is lovelier than the sight of a mellowed terracotta rhubarb blanching pot? There are many ways to make picturesque virtue out of practical necessity.

LEFT: As this winter scene shows, the design of a potager can be a source of delight in summer and winter alike.

ABOVE: The shapes and textures of garden artefacts often prove an excellent foil to plant vegetation.

GETTING STARTED

THE SITE

In practice, we rarely have much choice about where to grow our vegetables, herbs and fruit. We have to make do with the garden that comes with the house or, in the case of community gardeners, whatever plot is allotted to us. Within existing constraints, however, vegetables, and to a lesser extent fruit, should get the best site available (see the 'perfect plot' described below). If they are grown in a really unsuitable place, making them productive and attractive becomes a herculean task. If this is true in a standard kitchen garden, where aesthetics are not a priority, it is absolutely critical in a decorative situation. Vegetables must flourish if they are to look good and radiate a healthy glow. There is nothing beautiful about unhealthy, unproductive, struggling crops.

The perfect plot is level, open in the sense of not being heavily shaded by buildings or, more importantly trees, sheltered, and has fertile, well-drained soil. A level site is obviously the easiest for the gardener to work, but there are always exceptions. Gentle slopes that catch the sun can be wonderful for bringing on early crops, while in areas prone to frost, slopes allow potentially lethal frost to drain away downhill through a gap in the lower hedge or fence, rather than sit in a frost pocket, which may damage the crops. On a steeply sloping site moisture and nutrients are lost in drainage, and on a very steep slope there is a risk of soil erosion. To minimize these effects, steep slopes should either be terraced, which can make a

very dramatic garden, or at least be cultivated in the main with rows running across the slope to keep the soil in place as much as possible.

While some vegetables and fruits tolerate dappled shade, a reasonable amount of sunlight is a prerequisite of healthy growth, hence the need for an open sunny site. In a newly acquired garden, take time to observe which parts of the garden are most shaded and avoid these areas for growing vegetables. Instead plant spring bulbs or shade-tolerant ornamentals or, if feasible, use them for structures such as a garden shed, or compost bins and rain butts.

The requirement for shelter may seem incompatible with the need for an open site, but this is not the case. In fact shelter from wind is probably the most undervalued factor in vegetable growing. Protection from even light winds has been proven more effective in increasing yields than optimum watering and optimum fertilizer use. So most vegetable plots will benefit from having some sort of windbreak. Ideally this should not be a solid barrier, but a permeable barrier that allows the wind to filter through and reduces its force, without casting any significant shade.

The most important factor affecting the success of a vegetable plot is soil fertility. The broad definition of a fertile soil is one that is well drained (waterlogging is the kiss of death

RIGHT: **Hard work has created this garden from what was poor soil. Optimum use is made of the site by growing herbs on the poorer part and vegetables in the fertile half.**

22

for vegetables, herbs and fruit), with a slightly acid to neutral pH (soil testing kits can be used to measure this), and a crumbly soil structure that is rich in plant foods or nutrients and retains moisture. It is a complex subject, but the quickest and most effective way to improve fertility is to work as much organic matter into the soil as possible, with well-rotted manures and garden compost being the most appropriate sources.

Don't despair if you find yourself with a garden of low fertility. Start by creating 'pockets' of fertility. Dig shallow trenches 15cm (6in) deep, fill them with used potting compost, or even good commercial potting compost straight from the bag, cover this with a thin layer of sieved soil and plant out (or sow) any shallow-rooting vegetables such as dwarf beans, lettuce, seedling salads or spring onions in them. Getting something to grow is the first step along the road to fertility, as it kick starts the biological activity. (For further reading on shelter and soil fertility, see p.201.)

THE STYLE

The choice of style for a vegetable garden, of course, is a personal one, and some of the many possibilities are discussed in chapter one. Is your idea of beauty the military precision of well-defined, wood-edged beds separated by white gravel paths? Or does that seem clinical and cold? Is your dream plot irregularly shaped with edges softened by creeping herbs tumbling over onto the paths? How high a priority

is productivity? Box edges and elaborate paths take up precious space that could be used for growing vegetables, herbs and fruit . . . can it be spared, especially in the smaller garden? Do you have the time to look after formal edges, hedges and topiary features on top of the normal demands of vegetable growing, which are not inconsiderable?

To some extent the size of the plot affects the decision. Perhaps the only general rule is that the smaller the site, the simpler the plan should be. An elaborate formal potager must have a large site. Yet a very small plot can be equally well served by a simple, formal plan or a totally informal layout. I think of vegetable gardens as small, medium or large. Small is typified for me by my two potagers, both about

ABOVE: **While a classic design is the basis of this potager in upstate New York, the wooden fencing, gravel paths, stone edges and decorative centrepiece are made from low cost, local materials.**

29 sq m (35 sq yd) in area. The playing area of a tennis court, 260 sq m (312 sq yd) represents a medium-sized garden and anything larger than a tennis court definitely qualifies as large.

The shape of the site must be taken into account. A triangular design would sit naturally in a triangular plot. A narrow rectangular garden would be the ideal setting for a formal grid of rectangular beds, but equally a network of gently curved beds on either side of a meandering central path could form the framework for an informal, imaginative garden.

DRAWING UP THE PLAN

Very few people have the talent to walk into a garden, visualize what they want, put in a few marker canes linked along the ground with a bit of hosepipe – and there it is, it works. For ordinary mortals it is still surprisingly difficult, even in a small garden, to visualize how everything will fit together when you are in the midst of it. The alternative is to design the plan on paper and, in the vast majority of cases, this is the better approach. Professional designers all seem to agree that if it looks good on paper, it works on the ground.

Before going to the drawing board, spend as much time as you can in the garden to be, picturing the various possibilities. Position a plank to represent a garden bench; put in canes to indicate the ultimate height of any fruit trees you plan to plant; watch carefully for shadows cast by nearby trees or buildings. If the garden is visible from the house, consider what it will look like from the downstairs windows, and the pattern it will make when seen from the first floor. Imagine linking it to the rest of the garden with arches or tunnels of fruit and climbing vegetables. Keep these factors in your mind as you set about the design.

There are four stages in designing a garden:
1 Surveying (measuring) the site and preparing a sketch.
2 Making the scale drawing.
3 Designing the garden on the scale plan.
4 Setting out the design on the site.

Surveying the site The key tools are a 20m (60ft) builder's measuring tape, ideally with a hook on the end that can be fixed around a spike or dug into the ground, a rubber, pencils, a large pad of paper and several long wooden canes. It goes without saying that it is a great deal easier to carry out this job when two people are involved.

To get an accurate plan of the area, every key measurement should be made from two directions, i.e. from both ends of a fixed line (see diagram 1). In this diagram the fixed line AB is an existing hedge, separating the house from the area where the potager is being made. To ensure that the information being recorded is as accurate as possible, the position of every key feature, such as the bed edges or the centrepiece, should be measured from two points, in this case from both ends of the fixed line AB, to give a pair of measurements. Measurements can also be taken from existing features such as established trees. If a boundary fence is a straight line (LM on the diagram), it can be measured out in equal sections, approximately 3m (10ft) apart, marked with long canes to give an extra set of reference points (L1, L2, L3). Or you can establish an additional line yourself with canes. It is important to make a note of changes in level on the site that might affect your design, the direction of north and south, the areas of deepest shade and any variation in soil type and drainage. This information will help you to decide on the positioning of features and plants in the garden.

Making the scale drawing Once you have recorded all the measurements on your sketch, it is time to make an accurate scale drawing of the site. It is best to draw the plan on tracing paper, which should be fixed to a board or desk top with masking tape. Draw in pencil so you can rub out. The task is much simpler if you have a scale ruler (purchased in art supply

LEFT: **A potager in the making in Wales. Although trees, shrubs and perennial herbs take a year or so to become established, a garden can look pleasing in its first year.**

ABOVE: **Elaborately sculpted box forms the centrepiece of this elegantly designed garden on the west coast of the United States.**

mind, remember it is a working garden so do not overlook the practical considerations. Beds should be a manageable size with good working access. If they are much wider than 1.2m (4ft) it is hard to reach the centre from the surrounding paths. Beds situated against fences are awkward if more than 60cm (24in) wide. Some of the paths should be wide enough for manoeuvring heavily laden wheelbarrows. Play with practical shapes first, then develop what looks good.

Indicate all measurements that you have worked out clearly on the final version of the design. These will be the basis for setting out the design on the ground. If the plan is to scale, you can measure any required distance with the scale rule as you go along.

THE SITE PLAN

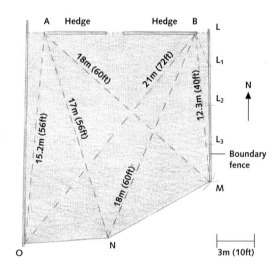

1 The first stage in drawing up a garden plan is to measure the site accurately, so that a scale drawing can be made. In the above case an existing hedge, AB is used as the fixed line of reference. To pinpoint the boundary corners and key features precisely, measurements are taken from points A and B, or other existing features such as trees. Draw the site plan on tracing paper. A scale ruler is a useful aid for making a scaled drawing of the site plan.

shops). If not, lay the tracing paper over graph paper. For an overall plan of the whole garden, a scale of 1:200 or 1:100 is practical. If you decide later to make a detailed planting plan use a scale of 1:50 or 1:20. Write the scale on the side of the plan, with arrows to show the points of the compass.

Draw in the fixed line first, and use it, as you did outside, to determine the other key points on the site. Use compasses and the paired measurements you made outside to position boundaries and key points accurately on your scale drawing. For example, to get the exact position of the corner M in relation to your fixed line AB, take the pair of measurements from your sketch: point A to point M =

18m (60ft), and point B to point M = 12.3m (41ft). Set the compasses to the scaled-down size of A–M, set the point on A and draw an arc on your plan in the general area of point M, then set the compasses to the scaled down B–M, set the point on B and draw another arc. Point M is where these arcs intersect.

Continue in the same way for all the other measurements (points N and O). When you have completed the scale drawing, cover it with a clean sheet of tracing paper, and make a fresh pen and ink copy. It is a good idea to use a heavier line for the more important features. This is your scaled site plan or survey drawing. **Designing the garden** Put a clean sheet of tracing paper over the site plan, and start working out ideas. You can overlay one tracing on another to make gradual changes, or start again with a clean sheet of paper if necessary. However romantic the garden you have in

25

Setting out the design on the ground For this stage you need the long measuring tape, string and the marking pegs: hooked metal pegs, or substantial wooden pegs are ideal for this. A 25cm (10in) wooden peg with a 7.5cm (3in) nail hammered into the top of it for attaching string makes a highly visible marker. Flexible hosepipe is very useful for marking out beds with curved outlines, alternatively trickle dry sand out of a bottle.

Let's look specifically at marking out three features in the design shown in Figure 2: the circle centred at X, the straight line C–C5 that backs the three easterly beds, and the curved edge G3–G4.

To position the mid-point X of the circle (Diagram 2):
1 Measure the distance from A–X on your plan, and use the scale to convert it to the distance on the ground.

SETTING OUT THE DESIGN

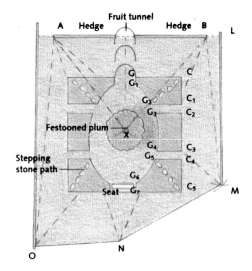

2 With the scale plan as a guide, the key points can be laid out in the garden as above. Measure the distance on the plan and use the scale to convert it to the distance on the ground. Flexible hosepipe can prove handy for marking out curved beds.

2 Insert a peg at point A at the west end of the hedge, attach the tape measure to it and measure out the scaled-up distance. Mark an arc in the ground at the point where X will be.
3 Do the same from point B. Where the arcs intersect will be point X, the centre of the circle. Mark it with a peg.
4 From this central point measure out the radius of the circle, and, keeping the tape taut draw out the circumference. Mark it with pegs and string, or with a trickle of sand.

To establish the straight line C–C5:
Use the same method as outlined above. Again, take the measurements on the plan as the basic reference, and convert them into measurements on the ground.
1 For the first corner C, take measurements from points A and B.
2 For C1 take measurements from A and B, and so on.
3 When the line C–C5 is completed mark it out with pegs and string. It can be used as the basis to mark the curving inner edges of the individual beds between G1 and G6.
4 Use the same method to establish the outer corners of the beds G and G7. Use A and B as reference points, or points on the line C–C5 if this is more convenient.

To position the curved edge G3–G4 (Diagram 3):
The simplest way to do this is to take parallel 'offsets' – the lines Z1–Z2, Z3–Z4 and Z5–Z6 – at right-angles from the fixed line C2–C3 (see Diagram 2). Use a T-square to get the right-angles. You can make a rough one by nailing together a wooden triangle with sides of 5:4:3, with practical dimensions of 20, 16 and 12cm (10, 8 and 6in).
1 Put markers at Z1, Z3, Z5 along the baseline at 1m (3ft) intervals. The more markers

RIGHT: **In summer the underlying plan of the potager at Ballymaloe Cookery School, southern Ireland, is hidden under a panoply of vegetables, herbs and edible flowers.**

you have the more accurate the final shape will be. Indicate them on your scale plan.
2 Measure the distance Z1–Z2 on your scale plan. Measure the equivalent distance on the ground, starting with a right-angle at Z1. Put in a marker at Z2.
3 Repeat for Z3–Z4 and Z5–Z6.
4 Finally link the small gaps between the marker pegs by eye, marking the curves on the ground. Provided there is a straight line you can use as a basis, taking parallel offsets is a useful way of marking out irregularly shaped beds.

Needless to say, if the curved edges were designed as segments of a true circle, the procedure would be easier. It would be a question of tracing a larger circle from the central point X.

POSITIONING CURVED EDGES

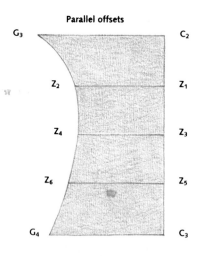

Parallel offsets

3 Setting out curved edges can be tricky. The best way to do it is to establish a straight edge (C2–C3) and then take parallel offsets from it. Place markers at intervals along the fixed line and then link the gaps by eye, forming the curves on the ground.

PLAN OF A FORMAL POTAGER

The set of beds in the plan opposite forms part of the formal potager at The Old Rectory, Northamptonshire, central England. There are seven beds in all of varying patterns, shapes and sizes. Some are connected to their neighbours with arches or shared L-shaped bed, others are segregated by a trellis of espalier pears. They are all enfolded by a framework of brick walls and a yew hedge. A network of brick and concrete paviour paths, laid in simple patterns, is another geometric element in the design.

Skilfully clipped box hedge provides the bold outline for the central square beds, each corner accentuated with a neatly trimmed box pyramid. (Pyramids proved easier to train than the rounded balls, which appear in the original garden plan.) While standard roses and red currants strike a note of elegant formality in the outer L-shaped beds, the rustic hazel arch in the centre, re-made every year, has its own distinct, cottage garden informality. Here, the cup-shaped, long-stalked green-purple flowers of *Cobaea scandens* mingle with climbing purple French beans. Everywhere herbs exert their charm. Creeping and carpeting thymes are tucked into every corner, rosemary, purple

sage and marjoram cluster at the entrances, lavender dominates the central path, densely planted chives are given a bed of their own, and clipped wall germander (*Teucrium* x *lucidrys*) makes a smooth rounded edging, which softens the overall appearance of the bed it surrounds.

The more sprawling vegetables such as courgettes, marrows, potatoes, tomatoes and chard are given fairly free rein in the outer beds, but striking patterns are created in the confines of the inner beds. In one of them, narrow bands of peas criss-cross the beds, with contrasting triangles of carrots and spinach within the arms. In another, double rows of leeks separate squares of red and green lettuce.

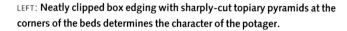

LEFT: **Neatly clipped box edging with sharply-cut topiary pyramids at the corners of the beds determines the character of the potager.**

BELOW: **The simple device of a central arch linking the beds enables edible and ornamental climbing plants to be grown together with dramatic effect.**

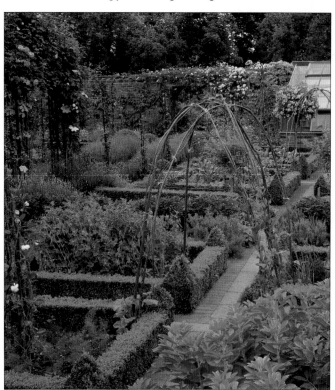

Sweet corn is surrounded by circles of radish, some of which will be allowed to flower and self-seed among the corn. A bed devoted entirely to globe artichokes demonstrates the effectiveness of planting these blue-grey, thistly plants *en masse*.

Where paths meet the boundaries, standard trees, such as variegated *Euonymus*, are grown to make a natural focal point. Elsewhere tender citrus fruits and olives, slightly tender vines, and a standard, fine-leaved box are grown in beautiful, large terracotta containers. These

are placed at key points on the boundaries of the potager or within small, box-edged beds in summer, then taken into the conservatory for protection during the cold winter months. Fragrant pelargoniums are allowed to tumble around the feet of the vines.

1	Wall germander (*Teucrium* x *lucidrys*)	13 Box
2	Chive	14 Purple sage
3	Red and green lettuce 'Salad Bowl'	15 Thyme
4	Courgette 'Goldrush'	16 *Rosa* 'De Meaux'
5	Standard red currant	17 Red lettuce butterhead 'Sangria'
6	Pea	18 Green crisphead lettuce 'El Toro'
7	Carrot	19 Leek
8	Spinach	20 Tomato 'Gardener's Delight'
9	*Cobaea scandens* (cup and saucer vine) and purple climbing French beans on an arch	21 Rosemary
10	Globe artichoke	22 Purple-flowered potato 'Charlotte'
11	Red and green chard	23 Sweet corn
12	Lavender	24 Radish
		25 *Rosa* 'Yvonne Rabier'

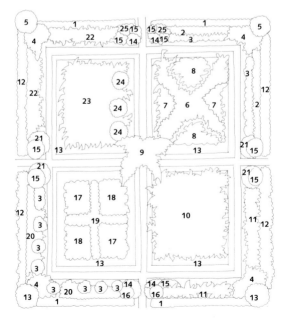

PLAN OF AN INFORMAL POTAGER

An informal, cottage garden style is often the most appropriate when it comes to creating a potager in a small, awkwardly shaped area. This is the case at Overstroud Cottage, in Buckinghamshire, central England, where the triangular plot is no more than 8m (27ft) along the front, with an average depth of 6m (20ft).

In the summer months the boundaries and paths disappear beneath foliage, flowers and fruit, only to reassert themselves in the autumn to spring period. An astonishing amount of fruit utilizes and forms the framework for this little potager. Besides the espalier pears and figs on the sunny wall at the back, there are standard gooseberries, black currant bushes in the corners, an arch where tayberries mingle with clematis and stepover apples undercropped with wild strawberries along the front edge.

Roses climbing up arches and into the conifers, and grown as standards and in pots in the centre, give the garden the rich fragrance and colour of a cottage garden. The herbs include parsley, chives and lemon verbena, which is grown in a tub, the gold-leaved sage *Salvia officinalis* 'Icterina', the vigorous lavender 'Grosso', several grey-leaved herbs, pennyroyal mint and 'Treneague' camomile, which creeps between the paving stones. Borage, pinks, primulas, pulmonaria, scented pelargoniums, sweet peas and tulips are typical of many cottage garden plants.

BELOW: **A blurring of line and colour is a feature of the informal cottage garden approach, but there is still a role for contrasting topiary and standard fruit trees.**

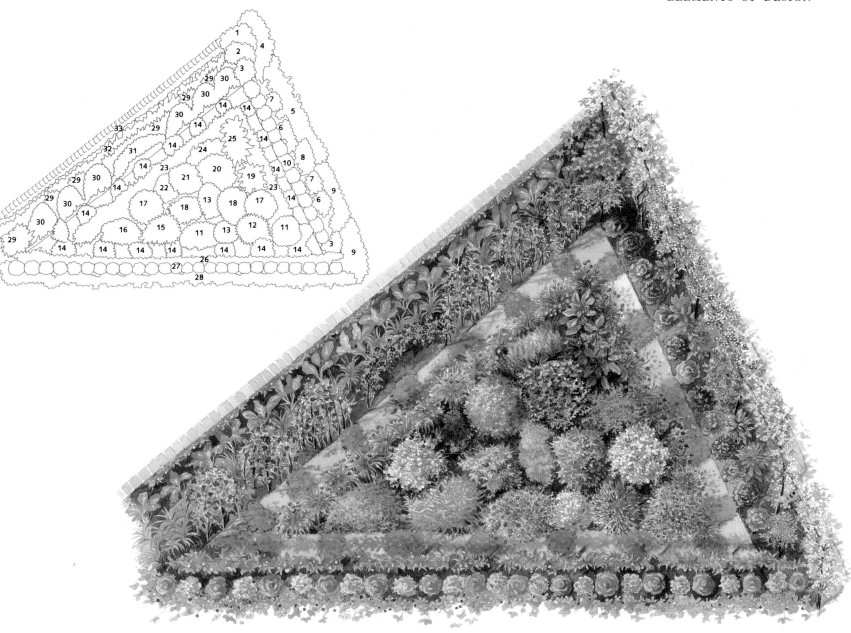

1 Fig	7 Lungwort	13 Thyme	20 Scented	26 Stepover apples
2 Black currant	(*Pulmonaria rubra*)	14 Camomile	pelargonium	'Jester', 'Jupiter',
3 Standard gooseberry	8 *Rosa* 'Celestial'	15 *Artemisia*	21 Rue	'Bountiful' and
'Whinham's Industry'	9 *Rosa* 'Rambling	*ludoviciana*	22 Oregano	'Greensleeves'
4 *Rosa* 'Blairii Number	Rector'	16 Marjoram	23 Chive as edging	27 Lettuces 'Cos' and
One'	10 Ornamental cabbage	17 *Rosa* 'Nozomi'	24 *Artemisia*	'Lollo Rosso'
5 *Rosa* 'Kew Rambler'	11 Pinks (*Dianthus*)	18 Sage	*arbrotanum*	28 Wild strawberry
6 Comfrey	12 Lavender	19 Salad burnet	25 *Borago pygmaea*	as edging

29 Shallot as edging	
30 Sweet pea on hazel	
wood arches	
31 Tayberry and	
Clematis viticella	
on arch	
32 Swiss chard	
33 Espalier pear	

PLAN OF A SMALL, URBAN POTAGER

The Barnards' highly productive vegetable garden in Portland, Oregon, west America, feels remarkably uncluttered, yet contrives to fit a lot of edibles into a small space. It was originally a narrow, gently sloping strip about 7.8m (26ft) long and 4.8m (16ft) wide, planted with grass and a few shrubs – in effect a typical urban passageway between the street frontage and the secluded area behind.

Clever terracing on three levels makes the best use of the site. At the highest level three raised beds of different widths, crisply edged with cedar board, jut out from the house. Raised brick paths bridge the gaps between them, stepped down to the level of the middle terrace. Sunken beds flank the sunniest side of the central patio area, and their wooden edges are flush with the bricked terrace. It's a 15cm (6in) timber-edged drop to the lowest level, a mere 60cm (24in) wide strip running parallel to the boundary picket fence.

The beds beside the house are densely planted in orderly squares, smothering weeds and highlighting the complementary textures and colours of cabbage, carrots, chives, leeks spinach and many types of lettuce. Bare ground is abhorred, so a lemon cucumber may be planted among Swiss chard, or an eggplant or pepper slipped into a convenient gap. On the lowest level peas are followed by corn and tomatoes, and squashes and corn may take over from the beans in the tepee bed. Rocket and celery are left to flower and seed into the winter months, but otherwise flowers, the majority edible, are restricted to pots. These are grouped to great effect around the garden: a blueberry in one, rosemary in another, sorrel and nasturtiums in others. Creeping thymes, Corsican mint and self-sown toadflax fill the crannies between bricks, and trained plums and kiwis utilize the walls of the house.

LEFT: **The upper terrace, paved with mellow bricks from a dismantled chimney, serves as a patio. While the beds are packed with vegetables and herbs, the 'New Dawn' rose and 'Hortensia' hydrangea are purely decorative.**

BELOW: **The partly shaded beds suit spinach, kales and chard. Green and red lettuce make a neat edging, but a casual note is introduced by self-sown vegetables.**

1 Climbing French bean
2 Bush bean
3 Tomato
4 Corsican mint
5 Sweet corn
6 Aubergine
7 Lavender (topiary)
8 Strawberry
9 Pea
10 Rosemary
11 Mixed lettuces
12 New Zealand spinach
13 Carrot
14 Chive
15 Trained plum
16 Lettuce 'Cos'
17 Creeping thyme (dotted about)
18 Red cabbage
19 Globe artichoke
20 Blueberry
21 French marigold
22 Sorrel
23 Nasturtium
24 Potato
25 Leek
26 Salad rocket
27 Hydrangea
28 Rosa 'New Dawn'
29 Herb topiary
30 Creeping herbs

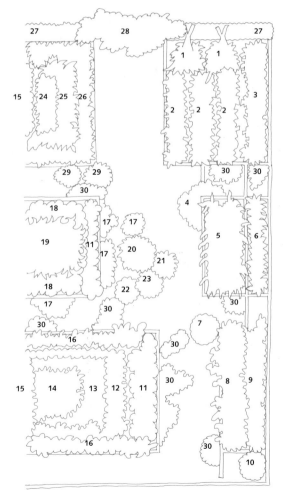

33

PLAN OF A LOW-MAINTENANCE POTAGER

The low-maintenance garden plan below, for an area about 6m (20ft) long and 1.5m (5ft) deep, is designed for a climate where winters are not severe. What is required of the garden is that there is always something colourful and pretty, always a few herbs for the cook, and as far as possible, a vegetable for the pot. Once established it should fulfil these demands with the minimum of care.

The backbone of the garden will come from perennial plants. Perennial vegetables, largely because they spring from a rootstock in the soil, tend to be ready in the early part of the year. Asparagus, globe artichokes, 'Good King Henry', perennial broccoli, perennial kale and rhubarb are typical vegetables of this type. Perennial culinary herbs include ordinary and garlic chives, Welsh, perpetual and spring onions, marjoram, thyme and large 'background' herbs such as angelica, lovage and sweet cicely. Daylilies, pinks and nodding onion are some of the many perennial edible flowers with a long flowering season.

ABOVE: **The hardy red chicory 'Treviso' is a trouble-free plant that often behaves like a perennial. Plant it at the back, and enjoy the tall, sky-blue flower spikes.**

BELOW: **The bronze-leaved fennel is an ideal plant for a low-maintenance garden, being pretty at every stage. It is self-seeding, but seedlings are easily pulled up if it shows signs of becoming invasive.**

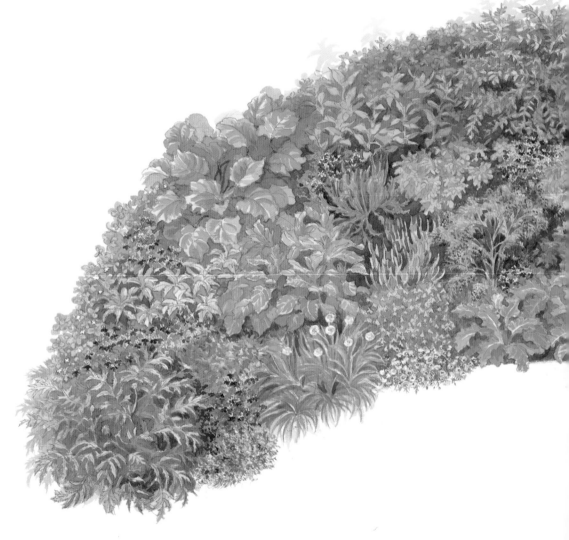

34

ABOVE: **Cardoon, with its silvery foliage and striking seed-heads, makes an excellent background plant. The related globe artichoke looks good at the front of the border.**

Another useful group are those herbs, edible flowers and vegetables that perpetuate themselves by self-seeding. There are the salad plants corn salad, land cress, rocket and winter purslane (in the main winter crops), herbs such as chervil, fennel, parsley, 'Parcel' and cutting celery and the spinach-like red orache, which is a boon in early spring. Among edible flowers borage, nasturtium and pot marigold are certain to produce colour throughout the growing season, but must be kept under control.

The main task, as far as garden upkeep is concerned, is to maintain fertility by giving the perennials a thick mulch of manure, straw or rich compost every spring. This will also help to suppress the weeds. Cut back all flowering seedheads on 'Good King Henry', rhubarb, seakale and sorrel to conserve the energy of the plants. The self-seeders may need to be thinned out, uprooted or transplanted into suitable situations if they start to be invasive. Every few years replace the perennial kale, broccoli and alpine strawberries, and plant in a different spot. Oca and red chicory normally need re-planting annually. Trouble-free vegetables such as Swiss chard and courgettes can easily be worked into gaps, and if there's plenty of space, plant cardoons in the background.

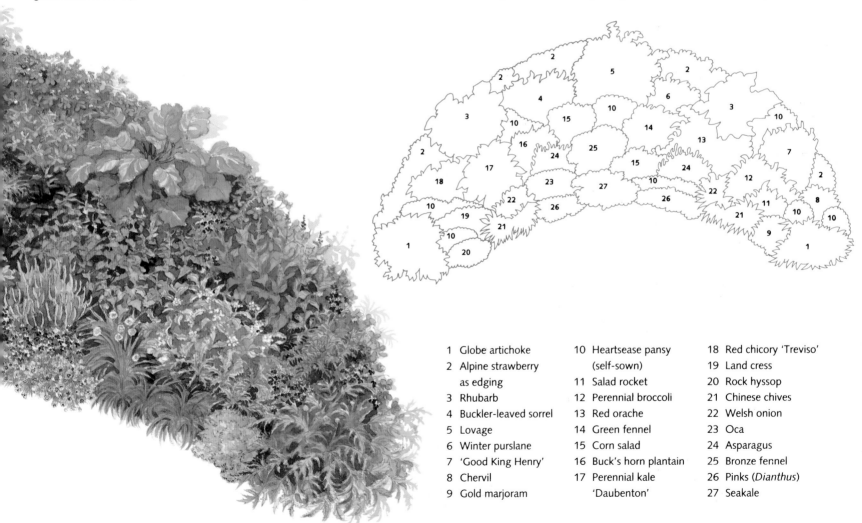

1	Globe artichoke	10	Heartsease pansy	18	Red chicory 'Treviso'
2	Alpine strawberry		(self-sown)	19	Land cress
	as edging	11	Salad rocket	20	Rock hyssop
3	Rhubarb	12	Perennial broccoli	21	Chinese chives
4	Buckler-leaved sorrel	13	Red orache	22	Welsh onion
5	Lovage	14	Green fennel	23	Oca
6	Winter purslane	15	Corn salad	24	Asparagus
7	'Good King Henry'	16	Buck's horn plantain	25	Bronze fennel
8	Chervil	17	Perennial kale	26	Pinks (*Dianthus*)
9	Gold marjoram		'Daubenton'	27	Seakale

PLAN OF MY WINTER POTAGER

My Winter Potager started life in 1987 as an overspill from the Little Potager. Its purpose was to group together and make a feature of the vegetables that retain colour and form in winter.

It was carved out of a corner of the kitchen garden beyond the Nissen tunnel, using a pattern copied from Villandry. It runs north to south, is flanked on the west by the orchard's net windbreak and a 'wall' of long-established rhubarb, and on the east by a path separating it from the rest of the garden. It was eventually enclosed on its north and south sides by trellises planted with clematis and evergreen honeysuckles, vines with colourful autumn foliage, Japanese wineberry and Oregon blackberry.

My feeling is that a winter potager is a practical proposition in climates where a reasonable number of vegetables normally survive winter in the open. Mine has taught me a lot about making a vegetable plot that has to look beautiful all year, even though its big moments come late in the season. A planting of this sort is bound to be a gamble. Some years mine retains its colour and vitality into late spring; but in others weather conditions have brought its beauties to a premature end in mid- to late winter. Whatever lies ahead, it is always glorious in autumn, when it is crowded with green and red chards, ornamental and curly green kales and the blue-green patterning of leeks.

It is essential for a winter potager to have a strong framework of perennials to support the winter plantings and to provide interest in the rest of the year. If background trees or shrubs are appropriate, choose evergreens or those with coloured winter twigs, such as willows or dogwoods. Fruit trees provide blossom in the spring, colour in summer and, if the trees are trained, form in winter. There's a case for establishing edges of evergreen hedging plants or topiary, or the more flexible edging of winter marjorams, thyme or strawberries. Garlic chives, with their bright starry white flowers, can be planted along the outer edges. Perennial vegetables with architectural leaves or striking seedheads (see pp.81–85) more than earn their keep wherever they are in the winter potager.

The key to long-lasting success is to focus on the vegetables that are most reliable in your winter conditions. It is a good idea to plant the vegetables a little closer than usual to offset the 'shrinkage' that seems to occur where plants are exposed to winter winds, frost and rain.

LEFT: **Creamy heads of overwintering cauliflower make a striking contrast with the seeding red kale in spring.**

BELOW: **From spring to autumn, broad rhubarb leaves prove the ideal background for the winter potager.**

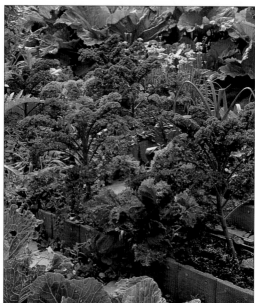

During the course of a year each section can, potentially, be home to two crops. Summer is the planting time for the main winter vegetables. Where the previous winter crop is cleared by early to mid-spring, there is time for a catch crop first (see p.200). My favoured options are lettuce or endive started off indoors, a green manure (see pp.137–8) or cut-and-come-again seedlings (see pp.110–13). Quite often the last few overwintered leeks, chicories, brassicas or self-sown salsify are left to run to seed, and cleared just before the summer planting.

1 *Clematis armandii*
2 Kale 'Peacock'
3 Carrot
4 Parsnip
5 *Vitis* 'Miller's Burgundy'
6 *Lonicera japonica* 'Halliana'
7 Kiwi 'Issai'
8 Chinese chive
9 'Grumolo' chicory, red Brussels sprouts and 'Black' kale
10 Hamburg parsley
11 Common chive
12 Beetroot 'Bull's Blood'
13 Winter savory
14 Winter pansy
15 'Ballerina' apple trees
16 Corn salad
17 Leek
18 Thyme
19 Hardy cabbages interplanted with purple pak choi
20 Purple-leaved mustard
21 Green and red curly kale and curly endive
22 Cardoon and strawberry 'Ruby Glow'
23 Evergreen marjoram
24 Cauliflower 'Jerome' interplanted with purple pak choi
25 Celery 'Parcel'
26 Red chicory 'Treviso'
27 Oriental bunching onion 'Ishikuro'
28 Alternate red- and green-stemmed chard
29 Stepover apple
30 Pink-flowered strawberry
31 *Clematis cirrhosa*
32 *Vitis* 'Brandt'
33 Oregon blackberry
34 *Vitis* 'Teinturier'
35 Japanese wineberry
36 Rhubarb
37 Purple pak choi

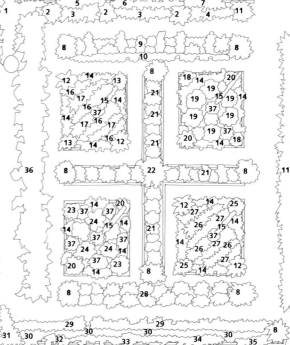

PATTERNS AND BED SHAPES

Few elements of the vegetable garden design have more impact on its character than the patterns of the beds. In very informal, cottage gardens the pattern may be barely discernible, but where vegetables are being grown on any scale, as opposed to being popped in among the perennials, there needs to be some kind of framework – visible or invisible.

The choice of patterns is enormous, from a plain square plot at one extreme to curlicues of a knot garden at the other, and both can be equally valid in a decorative vegetable garden. With very simple designs, the creativity lies in imaginative and skilled planting within the bare frame. With an intricate design, much of the beauty is inherent in the patterns and the plants or materials used to outline them.

LEFT: **Some of the beds in the herb garden at Ballymaloe Cookery School, Ireland are grouped in quartets, but an unusual effect is created by their scalloped outer edges.**

The potential tapestry of a complex design is alluring, but think hard before embarking on it. Consider the practicalities of manhandling hoses and wheelbarrows between the beds, and don't overlook the work involved: the more intricate the design, the more edges there will be to maintain, and the more path footage to lay and look after. It is no easy task to get the uniform look of the classic parterre or park bedding scheme with vegetables as the principal players. More than most garden plants, their performance, and hence appearance, is at the mercy of weather and pests. This type of complex design can be lovely when it works, but it can be something of a gamble. To play it safe, elect for a simple design that will be enhanced, rather than ruined by unpredictable behaviour on the part of the vegetables.

There's plenty of room for compromise. A garden can encompass a set of formal patterned beds and an informal area. Equally one can take a segment of a complex design, such as a corner of a square at Villandry, and make use of it in a simpler setting. Conversely, the basic bed shapes of squares, triangles and circles can be manipulated and integrated into satisfying, moderately complex designs.

SQUARES

The traditional square or rectangular plot is the basic building block of a host of kitchen garden designs. The simple geometry of a grid of identical, evenly spaced beds can be elegance itself. A Normandy farmyard garden designed by the French landscape architect Pascal Cribier is made up of 36 square beds in three ranks, dropped neatly into the rectangle embraced by the old farmhouse, barns, outbuildings and rustic fencing. The majority of the beds are planted with a single crop, which emphasizes the chequerboard effect. That's not so very different from the layout adopted by the famous diarist and gardener John

LEFT: **The nine main squares at Villandry exhibit a range of patterns, which have been the inspiration for many smaller-scale domestic vegetable gardens.**

ABOVE: **Rectangular beds have an elegant simplicity and are practical to work. The beds here are of varying lengths, and are grouped in a loose but pleasing pattern.**

ABOVE: **The classic four square bed in The Old Rectory, Northamptonshire. For the same shaped beds linked with a central arch, see the Formal Plan, pages 28–9.**

ABOVE: **Another variation of the diagram below, with the outer beds becoming L-shaped to accommodate a central square bed. This is an easily managed design.**

Evelyn in the seventeenth century. A plan of his garden at Sayes Court, near Deptford, south London shows a double row of 20 rectangular beds side by side, running due north and south.

In a garden based on this simple format, an exuberant planting of vegetables, herbs, flowers and shrubs will completely hide the rigid formality of the underlying plan, but it will still hold everything together. Alternatively, the same design of narrow beds, planted neatly with one crop or a single crop with a contrasting edge, will create a crisp, ordered, formal appearance. Another essentially simple device is to divide the space into small square beds each, perhaps, with a fruit tree at the centre linked with a series of long narrow borders.

Another good basic design is the quartered square or rectangle, often seen in centuries old walled kitchen gardens. On a grand scale, the quarters can be separated by crossing grass or gravel paths lined with espalier fruit. Cover the paths with arches, and the beds can be linked by tunnelled alleys of climbing fruit, beans, squashes or sweet peas.

This essentially simple format is also ideal for a small garden. My Little Potager started out as a quartered oval, but slowly became

PATTERNS AND BED SHAPES

BASIC GRID: The grid of rectangles or squares is one of the oldest layouts used for vegetable gardens, but it can still be dramatic in a modern setting.

QUARTERING A SQUARE: One of the most basic designs is the square and rectangle, subdivided into four smaller squares or rectangles separated by paths.

SQUARES WITH A CENTRAL CIRCLE: For a more complex pattern four square beds can be grouped around a circular bed, and the sides curved to make a natural fit.

39

LEFT: **This simple approach of criss-crossing paths forms a suitable framework for the numerous plots in one of the New York Community Gardens.**

Put a bed in the middle of the rectangle or square, and a new range of designs is possible. Most popular perhaps is a central circle, with the inner sides of the surrounding squares curved to fit around it (see diagram, p.39). With a square in the centre, the outer beds naturally become L-shaped; with a central cross they can be neatly stepped on the inner side, as in the centremost square of the potager at Château Villandry. Yet another option is to have a set of four squares in the centre.

Further possibilities stem from pushing the squares further apart and setting beds between them along one or both axes. They can be single beds, or pairs of narrow or broad beds. These last two patterns are used at Villandry in the south-eastern square and the eastern square in the central row. Another variation on the theme is to set the four squares in the arms of a cross. This is the core of the design for my Winter Potager (see the Plan of My Winter

moulded into a rectangle with gently rounded corners and an arch in the middle. Indeed, the quartered square or rectangle cries out for a straddling archway as a centrepiece. Whether a permanent feature or a utilitarian hazel, willow or bamboo structure made anew each year – it's the perfect focal point for a vegetable plot.

The centre squares in the Old Rectory potager in Northamptonshire, central England, are all linked this way, the arches home to a colourful mix of purple-podded climbing beans and climbing squashes, intertwined with the showy green-purple flowers of the cup and saucer vine, *Cobaea scandens*.

WAYS OF QUARTERING A SQUARE DIAGONALLY

Where a square is quartered on the diagonal, rather than at right angles, a different pattern is made. The result is four large, essentially triangular beds.

For a more rigid and formal design, subdividing the square with straight central paths creates a set of eight four-sided beds.

Redividing the diagonally quartered square with a circular band makes a complex pattern. The curved edges look best planted with salads or herbs.

DIAMONDS AND TRIANGLES

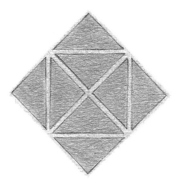

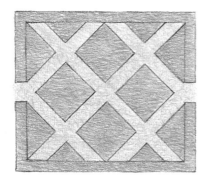

Shifting a square by 45 degrees converts it into a diamond, which, with a set of four right-angled paths, can become four, neatly paired triangles.

A series of head to toe triangles can be fitted against a wall. The format is ideal for growing differently coloured and textured seedling crops.

Quartets of diamond-shaped beds form a strong, bold pattern, with plenty of scope for contrasting planting in the surrounding triangular beds.

Potager, pp.36–7), which I copied from the central-eastern bed at Villandry. A lay-out of a long rectangular bed in the centre, with an L-shaped bed around each corner, is a suitable alternative for a rectangular plot.

Completely different effects are created by quartering a square diagonally, rather than at right angles (see diagrams opposite). At its simplest, this creates four large triangles. Set them around a central circle with the triangle tips rounded into curves, and you have another classic pattern. For something a little fancier, bisect each bed with a circular band following the outline of the central circle, or a straight path parallel to the outer edge. Either of these designs will make eight, attractively shaped sections. This last, essentially, is the Lawson design adopted by Rosemary Verey for her apple and pear goblet beds at Barnsley.

While on the subject of diagonals, consider having paths radiating from the main axis at a 45 degree angle rather than a right angle. Not only does it give a garden character – a series of diagonal paths creates a 'fish bone' look – but it also allows plenty of scope for varied and irregular bed shapes and patterns.

DIAMONDS AND TRIANGLES

Some of the most striking effects can be created with diamond-shaped beds as the basic unit. Set them point to point, as American designer Ryan Gainey has in his romantic vegetable garden; box-edged with a standard rose in the centre of each, they make a wonderful spine to his garden. The core of the potager at the Ballymaloe Cookery School, near Cork in southern Ireland, is four large diamond beds in the centre of a square, with an outer rim of triangular beds against the garden boundaries (see diagram above right). The narrow zigzag of diamond beds in the south-west corner of Villandry creates a dazzling effect. A diamond shape is a natural for a central bed. I saw this twice in communal gardens in Boston. In one, a diamond bed with the sides curving inwards was prettily offset with an outwardly curving brick path. In the other an elevated diamond, edged with granite cobble stones, added a second level to a tiny plot.

RIGHT: **The zigzag of diamond beds at Villandry is planted with ornamental kales, but looks equally dramatic planted with architectural plants such as globe artichokes.**

A pattern of triangles is easily developed from a square or diamond base. Divide a square both at right angles and diagonally and eight neat triangles emerge. Or quarter a diamond shape with diagonals, bisect each quarter across the corners and a pleasing pattern of triangles emerges, four in the centre and four tucked into the corners. Triangles also fit well together head to toe, so to speak. The ribbon of brick-edged triangles intended for herbs in the St Jean de Beauregard potager in the Essonne, south-west of Paris, would make a lovely pattern planted with salad plants.

CIRCLES

The inherent grace of a circle is easily adapted to the vegetable garden. A softer outline than a square, it is often the first choice for anyone carving a small vegetable area out of a lawn. Larger gardens, too, are bequeathed an essential elegance if enclosed within a circle. Most of the basic permutations on a square can be applied to a circle, commonly creating beds with a curved outer edge. Square designs can be fitted into a circular frame, the two linked with a ring of semicircular beds (see diagram below left). Dissecting a circle with two paths, crossing naturally in the centre, will create an apple pie-shape of four triangles (see diagram below), or three paths to create six triangles, again an adaptable framework for vegetables.

Small round beds can look very effective, either scattered at random in a lawn, or flower garden, or worked into the formality of a more

ABOVE LEFT: **All the paths in the potager radiate from a central circle outlined in clipped ivy.**

ABOVE: **An eyecatching golden-coloured circle is created with the simple device of an edging where *Tagetes* 'Lemon Gem' and 'Golden Gem' are alternately planted, about 40cm (16in) apart.**

OPTIONS WITHIN A CIRCLE

An outer circle can be linked with an inner square, with a ring of semicircular, half-moon beds. There is great scope here for contrasting planting schemes.

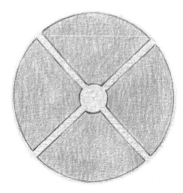

The 'apple pie' is one of the simplest designs suited to any style of planting. Increasing the number of dissecting paths makes the pattern more complex.

ABOVE: **One set of rectangular beds at Sooke Harbour House, Vancouver Island, forms a natural, semicircular edge against the lawn.**

BELOW: **The gentle curves of circular borders are ideal for planting with edible flowers, as here at Fetzer Winery, California, with daylilies, nasturtiums and pansies.**

contrived pattern. They look most dramatic if planted boldly with one type of vegetable, or even a single plant such as a globe artichoke or courgette. Semicircles and arcs are gentle shapes, easily moulded into the outlines of gardens large and small. Paving stones carve a semicircular path around Susan Brooke's tiny potager (see the Plan of an Informal Potager, pp. 30–1), within the frame of stepover apples and roses intermingled with fruits. At Sooke Harbour House, Vancouver Island, rectangular vegetable beds, all of different lengths, are grouped so that at one end they make an arc.

UNCONVENTIONAL PATTERNS

Over the years gardeners have had a lot of fun with more bizarre designs, in which symbolism has played its part. Edible landscaper, Robert Kourik, maintains that a lot of 'mandala' gardens – typically circular symbols depicting the universe – were created in the past, though few survive. The religious symbolism of the maze has also found expression in vegetable gardens. In the southern-central bed at Villandry there is the Greek maze: its narrow coiled beds strike a brilliant note when simply planted with red

lettuce or ornamental kales. The priory garden at Orsan in central France has a 'potager labyrinth', but my favourite is a 'sunray' garden in Wales. A small corner bed is planted with brilliantly coloured orange and yellow flowers to represent the sun, and a fan of ray-like beds, edged with upright black slates, radiate outwards for vegetables.

MINIMAL PATTERNS

A creative vegetable garden doesn't have to have patterns. Take a small plot with a meandering path from the house to the back fence: vegetables can look perfectly at home in the casual borders alongside the path. They can be grown in beds of all sorts of shapes and sizes, fitted into the natural contours of any established garden. It is just a question of overcoming our preconceived ideas about how they should be organized and segregated.

BELOW: **A series of raised beds of varying shapes and sizes makes optimum use of a sloping urban site.**

BOUNDARIES

Traditionally, the vegetable plot was enclosed or separated off from the rest of the garden. The age-old practical reasons for doing this still hold good, the most important being the need to protect the produce from pests. What feeds us, feeds them, and anyone who has suffered from the attentions of rabbits or deer will need no persuading of the need for an enclosure. It is almost as important to protect crops from the ravages of the elements. Vegetables need a degree of shelter from wind if they are to grow well, but the art is to provide the protection without creating a completely airless atmosphere in which pests and diseases will flourish.

The enclosure can be more than a means to an end: it can be an end in itself. What a wonderful backdrop a stone or brick wall can be, especially when ornamental climbers or fruits are trained against it. What can compare with a long-established hedge? If you are one of the fortunate few with a mature setting for your garden, count your blessings. For the rest of us, constructing or planting the surround should be the top priority. It needn't be complicated: some of the loveliest modern potagers are created within the simplest of fences.

BELOW: **The traditional picket fence merges into a rural setting, and will keep out most small animal pests. It is strong enough to support the less rampant climbers.**

The first choice is between a 'man-made' or a living boundary. The advantages of walls or fences over hedges or other boundary plants are that they take less space, don't compete for sun, nutrients or moisture, may provide support for ornamental climbers and trained fruit, are easier to make animal proof, in most cases require only minimal maintenance and, of course, you don't have to wait for them to grow. The drawbacks are the initial cost, a limited life in some cases, and their visual sterility compared to the ever-changing colour, texture and form of a living boundary.

The second choice could be summarized as 'solid' versus 'see-through'. With a solid wall, fence or even close-knit hedge, the feeling of intimacy is complete, but something is lost by not being able to see in or out of the vegetable garden. Partial barriers filter the wind, reducing its effects but still allowing air movement. Technically, a solid barrier blocks and diverts the wind, potentially creating a turbulent zone elsewhere in the garden. It will also cast shade. On the other hand, there can be a lovely cosy spot along the foot of a wall or fence on both the windward and the leeward side for early vegetables and tender plants.

MAN-MADE

All sorts of materials and structures can be used to make boundaries, from chains slung between posts to concrete block screening. Anything that can double as a screen and support for climbing plants is a candidate.

Paling fence Traditional picket fences of pales, posts or rustic stakes sit very comfortably around a vegetable garden. They tend to be about 1.2–1.5m (4–5ft) high, with the pickets spaced 5–7.5cm (2–3in) apart, and nailed to horizontal backing rails. This makes enough of a barrier to filter the wind, and also to provide

RIGHT: **A linked chain makes a pleasing boundary, but gives no protection against the elements. Roses, or fruits such as blackberries, can be trained along it.**

shelter for the crops. Styles range from the rough-hewn, which can be very appealing, particularly if used to form an uneven, undulating fence, to the well-manicured, which are often painted white. Pretty features can be made of the wicket gates, with gate posts carved or decorated with finials, while the top of the gate can be scooped or bowed. Palings can be bought as panels for easy erection; buy them pressure treated. Light-weight climbing plants, such as semi-dwarf sweet peas, will sprawl over a picket fence. To give them extra support, wire-netting can be attached to the fence.

In California I saw an excellent example of a dual-purpose, double deer fence around a small sloping vegetable plot. The outer ring was a palisade of uneven redwood grape stakes. Some 1.2m (4ft) inside was a wire-mesh fence 1.2m (4ft) high. The deer, because they like to

see where their feet will be landing, kept away, but climbers grew happily on the inner fence.

Post and rail This basic method of field fencing can be adapted to gardens, but is best suited to rural settings. It offers little shelter but wire-netting can be attached to the posts, making a support for climbing vegetables.

BELOW: **A simple post and rail fence serves as little more than a frame to the garden. This more substantial fencing is better suited to enclosing vegetables.**

Retaining walls on slopes Gardening on sloping ground is an awkward business, and the answer, in many cases, is to make level terraced beds. To keep the soil in place, they will have to be edged with strong retaining walls. Stone, brick, concrete blocks, various types of timber such as planks, logs or railway sleepers, can all be used. Depending on the nature of the terrain, the terraces – and hence the walls – can be anything from 27cm (11in) to 45cm (18in) high. If necessary conceal ugly walls with trailing plants, but on the whole, terracing has an intrinsic beauty of its own. The earth-moving involved in terracing is extremely heavy work, and there may be structural and safety considerations that make it advisable to call in a professional garden contractor.

Solid fences These can be made of boards, split timbers or poles. Any wood that is not naturally rot resistant should be pressure treated to increase its lifespan. One of the simplest ways to erect a fence is to purchase softwood panels, normally sold in lengths of about 1.8m (6ft). They are nailed or fastened to posts, sunk at least 45cm (18in) deep into the ground, or concreted in if necessary. Posts can also be sunk into metal sockets, which are hammered into firm ground, or concreted in on shallow or stony ground. These protect the posts from water damage and make any eventual replacement easier. Panels will also last longer if they are attached at the lower edge to horizontal, pressure-treated gravel boards, which keep the base of the fence off the ground. These boards are fairly easily replaced if they start to rot. Horizontal wires can be attached to the fence to support fruit or climbing vegetables.

Trelliswork Wooden trellis can provide the perfect solution for enclosing a plot, combining a degree of windbreak and shelter with an excellent means of supporting trained fruit,

LEFT: **On sloping ground the retaining walls or fencing must be strong enough to prevent soil slippage. Rounded logs are often used for this purpose.**

BELOW: **Landscape designer Tom Berger used free-standing panels, sheathed with plywood and covered with grey cedar shingles to match the houses nearby, for a potager in Washington State, USA. Grapevines planted between the panels and trained on wires make a natural green wall.**

climbing vegetables and colourful climbing shrubs and annuals. Strips of trellis can also look very attractive attached to the top of walls and fences. The patterns of the trellising can be beautiful in themselves, especially when outlined with frost or snow; the blue oak trellis fencing at Villandry, with its elegant carved gateways, is an excellent example. The squares or diamonds of the lattice work can be anything from 10cm (4in) to 27cm (11in) across. Make the trellis as durable and strong as you can. We originally enclosed one side of our Winter Potager with expandable trellis from a garden centre, but its flimsy laths soon needed reinforcing. When we later erected trellis on the most exposed side, we used sturdier 3cm (1in) slats, 5mm (¼in) thick, and concreted the posts into the ground. They will take far more weight and last much longer.

Walls Building stone or brick walls is skilled work and can be costly, both in terms of labour and materials. Where there is plenty of local stone available, an old-fashioned field wall of roughly laid stones can make an appropriate background to the garden. Dry-stone walls, which are double-layered with an in-fill of soil and rubble, allow trailing vegetables to be planted along the top, provided a little manure is worked into the soil. Alpines and Mediterranean perennials can find a well-drained foothold in soil pockets on the sides.

ABOVE: **Where space is limited, especially in urban settings, wooden trellis gives a sense of privacy with no loss of light, and provides valuable support for climbers.**

RIGHT: **After earlier failures, sturdy homemade trellising was erected around my Winter Potager. Slats can be arranged to make pretty diamond and square patterns.**

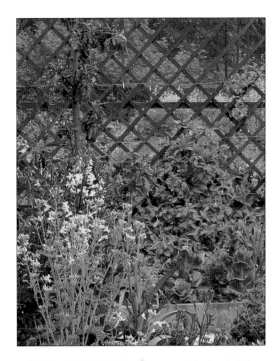

RIGHT: **A solid flint wall is not only the perfect backdrop for a kitchen garden, but provides the ideal environment for growing trained fruit, such as espalier apples, apricots and pears.**

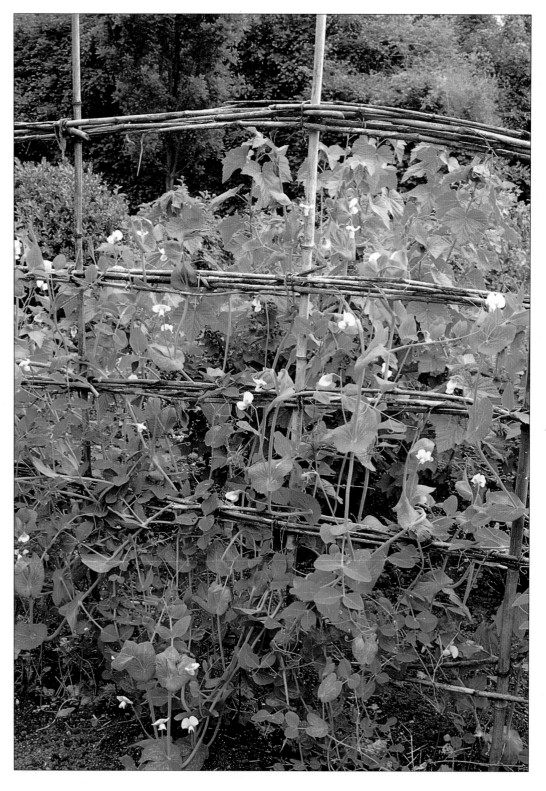

Woven hurdles and fencing Weaving hurdles and fences from supple woods such as willow, hazel and ash is an ancient craft. The soft, subtle colouring and texture of wood makes it the perfect backing for colourful vegetables. The drawback is its relatively short life. For this reason, hurdles are best used as temporary windbreaks or to block out eyesores, to be replaced periodically as necessary, and for fences as a short-term enclosure while a hedge is maturing. A well-constructed willow fence may last from between five and seven years before it starts to subside gracefully. If shrubby climbers have been established on it, this may not matter unduly as they will then more or less support the fence.

Portable fencing hurdles are normally up to about 1.8m (6ft) long, as anything larger than that becomes unwieldy to handle. Hazel and ash are more rugged, and hence slightly more durable, than willow. They are woven with cleft wood, presenting a rounded bark texture on one side and a lighter-coloured, flatter surface on the other. Hazel hurdles last up to ten years if treated with a wood preservative that is safe for plants, otherwise disintegration may start within four years.

One of the joys of woven willow fencing is how it can be made to fit the site. In 1994 a young basket maker, Martin Nunn, wove an undulating willow fence around my Little Potager. It was an experiment for us both, but it worked beautifully. Its outstanding characteristic is that it seems to flow from one side to the other. The front is low, no more than about 60cm–1m (2–3ft) high, allowing you to see

LEFT: **Climbing supports can double as boundary fences. In Hadspen Gardens, peas are growing on a bamboo frame, the uprights made from *Pleiobastus auricoma* and the more flexible cross-pieces of *Sasa palmatum*.**

over it into the garden. The back rises to about 1.8m (6ft) at the centre, hiding the polytunnel in the background. An arch leads through to the rest of the garden, strong enough to support a crop of marrows. At 2m (6½ft) intervals the fence is reinforced with stronger hazel posts. For an exceptionally strong fence, upright metal piping can be used. The highest points of the fence are the most susceptible to the combined effects of wind and the weight of climbers.

We found ideas evolved as it was being made. Cutting off the front corners with a low band of willow created two raised corner beds, which gave welcome height in this all-too-flat garden. (To protect the willow from moisture, the beds were lined with heavy black plastic before being filled with soil.) Two smaller 'baskets' were made on either side where the central path abuts the fence, with just the right amount of room for a pair of red peppers or dwarf tomatoes interplanted with trailing lobelia. As a finishing touch, small willow hoops were pushed into the top edges of the beds and along the corner curves of the fence, providing extra height for climbing beans and squashes. In the second season, an arbour and a seat were constructed at the back of the potager, with baskets on either side in which I planted ground-cover 'Flower Carpet' roses and sweet peas.

RIGHT: **The pocket beds woven into the willow fence around my Little Potager have added enormously to the charm. They are lined with heavy polythene film to separate the willow from the damp soil and extend its life.**

Much of my willow fence runs alongside the path that encircles the potager, so it is impossible to plant against it. Vigorous tendrilled climbers planted at the back pushed through from one side to the other, so the gaps purposely left in the first year proved unnecessary. Nevertheless, the fence looks best with plants right against it. On the whole, squashes climb without additional support, but beans need guiding strings or wires. One of the things we learnt was not to be too tidy about trimming off the stubby willow ends after the fence was made. They proved to be the ideal 'handles' for the tendrils of the climbing plants.

Willow weaving requires considerable skill and physical strength. If you can't manage it yourself, it is advisable to get professional help.

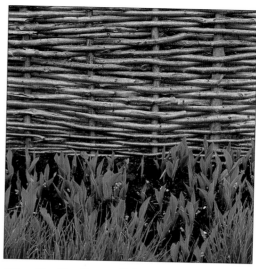

ABOVE: **Hazel hurdles usually last up to ten years, and are invaluable for temporary fencing to protect young shrubs from wind and for concealing eyesores.**

LEFT: There is no disputing that a tall boundary hedge, such as the beech seen here, makes a beautiful background, but think carefully before planting one in close proximity to vegetables. It casts shade, and the roots spread far, competing for nutrients and water.

HEDGES

The traditional 1.5–1.8m (5–6ft) boundary hedge is a luxury in terms of space. When mature it may well be at least 1m (3ft) wide at the base, potentially stealing nutrients and moisture from up to 1.8m (6ft) on either side, so any hedge planted around a vegetable plot must be there for a good reason. Besides providing shelter, it should either complement the design or produce edible flowers, attractive coloured leaves, fruits or shoots.

Clipped evergreen hedges are the classic boundary for a formal potager, providing a strong background all year. They can also be an excellent vehicle for decorative features. Bare-stemmed, round-headed hollies, yews or hornbeams look superb coming up through the evergreen. Deciduous and informal hedges set a different tone. Choose those with colourful blossoms, berries or fruit: at some point in the season they'll create a colourful backdrop for the vegetables. Space permitting, the perfect frame for a winter potager would be those species of willow, dogwood and the blackberry family with brightly coloured winter branches.

As a hedge will be there for a long time, it is crucial to make the right choice from the large number of potential hedging plants. Soil, climate and location are key factors. In narrowing the choice, consult good catalogues and reputable local nurserymen (see Suppliers, p.201). Information on a few of the most suitable hedges in a vegetable garden setting are given on pages 52 to 54 (for dwarf hedges, see pp.63–5 and for hedge topiary, see p.69).

The chosen site must be thoroughly prepared prior to planting. If feasible, dig a 1m (3ft) wide strip, two spades deep, and work in a generous amount of well-rotted manure (see p.131). Hardy species can be planted between autumn and spring, provided the ground is workable – neither frozen nor waterlogged. This is also true of conifers, the proviso being they are good nursery-grown plants and are still dormant; otherwise delay planting until spring. Never skimp on plant quality: select sturdy, healthy, one- to three-year-old plants, with plenty of shoots emerging from low on the stem. Plant them in firmly. Waterlogged ground should be avoided, but if conditions are wet, plant on a mound; conversely, plant in a basin 7.5–10cm (3–4in) deep in dry situations. Mulch after planting with heavy plastic, carpeting or an organic mulch such as straw or compost applied in a layer at least 5cm (2in) thick, but not in contact with the stem. It is essential to keep the young hedge weed-free and prevent it from drying out in the first two or three years. Protect evergreens in exposed positions with temporary windbreaks until they are well established.

To encourage compact, bushy growth the rule of thumb is to cut back deciduous hedges and evergreens (other than conifers) after planting to within 30cm (12in) off the ground. (If they have plenty of shoots coming up out of the base, this is unnecessary. Leave them for a year or so, to build up a strong root system before pruning.) In the following summer, cut back young growths of deciduous species by about half; trim evergreens lightly the following winter. Most conifers should be left unpruned until they reach the required height, when the leading shoot is pruned back.

All except informal hedges need to be trimmed regularly in order to keep them looking tidy and in shape. Taper the sides evenly so that the hedge is wider at the base than at the top; otherwise the lower parts get shaded and sparse. Most established hedges are clipped annually in late summer to early autumn, unless otherwise stated, although flowering and fruiting hedges may have to be pruned after they have 'performed'. Solid hedges can be trained over gateways or into archways, or even have 'windows' cut out of them. Unless growth is very vigorous, work in a general fertilizer, or mulch heavily with compost after trimming. The roots of a well-fed hedge will keep close to the hedge rather than spreading.

ABOVE: **This formal potager in Washington State, USA, has been dubbed the 'secret garden', as there is no obvious entrance. It is the multi-layered perimeter that catches the eye, with grapevines standing out against the formal yew hedge behind, beautifully matched by the topiary box hedging in the centre and around the beds. Most of the vegetables are grown in the raised beds in the foreground, only just visible in the picture.**

Hardy evergreen hedges *Buxus sempervirens* (Common box or boxwood) and the variegated box, *B. s.* 'Elegantissima', are small, shiny-leaved boxes that make slow-growing, dense, long-lived, medium to tall hedges. They are also used for dwarf hedging and topiary as they respond well to clipping. Set the plants 20–30cm (8–12in) apart. Box is a greedy plant and develops a huge root system that can be periodically chopped back with a spade. I saw a lovely hedge of 1m (3ft) high common box interplanted with variegated box, which was allowed to billow out sideways into contrasting 'balls' along its length.

Ilex aquifolium (Holly) is a slow-growing, dramatic hedge, with many beautiful forms, including the silver-edged 'Handsworth New Silver' (a female variety) and the variegated gold-edged 'Golden Queen' (a male variety). The cultivar 'J. C. van Tol' is self-pollinating and almost spineless. Set the plants 30cm (12in) apart. Trim with secateurs in late summer. For berries, plant male and female plants in the ratio of 1:5. Be warned, the sharp fallen leaves make weeding near the hedge a nightmare.

Lonicera nitida (Evergreen honeysuckle) makes a small-leaved, vigorous, fast-growing hedge that is best restricted to a height of about 1.2m (4ft). It tolerates most soils but is a greedy feeder. Set the plants 30cm (12in) apart. It needs frequent clipping from late spring to late summer, keeping it well tapered. Don't plant it in exposed situations. Deer, incidentally, won't touch it.

Taxus baccata (English yew) is an exceptionally long-lived, deep green plant considered the aristocrat of hedges. If well-watered and well-fed it is faster growing than is generally supposed.

RIGHT: **Box is a popular edging for potagers, but suitable varieties make excellent medium- to tall- boundaries. They will require feeding if they are to flourish.**

Set the plants about 45–60cm (18–24in) apart in well-drained soil. 'Elegantissima' is a wonderful golden form. Yew should not be cut in its first year after planting, but mature yew can withstand severe pruning. Prune in late summer or early autumn.

Thuja has a number of species that trim well to make handsome hedges. Recommended are the following: *T. occidentalis* (American Arbor-vitae), its compact form 'Smaragd', the more feathery, slower-growing *T. orientalis* (Chinese Arbor-vitae) and *T. plicata* 'Atrovirens' (Western red cedar). Set the plants about 60cm (24in) apart. Delay pruning until the second season and thereafter prune annually in late summer.

Viburnum tinus (Laurostinus) makes the ideal background hedge for a winter potager, as it produces small, flat heads of pretty white flowers from autumn to spring in all but the coldest areas. Set the plants 60cm (24in) apart. After flowering, trim it back hard into a square, formal shape for the summer months.

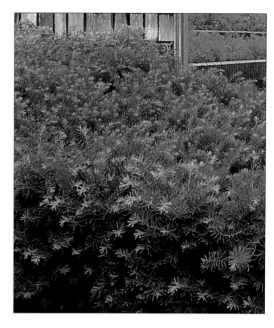

ABOVE: **Yew is one of the finest hedges. The deep green leaves make a superb foil to colourful planting.**

BELOW: **Alternating gold and green forms of tall Leyland's cypress form a substantial windbreak, while 1m (3ft) high box provides a more intimate frame.**

ABOVE: **The patterns of light and shade, and contrasting colour in a tapestry hedge arise from interplanting species such as yew, holly, and copper and green beech.**

RIGHT: **The entrance to the herb garden at Ballymaloe Cookery School is through an arch in a beech hedge.**

Deciduous hedges *Carpinus betulus* (Hornbeam) is an excellent year-round hedge as the clipped young growths retain their coppery leaves in winter and it is most suitable for a formal setting. It resembles beech, but tolerates wetter soils. Set the plants about 45cm (18in) apart. Prune in mid- to late summer.

Crataegus monogyna (Hawthorn, Thorn, May) is a traditional robust, prickly hedge producing spring blossom and autumn haws. Set the plants 45cm (18in) apart. Hawthorn can stand severe cutting back. The hedge can be punctuated with single standards crowned with closely clipped thorn 'balls', and these look superb when brightly coloured or double-flowered varieties such as *C. oxycantha* 'Paul's Scarlet' are used (see Topiary, p.70). Prune in summer and, if necessary, again in autumn.

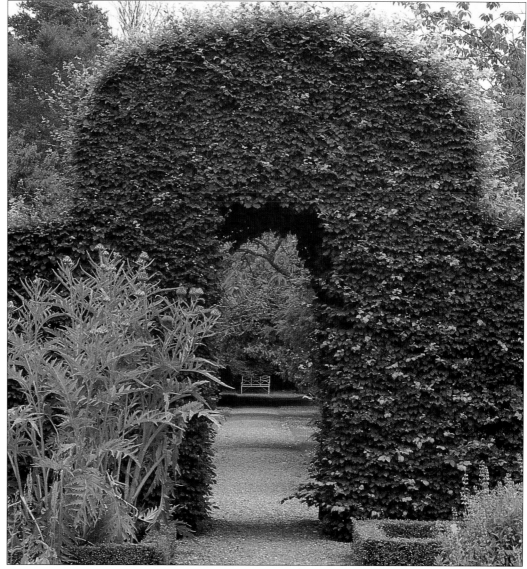

Fagus sylvatica (Beech) forms a handsome green hedge that keeps its leaves well into winter, but it performs poorly if the soil is heavy and wet. Set the plants 45cm (18in) apart. The purple form, 'Riversii', makes a dramatic background. The two can be interplanted, two greens to each red works well to make a tapestry hedge. Beech is best left for a year after planting to establish and then it should be cut back if the base is bare. Prune in late summer.

Rosa sp. (Roses) make colourful hedges where space allows. Suitable hedging species include the purple-leaved *R. glauca* syn. *rubrifolia*, which has purplish stems in winter. It can be pruned back in spring to a formal hedge. Also excellent are the various large-hipped *R. rugosa* species, *R. rubiginosa* (Sweet Briar), and *R.* 'The Fairy', with its double pink flowers and box-like foliage. Set the plants 45cm (18in) apart. Trim in winter or early spring if necessary.

53

Edible hedges With imagination, a huge range of plants can be called into service, including edible species of bamboo and cactus, the slightly tender *Laurus nobilis* (bay laurel), the semi-evergreen *Atriplex halimus* (tree purslane) with its edible shoots, nut trees such as hazel, and a host of fruits, from *Acca sellowiana* syn. *Feijoa* (pineapple guava), *Mahonia aquifolium* (Oregon grape), and the evergreen *Vaccinium ovatum* (huckleberry) to those traditional hedges in the plum family, *Prunus spinosa* (sloes) and *P. cerasifera* (myrobalan or cherry plum), and of course, grape vines.

INSTANT BOUNDARIES

Traditional hedges can take from two to six years to reach the required height, but a nearly 'instant' boundary or screen can be made in a number of ways. One method is to erect a simple fence of chainlink, plastic netting, wire mesh or cleft chestnut paling and cover it with evergreen or semi-evergreen climbers planted at the base. Choose variegated types for added interest, such as the honeysuckle *Lonicera japonica* 'Aureoreticulata' or an ivy such as *Hedera colchica* 'Sulphur Heart' (syn. 'Paddy's Pride').

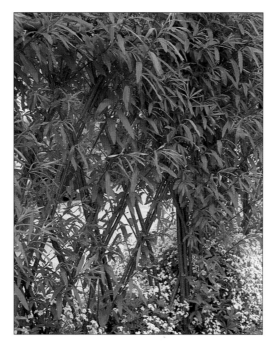

Making a 'fedge' Another option is to use inexpensive, fast-rooting young willow stems to make a fence-like hedge, which is endearingly dubbed a 'fedge'. A fedge made in spring will be a beautiful green wall by summer. I learnt something of the art of willow fedge-making from Steve Pickup, founder of the Willow Bank in north Wales (see Suppliers, p.201).

ABOVE: **With its shiny leaves, flowers and edible berries, Oregon grape is an excellent shade-tolerant hedge.**

LEFT: **The diamond weave in a fedge makes a lively pattern in summer and winter.**

The following is one of several ways to make a willow fedge. (In the diagrams below the entire fedge is made in a diamond weave.)

1 Make the fedge in late winter to early spring. Use fast-growing varieties that produce long straight rods. All varieties of *Salix viminalis* are ideal. Incorporating coloured-stemmed varieties makes it more decorative.

MAKING A WILLOW 'FEDGE'

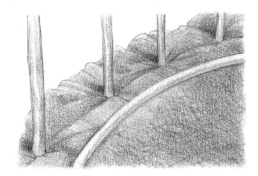

1 After the outline is marked, willow rods are pushed into 20–30cm (8–12in) deep holes. Planting through polythene keeps down weeds.

2 The weavers are put in at a 45 degree angle between upright rods, facing opposite ways. In a standard weave they are parallel to each other.

3 The top edge pairs of weavers are twisted horizontally between the rods. The ends of the main weavers are woven into the edge.

2 Mark the proposed outline with hosepiping. Allow a 1.8m (6ft) gap behind vegetable beds, as willow roots spread and 80 per cent of the rooting is in the top 30cm (12in) of soil. Unless the ground is very hard, special preparation is unnecessary beforehand. By planting through a 1m (3ft) wide strip of heavy black mulching material, the fedge can be made directly on grass. This will allow moisture to permeate but will keep back weeds, therefore preventing as much competition as possible.

3 The uprights are made from strong, straight, knot-free, two-year-old rods of roughly 2cm (³⁄₄in) diameter. Make 20–30cm (8–12in) deep vertical holes through the black plastic mulch, using a crowbar if necessary, about 30cm (12in) apart down the centre. Push the uprights firmly into the holes (see diagram 1).

4 Lighter and more supple, but not flimsy 'weavers' of one-year-old wood are woven between them on the diagonal. Both types should be as long as possible, ideally 2.75–3m (9–10ft) long. For the weavers, make similar holes at a 45 degree angle, about 10cm (4in) apart for a standard weave, all angled the same way. Push the weavers in firmly, then weave them in and out of the rods, behind one and in front of the next. Never weave too tightly, or the sap flow will be obstructed and the tips will die back. Cut off any sideshoots but leave the ends untrimmed and weave together at the top.

5 For a diagonal weave, make holes at the same place, but further apart and facing in opposite directions (see diagram 2). If space becomes tight, start from the top, weaving downwards into the hole. Finally, tweak the rods so they are evenly spaced in each direction.

6 To finish off the top edge, take pairs of weavers or binders and weave them horizontally in and out of the tops of the uprights (see Figure 3), twisting them between each upright

to make a firm edge. Weave the tips of the original weavers into it. For a neat effect, cut off the tops of the uprights at fedge level. Finish the outer edge by bending ends around the last upright and back on themselves. Twist gently as you go to break the fibres; this actually prevents the stems cracking. After the fedge is established, prune back or weave in subsequent growth to keep it tidy. It will be less competitive if pruned hard whenever necessary.

Making a turf wall A wall built of turves or sods is a quick, traditional method of enclosing a working garden, particularly apt if you are carving a garden out of field or lawn. Its natural simplicity would appeal to any ecologically-minded gardener. Grass soon grows out of the original turves to green the edges and top, where self-sown wild flowers can add a touch of colour. A wall will last through a good many years – the more robust the turf the better – though it will slump and lose its shape with time. It is not recommended where rabbits and moles are a problem.

There is an example of a turf wall around the 'kail yard' at the reconstructed Robert Burns' cottage in Alloway, on the west coast of Scotland. It is just over 1m (3ft) high, tapering from a base of 65cm (26in) to 40cm (16in) across the top. A taller wall would need a wider base. This type of wall can be made with 10cm (4in) thick, 40cm (16in) square turves, laid on top of each other, grass-side up, with the joints overlapping in both directions. The final coping

RIGHT: **The turves or sods used to make a traditional turf wall at Burns' cottage, Scotland, were cut by hand from the lawn behind the house.**

BUILDING A TURF WALL

The wall is carefully built up with overlapping square turves. The sides slope gently and the final coping is made of upright turves.

is made from half-size turves standing on their ends (see above). The sides are trimmed as necessary, the trimmings being used to fill any cavities. To ensure an even and straight wall, wooden templates and plumb-lines are set up at each end, with fine guide-lines between.

PATHS

Whether the design of a vegetable garden is simple or complicated, it is given definition by its paths, while its character is strongly influenced by their style. There are many options – well-trodden soil, grass, herbs, mulches, brick, stone, gravel or wooden duckboards – but they must be practical, appropriate and beautiful.

Aesthetics apart, what are the crucial points to consider when deciding which to go for? Key factors are climate and soil. For example, if rainfall is high and the soil heavy, it is essential to have a dry, firm surface to work from. That rules out soft paths, at least within the

LEFT AND BELOW: **Imagination has been at play in laying paths in the demonstration garden at Seattle Tilth Association in Seattle, USA. In one, giant stones and bricks capture the feeling of a fast-flowing stream, while in the other an eye catching, radiant sun is created from keys surrounded by brightly-coloured mosaics.**

main working area. Cost and permanence are closely related factors: the more durable the path the higher the cost, and the harder it will be to alter or move. Another consideration is the availability of materials. If good stone is cheap locally, or if wood chips are being given away, make the most of the opportunity.

When planning the layout of the paths, remember their main purpose is to provide convenient access to the beds. Except where curves are part of the design, straight paths will prove more serviceable than meandering ones. Paths should lead somewhere, either to the centre of the garden, or to enticing features on the boundaries such as a seat, well-trained fruit, or a handsome pot planted with a topiary herb. Decorative patterns and features can be created in stone and brick paths most easily where paths intersect. Imaginative mixing of the textures of concrete paviours, stone and brick within a path can be very effective, while herbs and flowers allowed to self-seed in cracks and gaps turn paths into rivulets of colour.

Path width is inevitably influenced by the size of the garden. Where space is scarce, wide paths are a luxury. The minimum practical width is 30cm (12in), with occasional wider paths, up to 70cm (27in), being essential for manoeuvring wheelbarrows, and setting them down with both legs on the path.

SOFT PATHS

Clover paths The white clover, *Trifolium repens* makes a dense cover, and it can even be mown if you don't want it to flower.

Grass paths Mown grass makes a handsome foil for vegetable beds, providing it can withstand the traffic. Make the paths the width, or a multiple of the width of your mower.

Herb paths The scent of a camomile path while working is pure heaven, but keeping it

ABOVE: **Earth paths are the essence of simplicity and are very beguiling in an unsophisticated potager. Avoid them on poorly drained or weedy ground.**

ABOVE: **Fragrant herbs such as thyme make a romantic path, but don't stand up to heavy traffic, so are best confined to out of the way areas.**

BELOW: **Grass provides the perfect foil for vegetables in all types of garden. In formal potagers, wide paths edged with herbs or flowers make a splendid vista.**

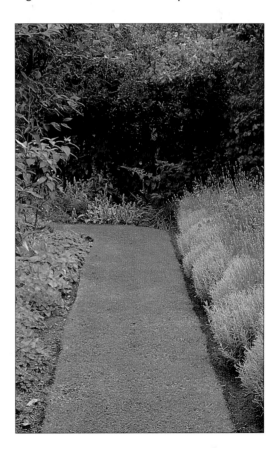

weed-free is extremely difficult. The same is true of all herb paths. If you succumb to the temptation, make herb paths on well-drained, weed-free soil in areas where traffic is light. For camomile use the non-flowering variety *Chamomile nobile* 'Treneague', with plants spaced 10cm (4in) apart. For thyme paths use the wild creeping thyme, *T. polytrichus* or the woolly thyme, *T. pseudolanuginosus*, setting the plants 20cm (8in) apart, or an evergreen, creeping variety such as *Thymus serpyllum*. The creeping mints prefer moister conditions. Suitable ones are *Mentha cervina*, with minute thyme-like leaves, planted 23cm (9in) apart, the vigorous pennyroyal, *M. pulegium*, also planted 23cm (9in) apart and the tiny-leaved Corsican mint, *M. requienii*, planted 10cm (4in) apart. Probably a better way to use herbs, however, is to grow them between paving stones or bricks.

All planted paths are relatively delicate in the early stages; don't walk on them until they are well established.

Soil paths 'Cheap and changeable' sums up the merits of a soil path. In the early days of designing a potager, it is worth keeping soil paths until you are sure of the layout you want.

ABOVE: **Bark chips look natural and are available cheaply in some areas. They will remain in good condition for several years, and can eventually be composted.**

ABOVE: **Old weatherproof bricks make very attractive paths. They can be mortared to prevent weeds and self-seeding plants establishing themselves in the cracks.**

ABOVE: **Bricks can be laid in simple or complex patterns, to enhance or reflect the overall design of a potager. Rough edges are easily hidden by overhanging herbs.**

MULCHED PATHS

For every type of garden there's a suitable mulch. At one extreme, thick layers of straw or hay look right in ecological and organic gardens, while at the other glistening river sand, raked Japanese style, adds the perfect note of elegance to the paths in the Villandry potager.

Gardeners now have access to several mulching materials derived from wood. These range from sawdust and wood shavings to wood chips, ornamental bark mulches and 'forest biomulch' (blends of wood, bark, twigs and leaves). They can all be serviceable and attractive. I have an ornamental bark mulch around my Little Potager, and the more rugged-looking 'forest biomulch' on the outer paths of the Winter Potager. At the recommended depths of 5cm (2in) and 7.5cm (3in)

they should last over two and over three years respectively. The last remnants can always be raked off and composted.

The best results are obtained by laying mulches over a landscaping mulching fabric, geotextile cloth or woven polypropylene material, all of which allow water to drain away but suppress weeds. As a general rule, lay a mulch as thickly as you can afford.

LAYING A SIMPLE BRICK PATH

1 Dig out the ground to a depth that allows for a 5cm (2in) layer of sand and the width of the brick. Generally there is no need for a more solid foundation.

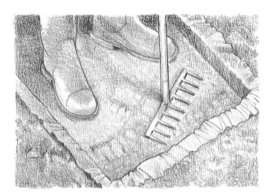

2 Lay a thick sheet of polythene film the width of the path beneath the sand. Smooth the sand so it forms an even base for the bricks.

3 Lay the bricks on a sand base, tamping them down with a club hammer, with a piece of wood over the bricks to protect them.

HARD SURFACES

Brick paths Purpose-made brick paviours and weatherproof 'engineering' bricks are suitable for outdoor paths, but ordinary bricks crumble on exposure to the elements. Old weathered bricks, with their soft shades of red, grey and blue are perfect for potagers and lend themselves to creative patterning.

In the average vegetable garden with a firm soil base, foundations are unnecessary. Simply lay the bricks on a 5cm (2in) deep layer of compacted sand (see diagrams opposite). To keep down weeds, line the trench with heavy polythene or, in areas of high rainfall, one of the permeable fabrics mentioned on page 58. Use a line and spirit level to keep the surface level. To stabilize the path brush dry cement into the cracks or point with mortar. This will prevent weeds growing, but will also preclude their use for herbs and self-seeding flowers.

Gravel The self-setting gravels, which need to be laid at least 4cm (1½in) deep, work into a fine, smooth, working surface. Loose gravels, such as white limestone chips, can make superb contrasting paths, but they must be kept in place with a wood, stone or brick kerb. The

BELOW: **White limestone chip gravel sparkles in the sun. It looks wonderful with herbs growing through it, and is ideal for plants that require good drainage to thrive.**

ABOVE: **The inherent harshness of modern concrete paviours is soon softened by establishing herbs, such as camomile and creeping thymes, between them.**

gravel should be laid about 1cm (½in) deep on a fabric base to prevent it working into the soil.

Stone Real stone is beautiful but exorbitant in price. Fortunately, modern concrete paviours are an excellent substitute. Lay them in the same way as for brick paths (see opposite), but dab a small amount of cement on each corner and in the centre to stabilize them. Tamp them down with a club hammer to level them. For a firm path of close fitting blocks lay them onto the sand, and bed them in with a hired plate vibrator. Leave gaps between the paviours for planting; in my Winter Potager a lovely effect was created by putting pebbles between them and planting herbs among them.

Wood duckboards These are made from standard pressure-treated gravel boards 1.2m (4ft) long, 15cm (6in) wide and 2.5cm (1in) thick. They will last twenty years, and are easily moved to new sites if necessary. To make a 30cm (12in) wide duckboard, place two gravel

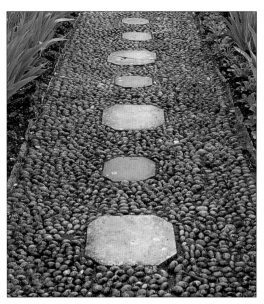

ABOVE: **The varying combination of rounded pebbles and flat stone slabs, of different shapes in this case, creates a striking path ideally suited to a formal potager.**

boards side by side, and fix them together at the ends and in the centre by nailing on three 30cm- (12in-) long cross pieces made from the same type of board, using 5cm (2in) galvanized nails put in at an angle. If the boards are slippery, staple strips of fine chicken wire across them.

BELOW: **Gravel is a hard-wearing and often beautiful material, but is best used where the beds have solid edges, to prevent the chips straying into the soil.**

EDGES

In a vegetable garden with any character the beds are edged, and the choice of edge reflects that character. Orderly edges of clipped low hedges or brick and stone suit formal designs. Wooden board edges and common culinary herbs typify workaday gardens, while rustic log edges, billowing lavender or colourful borders of scented pinks signify a more romantic approach to the vegetable garden.

At the most practical level a solid edge serves to keep the soil in the bed, and loose path materials such as gravel or bark mulch out of the bed. Where this is called for, an edge at least 5cm (2in) high is necessary. Space is a key consideration in deciding on the edging. Hard edges take the least room and, of course, offer no competition to plants, so in small gardens living edges must earn their keep, in which case culinary herbs, compact low-growing vegetables and edible flowers win out over decorative edging plants. In larger gardens, edging can be chosen purely for its decorative qualities. Good quality stone, brick and terracotta tiles are costly, as is establishing a classic dwarf hedge from nursery stock. The cost can be reduced by raising your own plants from cuttings and using recycled materials. Within these parameters the field is open for creating colourful, textured effects from whatever edging is chosen. Bear in mind that many of the plants or materials suitable for edging paths can also be used within large beds to divide them into sections.

HARD EDGES

Brick Raised beds are often edged with mortared brick walls up to 60cm (24in) high. Low brick edgings, like brick paths, must be made from weatherproof bricks, ideally from genuine old bricks, or well-made reproduction bricks, the colours of which range from blue-grey through buffs and pink to reds.

Single bricks can be laid flat, on edge, upright or upright but at an angle (see diagram opposite), with each brick leaning on its neighbour to give an attractive dogtooth effect. Where there's a hard path, pairs of bricks, set on their base side by side at ground level, make a smooth broad edge, easily draped with prostrate herbs or flowers. Edges can be several bricks deep; in one famous potager the lower sunken course is of cheaper bricks, with the visible upper layer made of decorative bricks, mortared to make a firm edge.

Where the path surface is firm and level, bricks can simply be butted together on the ground without the need for foundations to hold them in place. Alternatively, they can be laid in a shallow trough. For a firmer or permanent edging they can be set in cement or a fairly stiff concrete mix. Dry cement mix can be

ABOVE: **Tiny hurdles can be used to edge paths or divide beds. This hazel hurdle is 45cm (18in) high; nearby in the same garden even more diminutive 23cm (9in) high split ash hurdles were being used.**

BELOW: **Nicely weathered brick always makes a satisfying edge, at its simplest laid flat, but for a more striking effect, set at an angle (see diagram opposite).**

worked between upright bricks, or they can be mortared, to seal the gaps, which will also prevent weeds from getting the opportunity to take a foothold. Reproduction bricks are sometimes sold in solid units roughly 50cm (20in) long, which can be laid very quickly.

Hoops Simple, cheap and charming edges can be made from young stems of bamboo, beech, dogwood, willow or indeed any wood that is supple enough to be bent into an arch. They look best overlapping at the base. Stems can be trimmed or left with a lace-like network of twigs; or twist two stems together for a roped look. Willow hoops may take root during the summer, which doesn't matter, as it keeps them fresh and supple. Uproot them at the end of the season if you don't want them there permanently. Most hoops last for two seasons at the most, though bamboos may last for three. It is a good idea to dip the ends in preservative, as this will extend their life. Hoops can be any height, from low edges 30cm (12in) off the ground to taller hoops that can support climbing vegetables (see pp.86–9). Reproduction Victorian terracotta hoops are a permanent, but pricier, alternative.

Stone, masonry, concrete and bottles Loosely placed stones and rocks are probably the oldest type of edges with, once again, scope for recycling. I have seen granite setts from the Palais Royal in Paris and ornate stone masonry from demolished New York buildings keeping plots in shape. What an improvement on the modern pre-cast concrete edgings sold for the same purpose. Another recycling idea, seen at the Centre for Alternative Technology in Wales, is for upturned blue glass bottles pushed into the ground, neck first, to form an edging for a bed or border. Fern spores had colonized them to make an intriguing edge of natural bottle gardens.

ABOVE: **Here supple young beech stems are bent into low hoops to make a rustic, low-cost edge. The overlapping hoops create an attractive pattern.**

BELOW: **The ancient practice of using stones picked off the fields to edge vegetable beds, as seen here in a garden in upstate New York, has an appealing simplicity.**

LAYING A DOGTOOTH BRICK EDGE

Set the bricks on edge in a 7.5–8cm (3–4in) deep trench. For a more substantial edge set them in mortar, or work dry cement between them.

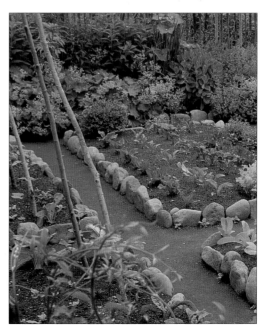

Tiles These impart an air of classical elegance to a vegetable garden. If you can find antique terracotta tiles, such as the rope-edged Victorian tiles, you are in luck. Modern terracotta tiles and good replicas are available and other types of tiling may be found locally. An informal effect can be achieved with unevenly shaped tiles: jet black slates can make dramatic, jagged edges, while giant, ceramic floor tiles can look wonderful placed at zany angles around a circular bed. Where tiles are used as an upright edge, set them in the same way as bricks (see diagram on p.61).

Timber An excellent natural edging for beds can be made from timber. Sturdy railway sleepers, half-sawn timbers or whole logs can be rolled or pushed into place, and nailed to sunken corner posts if necessary. For boarded sides, use boards 2.5–4cm (¾–1½in) thick. They can be any height from 7.5 to 10cm (3 to 4in) upwards, though they start to look gaunt if over 20–23cm (8–9in) high. Provided they are firmly secured, timbers can be laid on the surface, without being embedded in the ground.

For paths at bed level, a practical material is pressure-treated 8 x 4cm (3½ x 1½in) board

(widely sold as road fencing rail in 1.8m (6ft) lengths). The width gives the edge a substantial look, and the height is just enough to separate the path material from the bed, which will stop the soil from spilling onto the path. Nail the rails to 5 sq cm (2 sq in) pegs driven into the path or bed where the rails meet or at 1.8m (6ft) intervals. Boards can be painted colourfully or stained with any of the modern weatherproof preservative products available so they stand out or merge, according to the style of the garden.

ABOVE LEFT: **Golden feverfew elegantly spilling out over the rope-edged Victorian tile onto the path. These tiles are also made in blue-black with a metallic sheen, and make a pretty edging in formal and informal settings. Flowering chicory can be seen in the background.**

ABOVE: **My Winter Potager is edged with discarded roofing tiles nailed to wooden boards. The wavy tops of the tiles and the nails make a pleasing pattern.**

CONSTRUCTING A BOARDED EDGE

1 Set up stringlines and pegs to mark out the dimensions of the bed. With short-sided beds a peg at each corner is sufficient.

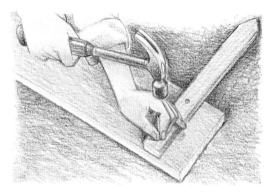

2 For the sides use pressure-treated boards. Nail them to 5 sq cm (2 sq in) posts or pegs, so the tops are below the top of the board.

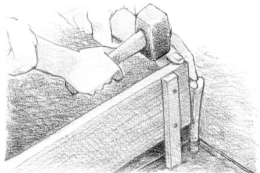

3 Drive the posts or pegs with the boards attached 30cm (12in) into the bed or path, using the string-lines and marker pegs as a guideline.

DWARF HEDGES

Dwarf hedges are the most seductive of edges. The bold outlines of evergreens, the softness of grey-leaved herbs, or the colour and contrasts of variegated or brightly coloured hedges are often at the heart of a potager's magic. They have their drawbacks, the most obvious being that they take up space and compete for nutrients and moisture. Even a neat low hedge may spread to 30cm (12in) or so, and create a dry strip on either side. It may provide shelter for beneficial insects, but will also harbour pests. Formal hedges need regular clipping to keep them shapely. In spite of these faults they remain attractive for straight and curved edges.

Choosing the most suitable hedge depends on the effect you want to create and on local conditions. Evergreen and shrubbier species, which are relatively long lived, generally require reasonably fertile soil. The grey-leaved herbs are shorter lived, but can tolerate poor soil, though good drainage is essential. It may be worth planting short stretches at first, to ascertain what is going to look right and flourish. Take plenty of cuttings to fill any gaps in the early stages or to use as later replacements. The following are some of the most suitable plants for dwarf hedging. (For more information about planting and trimming *Buxus* (box) and *Lonicera nitida* (evergreen honeysuckle) see Hardy evergreen hedges, p.52.)

Evergreen *Buxus sempervirens* 'Suffruticosa' (Dwarf box or boxwood) is easily trimmed, exceptionally long lived (though slow growing) and sweetly scented. This small-leaved form is deservedly the most popular of kitchen garden hedges. Use it for hedges up to 30cm (12in) high. Plants sold are variable and often misnamed so, if possible, select plants yourself, choosing dense, bushy specimens. Set the plants 10–15cm (4–6in) apart. Unless the plants are

bare-stemmed, with few sideshoots, allow the tops to grow unpruned for a year, then trim them level in late summer to early autumn each year until the required height is reached. 'Blauer Heinz' is a compact form requiring little trimming. Keep the plants well mulched and feed with a seaweed-based fertilizer in spring.

Many good strains of box can be found in gardens; it could be worth propagating your own. The simplest method is to snap off ripening sprigs about 7.5–10cm (3–4in) long, in late autumn or early winter. Bury them to half their depth in a seedtray of potting compost, and put them in a sheltered place, out of the sun, for the winter. They will have rooted by summer.

Hedera helix (Ivy) has some trailing and hanging forms that can make compact, low hedge-like edges and are much cheaper to establish than traditional hedges. The cultivar 'Ivalace' is recommended for this purpose, as it forms a stocky plant when clipped (see p.64). To establish a hedge quickly, set the plants 15cm (6in) apart. Trim in late spring and early summer. To propagate take semi-hardwood cuttings in summer or hardwood cuttings in late autumn.

Lonicera nitida (Evergreen honeysuckle) is a useful plant for making a quick dwarf hedge: 'Elegant' is one of the most suitable cultivars. Set the plants 20–30cm (8–12in) apart. It needs to be clipped frequently in summer. Propagate from hardwood cuttings in early winter or spring.

Rosmarinus officinalis (Rosemary) will form a beautiful hedge in mild areas on well-drained, preferably slightly alkaline soil. The cultivars 'Miss Jessop's Upright' and 'Primley Blue' are recommended for dwarf hedges. They flower early in the year, and can be trimmed fairly hard after flowering. Set the plants 45cm (18in) apart. Propagate from either 15cm (6in) long softwood cuttings taken in the spring, or semi-hardwood cuttings in summer.

BELOW RIGHT: **The bright yellow foliage of *Lonicera nitida* 'Baggesen's Gold' encircles the sweet corn neatly, while making a brilliant contrast with blue-leaved leeks.**

BELOW: **The small-leaved ivy, *Hedera helix* 'Ivalace' is a naturally stocky variety, and quickly makes a neat edge if trimmed hard between late spring and early summer.**

Teucrium x *lucidrys* syn. *chamaedrys* (Wall germander) is a classic knot-garden hedge, and with its glistening leaves and perky habit, it makes a beautiful 23–30cm (9–12in) high edge for the decorative vegetable garden. Set the plants 15cm (6in) apart in well-drained soil. It is one of the hardiest of the herb hedges. Clip it lightly in spring and again in early autumn, if tidiness is a top priority. To propagate, take cuttings from soft new growth in the spring. The variegated form 'Variegatum' is less hardy, as is the longer-leaved *T. fruticans*, which also makes a lovely hedge in mild areas.

Yellow and variegated hedges *Buxus sempervirens* 'Elegantissima' (Variegated box) can light up a garden. This silvery-edged cultivar makes a pretty, bright edging or dot plant. 'Gold Tip' and 'Latifolia Maculata' are also suitable varieties. Cultivate them like a standard box (see p.52 and p.63).

Euonymus fortunei 'Emerald 'n Gold' is an evergreen spindle that clips beautifully into a neat, bright green and gold hedge, turning bronzy-pink in the winter. 'Emerald Gaiety' is its green and silver counterpart. Set the plants about 30cm (12in) apart. Trim in mid-summer and late spring. Propagate from hardwood cuttings in mid- to late autumn.

Lonicera nitida 'Baggesen's Gold' is a variety of shrubby evergreen honeysuckle. It can form striking bands of yellow, provided it is planted in full sun. It also makes a brilliant square or circle frame within a large bed (see below).

Taxus baccata 'Elegantissima' can be clipped to form a striking low, golden-coloured hedge. Propagate this variety of yew from heeled semi-hardwood cuttings taken in late summer.

Thuja occidentalis (American arbor-vitae) has several slow-growing cultivars that can make a striking edge of golden-leaved hummocky plants, turning a lovely bronze colour in winter. The most suitable forms are 'Golden Globe', 'Rheingold' and *T. orientalis* 'Aurea Nana'. Set the plants 45cm (18in) apart. Clip gently in summer. Propagate from semi-hardwood cuttings taken in late summer.

Red-leaved hedges *Berberis thunbergii* 'Atropurpurea' is a deciduous, low hedge and it makes a colourful ribbon around beds, bronze in spring, and rich red in the autumn. Set plants about 60cm (24in) apart. The dwarf form 'Atropurpurea Nana' is slower growing but nearly thornless. 'Dwarf Pygmy' and 'Bagatelle' are other neat forms that are suitable for edging a decorative vegetable garden. Plant dwarf forms 30–40cm (12–16in) apart. Trim in late autumn. Propagate from heel cuttings taken in the autumn.

Grey-leaved hedges *Artemisia abrotanum* (Southernwood, Lad's Love) makes an excellent silver border for the potager, though it is only semi-evergreen. Set the plants 60cm (24in) apart. To keep it well-shaped, prune it hard in spring, but never in autumn. Propagate from semi-hardwood cuttings taken in late summer or raise it from seed.

Artemesia absinthium (Wormwood): the cultivars 'Lambrook Silver' and 'Powis Castle' are both evergreen. The bright, finely-dissected, aromatic leaves making bushy, shimmering edges. They will, however, require winter protection if temperatures are likely to fall below -5°C (23°F). Set the plants about 45cm (18in) apart. Propagate from softwood cuttings of young growth taken in early summer.

Helichrysum italicum syn. *angustifolium* (Curry Plant) is an evergreen herb with almost overpowering scent, but it can make a generous, billowing silver border. Set the plants 60cm (24in) apart. The cultivar 'Dartington' is dwarfer and more compact: plant it 30cm (12in) apart. Trim plants lightly in spring, and protect them in severe winters. *H. splendidum* is a shrubbier, reasonably hardy species that has small, oblong, bright yellow clusters of flowerheads. Propagate all types from softwood cuttings in spring or semi-hardwood cuttings in autumn.

Lavandula angustifolia (Old English Lavender) is the most typical cottage-garden grey-leaved hedge and is a reasonably hardy evergreen. For dwarf hedges use compact cultivars such as 'Compacta Nana' (syn. 'Munstead'), 'Folgate', 'Hidcote' (the dark blue and pink forms), 'Loddon Blue', 'Loddon Pink' and *L.* x *intermedia* 'Twickel Purple'. Set the plants 38cm (15in) apart. As a rule lavender should be replaced every four or five years, though some plants have survived for decades. Prune lightly in spring and after flowering. To propagate, take softwood cuttings in spring or semi-hardwood cuttings in summer.

Ruta graveolens 'Jackman's Blue' has evergreen blue-green foliage that makes an excellent edge and is particularly effective in winter. It is now, unfortunately, banned from my garden because of the skin-blistering effects of its sap. Set the plants 60cm (24in) apart. Trim it back hard in spring, but wear gloves and dispose of the clippings carefully. Propagate it from softwood cuttings or seeds in spring or early summer.

Santolina chamaecyparissus (Cotton lavender) is a traditional grey edging plant for knot gardens and parterres. It is a dense, evergreen shrub and has prolific flowers in early summer. The flowers are a muddy yellow colour in the hardier, standard form, but 'Lemon Queen' and *S. pinnata* spp. *neapolitana* 'Edward

Bowles' have prettier creamy coloured flowers and 'Sulphurea' has pale primrose-lemon flowers. Set the plants about 35cm (14in) apart. To keep them in good shape, trim fairly hard after flowering. Propagate from softwood cuttings in the spring. For more edging ideas, see Living Edges, pages 90–2.

ABOVE RIGHT: *Berberis thunbergii* **is notable for the brilliant colouring of foliage and berries. Use the more compact varieties for edging beds.**

RIGHT: **Cotton lavender** *Santolina chamaecyparrisus* **is an old established favourite for edging in herb gardens and potagers. Prune hard after flowering.**

FOCAL POINTS AND FEATURES

The romantic features that are used to give landscaped gardens structure, form, colour and, above all, height, rarely find their way into ordinary kitchen gardens. Arches and arbours covered with ornamental climbers, topiary and mophead standards punctuating the landscape, statues, fountains, containers, sundials and stone urns topped with flowers, create instant interest in ornamental gardens. Let them into the vegetable garden, and the transformation from functional plot to magical place is underway. The skill lies in integrating them with the truly productive elements of the garden – fruit, vegetables and herbs. What can be used, and how, depends on the character and scale of the garden.

LEFT: **A covered well built out of rubble graces this area in a New York Community Garden. Vegetables and flowers mingle together in many creative plots.**

Let's start with the entrance of the potager. In any garden, a wrought-iron or wooden gate can be lovely in itself. Straddle it with an archway clad with ornamental or fruitful climbers, and the vegetable garden beyond beckons irresistibly. Where there is plenty of room, a series of arches can be linked to make a tunnel: surely a fruit tunnel is one of the most perfect gateways to a potager? Or flank the entrance with pairs of trees or shrubs, or pots of topiary, herbs or flowers. Where appropriate, standard trees or straight-stemmed hawthorn balls can be trained to rise out of the boundary hedge on either side of the gate.

In formal vegetable gardens, the patterned pathways often radiate from the centre, and become decorative features in themselves. On a grand scale, a gazebo or summerhouse can be the hub of the garden, or a pool surrounded with flowers, or statuary encircled with clipped hedges. A specimen tree can also command this central space. In smaller gardens, the central spot is often adorned with a tall structure for climbing vegetables or ornamentals, or a single handsome specimen such as cardoon. Imaginatively planted pots can be grouped in the middle, or a still life centrepiece created with garden artefacts such as seakale and rhubarb blanching pots, old glass bell jars and leaded cloches. Even garden furniture can take centre stage.

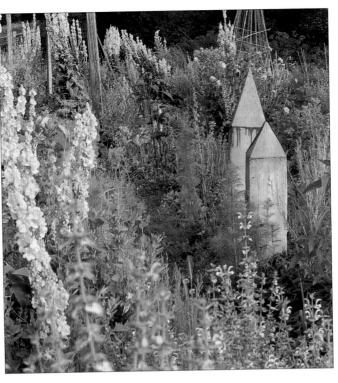

ABOVE: **Ceramic deva houses may be unusual features, but they fit perfectly into the ambience of the Occidental Arts and Ecology Center in California.**

It is the far side of a vegetable garden that most often cries out for a focal point of interest, such as a vista viewed down the main path. Any of the features suggested for the centre could be sited there, and it is the natural place for a seat or arbour or, if sunny enough, for espalier fruit trained against the boundary. At Ballymaloe Cookery School, southern Ireland, the potager is overlooked by a 'beech house' arbour. Copper beech has been planted all round its timber frame to form 'walls', and when it matures, 'windows' and 'doors' will be cut in it.

Don't overlook opportunities for putting decorative and architectural features into the beds. Metalwork obelisks for climbers, rod-like 'Ballerina' apple trees, elegant stonework, even scarecrows, can make a lively centrepiece. For

LEFT: **This long narrow Seattle garden with its zigzag of arches, cleverly set at angles down the central path and hung with lanterns, has a quality of its own.**

the romance of geometric structure, there's nothing to match dwarf hedges with topiary features – balls or more fancy finials – rising at the corners, nor, for pure prettiness, the simple device of linking beds with arches.

ARCHES

Arches can be made from all sorts of materials. Planed wood, plastic-coated tubular steel, rustic poles, trellis-work and wrought-iron are among the most common materials used to construct arches (see Supports, pp.71–3). If soft-stemmed and tendrilled climbers such as clematis, honeysuckle and climbing beans are to be grown up them, there will need to be some kind of mesh infill to provide support. Fruit trees, roses and hard-stemmed climbers can simply be trained to the bare framework.

Making a living willow arch is something of an experimental technique, but worth considering for a quick, green and unusual entrance. We made an arching willow gateway and were delighted with its rural charm, and the spiral pattern of the arch, even though several of the spirals failed to root in dry weather.

The arch must be constructed in early spring while the freshly cut willow is dormant. Use a vigorous willow cultivar such as *Salix viminalis* 'Bowles' Hybrid'. One bundle of 50 rods would be sufficient to make an arch of two linked pillars for a 1.15m (3ft 6in) wide gateway. The method is very similar to that for making a fedge (see pp.54–5). Mark out circles of 45cm (18in) diameter on either side of the gateway. Clear the ground of weeds, and lay heavy black polythene over the area extending 15cm (6in) beyond the circles. For the uprights of the pillars, select long straight rods about 1–2cm (½–¾in) thick. Trim off all sideshoots, and insert the rods into 30cm (12in) deep holes around the circumference of each circle, about 20cm (8in) apart. For the weavers, use thinner rods of 5mm (¼in) diameter. Make angled holes for them alongside, but outside, each upright. Weave them in and out of the uprights to make a spiral. The spiral can be fairly steep; aim to keep the willow vertical rather than horizontal and weave it loosely, so the sap flow is not restricted. It is easiest to start weaving from the top, working downwards. Push the weavers into the holes in the ground as deeply as possible. To keep the spacing even, twist loose ties around the points where rods and weavers overlap, but remove them later in the year to prevent growth being restricted. When the weaving is completed bunch the loose ends together as high as you can, and tie them temporarily.

For the overhead arch, the tops of rods on either side are twisted together. It may be easier to twist adjacent rods into pairs, then twist the pairs from opposite sides together. Tie them loosely until they knit together in the summer. Protect from rabbits if necessary, and keep the willows watered until they are well established. Twist in young growths in the direction of the spirals, using them to fill gaps.

MAKING A WILLOW ARCH

1 For a gateway pillar push long willow rods into the soil, and weave the finer stems between. The wood must be dormant at this stage.

2 To form the arch tie the uprights loosely near the top, and weave the ends together overhead. It is easier to work with paired stems.

SEATS AND ARBOURS

Seats and benches can blend quietly into the lines of a fluid design, but an arbour attracts attention and draws you to it – whether it is a seat beneath an arch or a nook enclosed in trellis. It can be the loveliest feature in the garden, and a vehicle for decorative climbing plants or climbing vegetables and fruit (see Climbers, pp.86–9). Build it from any of the materials used to make an arch, but it must be strong enough to support vigorous plants. Grow fragrant herbs, such as camomile and creeping thymes on the ground nearby or in the seat itself. For this the seat must have solid sides, of brick for example, so that it can be filled with rubble topped by 10cm (4in) of soil. Embed a couple of paving stones or short planks in the top to sit on, and set the plants between them. They will soon spread to cover the bare soil.

RIGHT: **Four years after it was planted this honeysuckle,** *Lonicera periclymenum* **'Early Dutch', had completely covered the back of the arbour seat in the Hatfield House knot garden, Hertfordshire.**

BELOW: **Potagers must be savoured in a leisurely way and there is no better way to do this than from a homely seat.**

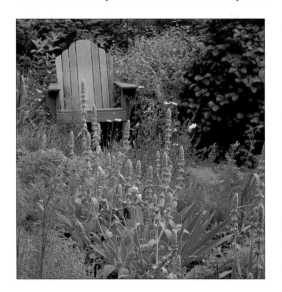

STANDARD TREES

A 'standard' tree is a small tree grown on a bare stem or 'leg' that is roughly shoulder height. A 'half-standard' has a stem about 1.2m (4ft) high. Trees that are suitable for growing in this way naturally form a branching head that can be kept small, or, alternatively, trimmed into a neat mophead or 'lollipop'.

Standards are elegant and decorative, and are easily fitted into gardens at key points in the design. For example, they can be planted down a main access or in the centre of a bed. Here standard fruit trees are the most appropriate and it is often practicable to grow vegetables and herbs around the stem. Evergreens make striking silhouettes: bay (both the golden and ordinary form), box, *Elaeagnus*, holly, Portuguese laurel and privet are commonly used. For colourful blossoms, honeysuckle, *Hydrangea paniculata* 'Grandiflora', magnolias, roses and wisteria are among many possibilities. For a subtle leaf colour, variegated *Euonymus* or grey-leaved willows such as *Salix helvetica*, with its catkins that appear in spring, can be superb. Buy standards from good nurserymen. Some have to be grafted to ensure strong stems or a weeping form. Rose standards, for example, are usually grafted onto a *Rosa rugosa* rootstock.

Training a standard mophead honey-suckle There are various ways of training honeysuckle standards. The method described below is used in the potager at Hatfield House, in Hertfordshire, south England, to form heads with a good combination of small branches and twigs, which retain a firm shape when clipped back after flowering. It has proved successful with all varieties of climbing honeysuckle, except the soft-stemmed variegated *Lonicera japonica* 'Aureovariegata'.

Start with a young plant in a 30cm (12in) pot. In spring select the two strongest shoots coming from the base and tie them to a cane. Remove the other shoots. (If there is only one weak stem, nip off the top leaving two buds. When shoots develop from these, tie them to the cane.) Allow the stems to grow to the height of stem you eventually require, usually 1.2m (4ft), making allowances for the depth of the pot. Then pinch out the top of the strongest shoot, and remove the other completely at the base. Two to four shoots then develop on the main shoot. When they are 10cm (4in) or so long, nip off the tips; each makes six to eight more shoots. Do this several times during the summer. Keep the plant in a pot over the winter, planting it out in its permanent position any time the following summer once the head is shaping nicely. Stake it with a 4cm (1½in) square pressure-treated post. It will be well established within two years.

Training a hawthorn crown 'on a leg' in an established hedge Hawthorn is fast growing, so a crown can be shaping nicely within two to three years. In spring select a strong shoot in the required position. If you want a leg of 75cm (30in), cut off the top slightly higher than this. Once the top is removed sideshoots will develop on the stem. Take off all of them apart from four near the top. As these

grow during summer, keep nipping out their tips when the new shoots are 10–15cm (4–6in) long, so they produce more sideshoots. It may be necessary to pinch out four times during the summer. Aim to keep the crown balanced and compact; it can gradually increase in size over the next few years. In the following season clip it to shape when the main hedge pruning is done. To keep it looking tidy this could be in late spring and early summer; otherwise clip it once in late summer.

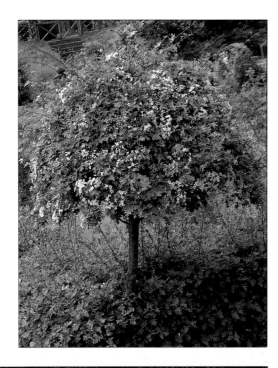

RIGHT: **The hawthorn crowns rising elegantly out of the thorn hedge are a dominant feature in the knot garden boundary at Hatfield House.**

BELOW: **Honeysuckle is a rapid grower and can easily be trained into an attractive standard feature, as seen here in the herb garden at Hatfield House, Hertfordshire.**

ABOVE: **In the winter evergreens reveal the bare bones of the garden and are a source of delight. At Barnsley House dark slender spires of fastigiate box contrast with the domed pyramids of common box, *Buxus sempervirens*, and the dwarf balls of golden box, *B. s.* 'Elegantissima'.**

LEFT: **Golden privet *Ligustrum ovalifolium* 'Aureum' is a fast-growing shrub, easily trained into eye-catching standards. It normally keeps its leaves in winter. Here it is elegantly paired with two-tiered *Buxus sempervirens*.**

TOPIARY

Simple forms of topiary – the art of clipping plants into decorative shapes – can be used to great effect in a formal or semi-formal potager. Free-standing forms can be grown at strategic points, topiary 'finials', typically cones and balls, can be trained to decorate dwarf hedges, while small topiaries can be grown in pots, to be moved around the garden or taken under cover in winter if necessary.

Of the many plants used in topiary, the most popular are evergreen hedging plants such as box, holly, ivies, juniper, privet, *Thuja*, yew and, in warm climates, bay, box and *Cupressus*. Myrtle, rosemary, sage and santolina are among herbs that can be clipped or trained into topiary shapes. A good topiary plant must have small supple leaves, the ability to recover quickly after clipping and, within reason, be relatively slow growing so that it retains its shape without the need for frequent clipping. Outdoor topiaries must be hardy. Of the hedging plants, box and yew are the easiest and most manageable to train.

Topiaries grow much faster in the ground than in pots, so those destined for pots can be started in the ground, then lifted and transplanted into the containers. The principles for creating simple topiary are illustrated here with box, but apply equally to other subjects. Basic shapes can be trained by eye, without the frames used for complex topiary, and are a good choice for a first attempt.

Box topiary *Buxus sempervirens* is the most suitable form for topiary, although the cultivar 'Suffruticosa', used for dwarf hedges, is too slow growing for all but the smallest pieces. So if corner cones are required in a bed edged with 'Suffruticosa', plant closely-matched plants of ordinary *B. sempervirens* at each corner.

Selecting good plants is the key to success. Whatever the final shape, look for naturally bushy plants, with plenty of shoots coming from low down on the stem. Discard thin tall plants with branches coming out at right angles, as they tend to go bare near the main stem and never train well.

To make a free-standing topiary ball, start with a bushy plant 23–25cm (9–10in) high. Start shaping in late spring to early summer when it is growing well. Working from above, clip back the shoots into a rough round shape, reducing it to about 15cm (6in) high. After the next flush of growth, later in the year, when it is beginning to grow out of its shape, clip it back again. Repeat this the following year. Once the ball has reached the required size it can be trimmed back harder to keep it within bounds which, in turn, helps it to become progressively more solid. A cone would be approached in a similar way, possibly starting with a slightly taller plant.

To train a shape out of an existing hedge, leave several shoots unpruned where the topiary will be. When they are 7.5–10cm (3–4in) long, prune back the tips to encourage them to branch out. Start to shape the topiary when there's a reasonable amount of bushy growth on which to work.

SUPPORTS

It is surprising how often the supports catch your eye in a vegetable garden, and this is not just because the plants on them are flamboyant, but because of their intrinsic texture or shape, and the patterns they can make. An arch, a trellis, criss-crossing bamboo canes, even a row of rough old stakes may be there for purely practical reasons, yet give a garden an elusive charm. A few ideas on combining practicalities and aesthetics will, therefore, not come amiss, focusing on the materials most commonly used for supporting decorative and edible climbers.

Bamboo The more rigid a bamboo cane structure, the better it looks. In the classic tepee, the canes are simply tied together near the top. If the tips are threaded through a metal or rigid plastic ring they stand more evenly, with less crowding at the top. Rows of closely spaced, crossed canes look striking but use a lot of canes. In Vermont I saw an elegant and efficient system based on sets of 'four-cane tepees' made up of two canes 60cm (24in) apart each side of the row with 60cm–1m (2–3ft) gaps between each set. The tops were linked with horizontal canes, while side supports were made from parallel rows of twine knotted around each cane. The strings were 10cm (4in) apart for lightweight crops such as peas, and 30cm (12in) apart for heavier climbers such as melons or cucumbers, which also required heavier and longer canes.

Long, crossed bamboo canes are a basic frame for supporting climbing beans. For an unusual effect, arrange the rows like the spokes of a wheel, or as dissecting diagonals across a bed. This can also be done equally with a metal or timber frame. To take the weight and height of the crop, canes should be 2cm (¾in) in diameter, at least 2.75m (9ft) long, and pushed up to 30cm (12in) deep into the soil.

LEFT: **Like spokes of a wheel, the bamboo cane structure criss-crossing a bed at Barnsley House makes a very theatrical support for climbers.**

BELOW: **The crisp patterns of a potager are lost if plants are badly staked. For a tidy look, secure tall tomatoes like 'Gardener's delight' to strong canes or stakes.**

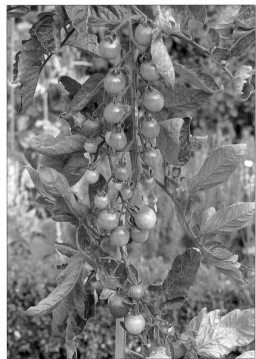

Ways with wood For a natural look, young stems and saplings of birch, hazel, willow or any wood supple enough to bend, make wonderful supports. Most of them become brittle with exposure, so are best made afresh each season. Young willow, which has a lovely gleam to it, and hazel, which is more substantial,

can be made into arches, screens, tunnels and tepees. Use thicker stems for uprights and thinner stems to weave a framework of horizontal supports, tying crossing stems where necessary. Basketry tepees of woven willow last four years.

Grow your own willows using a vigorous variety such as 'Bowles' Hybrid'. Push 30cm (12in) long cuttings of 1cm (½in) diameter into the ground in spring, leaving two or three buds above ground, spacing them about 1m (3ft) apart. Cut them back hard each year.

At Hatfield House, in Hertfordshire, south England, they have reinvented the medieval art of using untrimmed 2.5m (8ft) long birch saplings to make domed twiggy 'huts' as a support for sweet peas, and other ornamental and climbing vegetables. The secret is to make a circle with branches pushed into the ground leaning outwards: the tips can then be drawn together at the top and interwoven. Horizontal rungs are made by interweaving the slender side branches together.

BELOW: **An eerie 'Dream Catcher', made from string and Californian bay laurel (*Umbellularia californica*) at the Occidental Arts and Ecology Center in California, USA.**

Young stems of trees such as olives and bay can be plaited together as they grow to make a multi-stemmed plant: the stems eventually callus together where they touch. Hornbeams can also be trained in this way and the crowns clipped into stark spindle silhouettes.

Wood is often used for more permanent supports. Use short stretches of post and rail fencing to aid scramblers, or wooden obelisks for a formal note. Trellis work can be dramatic, whether used as free-standing arches, an arbour surround, a boundary fence, a screen or as a panel attached to a wall or fence. The size and shape of the patterning itself makes an impact: the effect of large 30cm (12in) squares is very different from that of tiny diamond screening.

Metal Metal structures have the advantage of durability, rigidity and a wonderful choice of shapes and silhouettes. For any soft-stemmed climber, there must be an infill to provide support. Fine-mesh steel lattice and black knotted twine net look best, although rigid and flexible plastic are available. For most edible climbers 10cm (4in) mesh is adequate. Soft options include biodegradable twine, which rots away at the end of the season, and even strong-ply wool, which can be woven between uprights.

Concrete reinforcing wire is by no means a glamorous product, but it can be used to good effect. Long strips can be cut with bolt cutters, stood on edge and overlapped at the top to make archways. A roll can be stood on end to surround and screen unsightly features or support tall tomatoes. It can be fixed to a wall at an angle to make a sloping frame, or attached to posts to make an upright trellis. It can even be arched over at ground level to make a low supporting tunnel for bush tomatoes. All sorts of farm fencing can be used as garden supports. Finally, edible, as well as decorative climbers can be trained up, and even over a fruit cage.

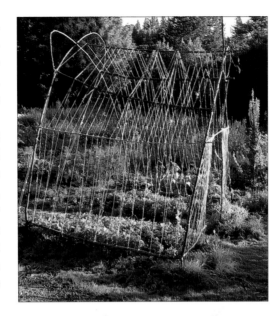

ABOVE: **Another structure made in a very different shape but from the same materials as the support shown opposite. Hops, pole or climbing beans and morning glory are some of the plants trained on them.**

BELOW: **The wigwam is one of the most widely used structures for climbing beans. It makes economic use of space, hence its popularity in small gardens.**

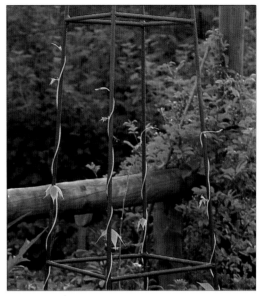

ABOVE: **The sunlight catches the tips of the runner beans, as they make their way elegantly up a slender obelisk frame, made of thin galvanized metal. The support is strong enough to take the weight of heavy climbers.**

BELOW: **Metal arches planted with cordon pears span a main axis in the restored four-square Victorian kitchen garden at West Dean, west Sussex, south-east England.**

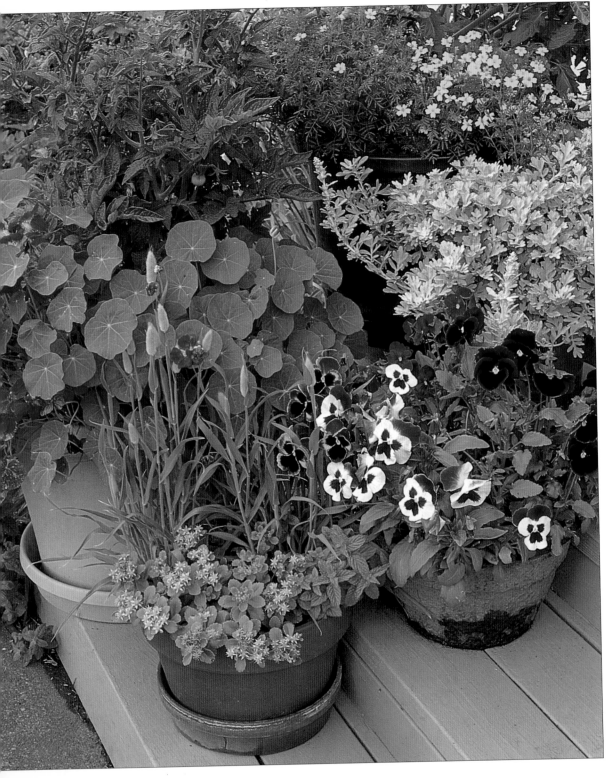

CONTAINERS

If your priority is keeping the larder shelves stocked with vegetables and fruit, growing them in containers will never be first choice. The bald facts are that productivity is low and a lot of work is required to get the best results. But where space is restricted and the 'garden' is a paved yard or rooftop, patio or balcony, the imaginative use of pots, tubs and window boxes to grow edibles is well worth the effort. And there is one advantage: tender plants grown in pots are easily moved to shelter in winter.

Beautiful pots also come into their own as decorative features. Unless they are too heavy to move, treat them as mobile focal points. The *pièce de resistance* of a potager is so often the right plant in the right pot in the right place.

A list of artefacts that can serve as planters would be very long. First to consider is the range of ordinary pots, tubs, troughs and boxes designed for gardening. On aesthetic grounds choose the best looking: handmade terracotta pots, for example, have a classiness that is never matched in mass-produced pots. On practical grounds go for the largest containers possible: the greater the volume of soil, the fewer the problems with drying out and feeding, and the better growth will be. Ugly containers can be concealed inside baskets of wicker or woven bark, or hidden behind a painted board or within a classic square 'Versailles' planter. Even the popular plastic growing-bags, which are never easy on the eye (unless sprawling plants are grown to conceal the plastic edges), can be made to look better if they are treated as panniers. Hold an unopened bag in the centre and shake the contents evenly to either end

LEFT: **In small gardens space can be saved and colour generated on doorsteps and patios by growing vegetables, edible flowers and herbs in pots.**

before straddling it over a strong rail or fence. Then cut planting slits on either side 7.5cm (3in) below the centre. All will be hidden with a crop of cascading 'Tumbler' tomatoes.

Provided they have good drainage (see p.77), improvized containers can be made out of anything from discarded domestic basins and sinks, to tyres, buckets, metal drums, chimney pots and wheelbarrows.

Plants for containers Among useful plants, herbs are most at home in the confines of pots, especially the undemanding Mediterranean herbs. Basil, marjoram, summer and winter savory, and thyme are happy in small pots, 10–12cm (4–5in) in width and depth; shrubbier species such as bay, juniper, lavender, lemon verbena, myrtle, rosemary, ordinary and pineapple sage, and tarragon require pots of at least 23cm (9in) in diameter and depth; they'll grow bigger in larger pots. Potentially tall herbs such as anise hyssop, fennel and sweet cicely can look wonderful in generous pots of 45cm (18in) in diameter and depth, but stake them subtly if necessary. Chives, lemon balm, culinary mints and parsley thrive in pots but need a moist and fairly rich soil, as do garlic chives and society garlic (*Tulbaghia*), which is a lovely flowering herb. Shallow containers, such as a standard seedtray 5cm (2in) deep, can be sown with caraway, dill, coriander and chervil, for cutting in the seedling stage.

With vegetables, the maxim 'the larger the pot, the better the crop' generally applies. Provided the soil is rich and well drained, nearly all vegetables can be grown successfully in containers, but some are more suitable than others. Many members of the *Solanaceae* family, for example aubergine, cape gooseberry, ground cherry, peppers, tomatillo and tomatoes, do well and look good in pots. Others have the foliage to make handsome pot plants:

ABOVE: **Many herbs thrive in the restricted environment of pots. Here** *Salvia officinalis* **'Berggarten' adds a decorative touch on the perimeter of a tiny potager.**

BELOW: **In the garden at Ballymaloe Cookery School a colourful pot of French marigolds (***Tagetes***) may keep whitefly away from the 'Tumbler' tomatoes nearby.**

BELOW: **A central cluster of pots, growing everything from an acid-loving blueberry to edible flowers, increases precious growing space in a small garden.**

the semi-tropical taro (*Colocasia esculenta*), with its arum-like leaves for one; silver-leaved courgettes for another. Climbing beans can get a foothold in a roomy pot then romp upwards. The ornamental kales and cabbages, with their wonderful spectrum of leaf colour, shapes and textures, are established favourites as autumn and early winter pot plants. Cut-and-come-again seedling salads (see p.110–13) look fresh

BELOW: **Room is found in this tiny garden for a large container crammed with colourful ornamental kales and sages. (See the Plan of an Informal Potager, pp.30–1.)**

and make excellent use of small containers and window boxes. For winter salads, grow salad burnet, corn salad, young spinach, land cress and 'Grumolo' chicory in shallow containers, and sorrel, Welsh and oriental bunching onions in deeper ones. Strawberries grow well and look pretty in pots.

Fruit trees make beautiful pot specimens, though skill is required to grow them well. Again, Mediterranean fruits head the list: grapes, figs, medlars, mulberry, olives and the citruses orange, lemon and lime. Hardy fruits including apples, blueberry, cherries, currants,

gooseberries, nectarine, pears and peaches can all be accommodated in pots, as can many exotic fruits, from persimmon to loquat. It is important to choose suitable varieties.

Pots and topiary marry well. The angular shapes of evergreens, typically box, or clipped grey-leaved santolina, can be shown off perfectly, as can herbs trained into round-headed standards. This works best with bay (the stem can be straight or dramatically twisted), lemon verbena, sage and rosemary. Some herbs, rosemary is one of the most willing, can be trained into eloquent spiral-shapes, spheres or layered

plants. A small tree specimen – weeping, half-standard or standard – can make a handsome centrepiece when grown in a fine pot or urn.

The quickest, easiest and most effective way to bring colour to containers is to grow flowers in them. Undemanding annuals such as convolvulus, eschscholtzia, lobelia, love-in-a-mist, nemesia, nemophila, to name a few, will happily co-exist with vegetables, or snuggle around the stem of a standard tree or herb. Mahogany-coloured French marigolds and parsley are a great combination. The purist can narrow the choice to edible flowers such as chrysanthemums, daylilies, fuchsias, nasturtiums, pansies, pelargoniums, pinks or pot marigolds. There are many more.

See the Plant Directory for cultivars of vegetables, herbs, fruits and edible flowers most suitable for containers.

Container practicalities Garden soil on its own is generally unsuitable for containers, as it tends to become compacted with the constant watering. For vegetables, it is best to use top-quality general-purpose potting compost, or good garden soil lightened with generous handfuls of well-rotted garden compost, potting compost (which can be once-used), worm compost, peat substitutes, coarse sand or vermiculite. For herbs, work in plenty of grit to ensure good drainage. For fruit and tree specimens, use good soil-based potting composts. As a rule, use fresh soil each season for annual crops. With perennial subjects at least replace the top 5cm (2in) of soil annually, repotting every two or three years.

With the general exception of herbs, plants grown in pots for more than a few months must have regular supplementary feeding. As a basic guide, feed vegetables with a general-purpose liquid feed or seaweed-based fertilizer every three weeks or so during the growing season.

Fruit trees need to be fed with a high potassium feed, such as a tomato fertilizer, roughly every two weeks from spring until the fruits start to ripen. Evergreen topiaries such as box should be top-dressed in spring with general-purpose fertilizer or blood, fish and bone, which supplies nitrogen and potash. During the growing season, feed every two weeks with a seaweed-based or tomato fertilizer.

One of the trickiest aspects of growing plants in pots is watering and drainage. Cover drainage holes with a good layer of crocks. With improvized containers, drill drainage holes of at least 1cm (½in) diameter in the bottom. Otherwise line them with a 7.5cm (3in) layer of crocks or charcoal to prevent waterlogging and to absorb moisture.

In hot and windy weather, pots dry out very rapidly. To conserve the moisture as much as possible, line the insides with heavy polythene, and mulch the surface with a layer at least 2.5cm (¾in) deep of gravel, stone or bark chippings. They may need watering several times a day: aim to keep the soil just damp to the touch. Where waterlogging through over-watering or high rainfall is a risk, raise pots off the ground on 'feet'.

New terracotta pots should be soaked before use, otherwise they will absorb a lot of moisture from the soil (unless they have been lined). Keep a saucer beneath them to conserve moisture in summer, but raise them off the ground in winter. Good quality pots are frost-proof, but if they are left empty in winter, store them upside down in a sheltered place.

Plants often look untidy in pots unless they are supported. Use wire or young stems of willow, dogwood or bamboo to make small domed mushroom-shaped frames. Put them in place soon after sowing or planting so the plants grow through to hide them.

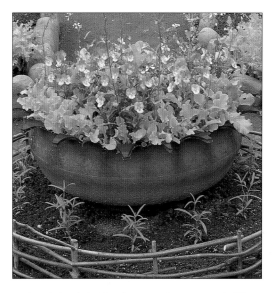

ABOVE: **A simple but lovely centrepiece to Dean Riddle's potager, upstate New York, is a large circular pot made from a tyre where violas peep over the top of salad rocket seedlings.**

BELOW: **Growing bulbs in tubs that can be moved around is one way of introducing colour to a vegetable garden in the bleaker months of late winter and early spring.**

DRAMATIC EFFECTS

DRAMATIC EFFECTS IN THE GARDEN are often associated with carefully designed landscaped vistas or ornamental displays. But drama in the kitchen garden? Nobody expects it, which may be why it has its own, special quality. You may work very hard to achieve drama, whether it's a crisp pattern of beds outlined with trimmed hedges or blue leeks interwoven with red lettuce. Yet sometimes nature takes a hand by sowing an uninvited seedling in a perfect spot, or enticing a runner bean to twine up a nearby stem. And the loveliest effects are so often unexpected: early morning sunlight on dew-laden dill or ruby chard leaves glowing with the sun behind them, or the towering silhouette of thistleheads on maturing cardoons. There's no infallible formula for creating drama in the potager, but this chapter looks at strategies that may help.

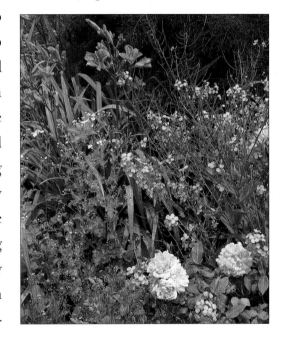

(See A–Z Directory pp.150–199 for detailed description, cultivation, further uses and cultivars of most plants mentioned in this chapter.)

LEFT: **Vegetables can be as dramatic as any decorative plants, once the rigidity of the conventional kitchen garden is abandoned.**

ABOVE: **The many edible flowers like daylilies, borage, pinks and roses can bring the drama of colour to the potager.**

PLANTING FOR EFFECT

Whether a kitchen garden will be conventional or 'creative' in character is determined by the way the vegetables are planted. As soon as planting for effect becomes a priority, the gardener will start to view and treat the vegetables in a similar way to herbaceous perennials or bedding plants, yet as one of Villandry's previous owners, François Carvallo pointed out, vegetables have a lot more to offer than mere flowers. Instead of having one burst of colourful flowering they retain their beauty over a long period, and in their gradual maturing they display infinitely varying colours. To support this view, he cites a red cabbage, grey-green at first, then bluish, and finally turning a sumptuous 'Veronese red'.

In my mind, the beds in a potager are framed canvases waiting for their paintings. Vegetables, with help from herbs and flowers, provide the palette from which we choose the colours and textures. As for style, you could say the choices break down broadly into the 'patterned' school and the 'landscape' school. The

former has its roots in the classical parterre. Here the impact comes from the juxtaposition of blocks of colour or strongly textured vegetables of even height, or from patterns made by planting visually complementary or contrasting types of vegetables near each other. These are essentially variations on formal bedding themes, so the style naturally suits a formal design, yet can also be adopted in informal settings. In the more informal 'landscaping' approach drama, more likely than not, will be provided by a strong focal point or feature. A single plant or group of plants of outstanding beauty, height or colour will draw the eye to the centre or far side of a

LEFT: **The simple device of planting or sowing on the diagonal instead of at right angles can be very effective in both small and large gardens. The colourful seedlings in the foreground are 'Russian' kale.**

ABOVE: **Individual plots in communal gardens are so small that vegetables are often tucked in behind cheery edgings of flowers and herbs with picturesque results.**

garden. The picture is completed by balancing and blending this pivotal feature with plants of different colours, textures and habit, whether climbers, ground-cover sprawlers, or sturdy-stemmed greens.

Whatever the approach, it is not usually necessary to make complex planting plans: rough sketches suffice. If you do want to keep to a precise plan, the main thing is to work out roughly how many plants you will need of each, then, if you're a pessimist (or perhaps a realist), raise about a third more. Given the vagaries of vegetable growing, it's a good idea to have some alternatives up your sleeve in case one crop fails. For example, red lettuce can be substituted for beetroot at the last moment, if needs be. I've so often found that a spontaneous approach to the potager has given rise to the loveliest, unexpected effects.

ARCHITECTURAL AND DRAMATIC PLANTS

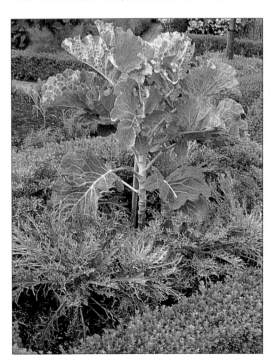

ABOVE: **Did this happen or was it planned? Whatever the answer, the sight of sunflower heads peering through the ripening sweet corn brings a smile of enjoyment.**

BELOW: **Jersey kale can grow to a height of 1.5m (5ft) dominating the skyline. Here it rises gracefully from a 'skirt' of ornamental kale, which conceals its bare stem.**

There is a handful of vegetables with such fine architectural qualities that it would seem almost criminal not to include them in a decorative vegetable garden. The trouble is that some of them are giants. For example, the cardoon (*Cynara cardunculus*) has beautiful purple, thistle-like flowers (see p.35) and blue-grey leaves but can reach 1.5m (5ft) tall with an equal spread. Where there is room to show it off, it makes a flamboyant centrepiece but otherwise it is best used as a background plant. Another handsome giant is the sweet coltsfoot (*Petasites japonicus*), grown for its edible stems and flower buds. But beware, it can be very invasive.

All tall vegetables have dramatic potential. The question is do they have the poise to carry it off? Among vegetables grown in temperate climates, sweet and ornamental corn are the most successful, Jerusalem artichokes and orache rather less so and the gaunt but lovable Jersey kale is a more awkward customer. It is surprising how effectively tall vegetables can be constrained within the confines of box-edged beds; even 2.5m (8ft) high Jerusalem artichokes can put on a well-mannered air. Giant kales can also be grown in this way but surround them with a 'skirt' of say kales or fennel to hide their knobbly-kneed stems. In climates with long, hot summers, tall-growing grain crops, such as grain amaranths, quinoa, sesame and sorghum, are the undisputed glamour queens. They produce magnificent, brilliantly coloured crimson to gold seedheads on mighty, some-times highly-coloured stems. Nor must we forget sunflowers, grown with such stunning

BELOW: **Jerusalem artichokes are normally banished to the garden boundary, where they can double as a windbreak. Yet here they have tremendous presence.**

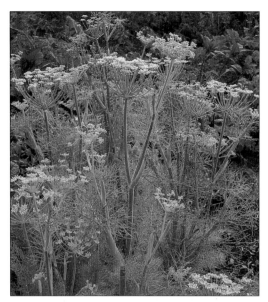

effect in so many vegetable gardens. Other less common tall vegetables and herbs include skirret, herb patience, lovage and angelica.

Tall vegetables can make wonderful and effective screens, effortlessly blocking out ugly walls and surfaces. Jerusalem artichokes and sunflowers can be grown as windbreaks, provided the sunflowers are planted closely in a band several rows deep. Sweet corn is a gift for the ornamental garden: as well as providing an effective screen at every stage of growth there is some feature that gleams in the sunlight – the leaves, the tassels, the silks. Among the most theatrical are some ornamental forms: clumps of 'Red Stalker' or 'Sugar Dots' against a blue sky are an unforgettable sight.

The statuesque vegetables of more modest dimensions, such as globe artichokes, rhubarb and the bush forms of courgettes, marrows and other members of the squash family, are easier to position in a garden. They all cut a fine figure and have beautiful leaves. Rhubarb, being a hardy perennial, makes a strong 'hedge' behind a vegetable border, although it dies right back in winter. Unless severe frost is the norm, a row of globe artichokes can make the most dramatic boundary. Both rhubarb and globe artichokes can also merge into a group blending best, perhaps, with feathery-leaved vegetables and herbs such as fennel, angelica and sweet cicely. With the squash family, it is worth studying varieties carefully so that you can make the most of their visual qualities. Courgettes with mottled grey leaves (see pp.184–5 for varieties) can be dotted around beds to provide highlights or, because the modern hybrids are even in height, planted to form a silvery curve through the garden. Single plants of 'Custard' or 'Patty Pan' marrows and 'Triple Crown' summer squash are large and handsome enough to serve as focal points in a planting scheme or, the ultimate accolade, to be given a small bed to themselves.

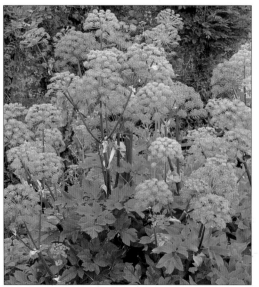

DRAMA FROM SEEDHEADS AND FLOWERING VEGETABLES

There is no doubt that some of the loveliest and often most unexpected effects in the kitchen garden come from vegetables, flowers and herbs that have run to seed. Some, of course, are grown for their seed, as is the case with the grain crops mentioned on page 81, sweet corn, and herbs such as dill, coriander, the herb celeries, fennel and caraway, where seeds are used for seasoning. Frequently plants run to seed at the end of their useful life. Sometimes, typically with beetroot, celeriac, lettuce or radish, they may do so prematurely (known as bolting) due to unfavourable weather. But there is also the option of leaving the plant unharvested simply for the delight of seeing the flowers and/or seedheads that eventually develop. This may seem an indulgence to the serious vegetable grower, but because leaving even one plant can have spectacular results, it is a practice that is easy to justify. I would also advise, in the cause of beauty, against clearing away old seedheads too diligently in autumn. Their fragile outlines can look marvellous in frost, and they provide valuable fodder for seed-eating birds.

Different botanical families produce particular types of flower and seedhead effects.

Umbelliferae Probably the most spectacular members of this family are those with laced, flat-topped seedheads, so often swarming with beneficial insects. The giants here are angelica and lovage, both of which become huge plants when seeding, so are best placed at the back of the border. To a lesser extent, this is true of sweet cicely and skirret. With the 'vegetable'

umbellifers, it is sufficient to leave a plant or two to run to seed where it has been growing. This works very well with celery and celeriac, parsnip, parsley, Florence fennel and carrots. They have such light, feathery foliage and flowerheads that other plants can continue growing around them, even beneath them. With some, notably parsley and hardy celery, a mass of seedlings will appear the following season and can usefully be transplanted into other positions. Dill deserves special mention, with its delicate seedheads that may reach 1.2–1.5m (4–5ft), turning slowly from fresh green to gold to bronze. It is a natural self-seeder too, but the sparkling carpet of seedlings should be left to grow where they appear, as they are too fragile

to transplant. The same applies to the seedlings of bronze fennel. Most of these umbelliferous seedheads can be used in flower arrangements.

Compositae The daisy family is full of surprises. Cardoons and globe artichokes have already been mentioned (pp.81–82), but how gorgeous the scaly heads with their fluffy purple rims look among the pompons of flowering leeks. The chicories form stunning spires of blue flowers when seeding. This is a classic example of a plant that is modest and low-growing in its vegetative phase, then bursts into

BELOW: **The giant fennel,** *Ferula communis,* **towers over seeding celery 'Parcel', in a garden where perennials and colourful herbs abound in the potager beds.**

ABOVE: **Like so many *Cruciferae* mizuna greens has edible blossoms, so is left to flower to create a bright patch in the garden and an extra ingredient for the salad bowl.**

a vast, multi-stemmed, flowering clump in late spring or early summer. It can reach 2.5m (8ft) high and over several weeks it is transformed, every morning, into a pillar of blue, though the flowers, which are a lovely addition to salads, have generally faded and closed by noon. One summer a corner of my potager was shared by a harmonious grouping of flowering chicory, blue hyssop, seeding leeks and red cabbage in its blue-tinted stage. They blended perfectly.

To most gardeners, a bolting lettuce is an unhappy sight, a sign of failure. But it undoubtedly has its compensations. Seeding lettuces,

which generally grow up to about 1m (3ft), make the most natural 'dot' plants, and look pretty over a surprisingly long period. Even if the leafy tufts are picked off for decoration, the stems continue to produce new flushes of leaves. On the whole, the red varieties have the dramatic edge over the green, though if they are interplanted the result can be a delightful bicoloured forest of miniature cones. The loose-headed 'Salad Bowl' types and, in particular, the deeply curled 'Lollo' varieties, seem to make the neatest spires, though I've also seen good effects with cos and crisp-headed varieties. Curly endive, too, makes handsome green spires when seeding and has pinkish flowers. I planted it one year as a dividing line across a bed, leaving alternate plants to run to seed. They turned into a very perky row of sentinels, each about 38cm (15in) high.

The constantly twinned root vegetables, scorzonera and salsify, both have colourful flowers – scorzonera, yellow and salsify, pale mauve – but their glory is in their powder-puff seedheads, which develop in autumn. The flower buds, incidentally, are

LEFT: **Spicy salad rocket runs to seed speedily, but should be left in place, as the flowers are dainty and colourful, and the seedheads that follow not only have their own charm, but enable the plant to self-seed.**

RIGHT: **Cauliflower looks dramatic in the winter potager in early spring, when most winter vegetables are on the wane. The plants are relatively slow to mature, but their stateliness makes them rewarding to grow.**

delicious, so if the stomach vies with the soul, eat some but make sure you leave a few to seed.

Cruciferae Being the backbone of a great many vegetable gardens, the members of the *Cruciferae* family, which embraces the cabbage family, have an image of worthy dullness. They are normally consumed or composted long before they have a chance to flower, but when they do so, usually as the result of neglect, they bring an unexpected blaze of colour to the garden when it is at its most bleak. Those with a reddish tinge to the leaves, which includes red Brussels sprouts, purple mustard and the reddish kales, are especially colourful. I love the

bright yellow, sweetly scented flowers of the oriental greens, shooting up to 1.5m (5ft) in spring in my polytunnel. Beautiful too are the flowers of seeding radish, which are sometimes pink and sometimes white. They can flower over many weeks. Keep picking the succulent young seedpods to use in salads and stir-fries: they're a treat. Cresses and salad rocket both make a very pretty bush when flowering. Use a few of the flowers in salads, then leave the rest to produce seed for sowing later or to self-seed for future pickings.

Allium In the onion family, it is leeks, with their creamy to purple, ball-shaped seedheads, which never fail to delight and attract the bees. Plant a few extra leeks here and there to seed. Whatever their neighbours, they never seem to clash, though letting them mingle with delphiniums is a particularly happy combination. My favourite in this family is garlic chives,

loved both for their pure white, starry flowers and their dainty seedheads. In some situations they self-seed into great snowy drifts.

Chenopodiaceae Some members of the beet family can be spectacular when they run to seed. With the sun behind them, the red-leaved and red-stemmed varieties glow like rubies, and the deeper the colour of the leaves, the brighter the glow, but even the green forms have quite a presence. Just leave the occasional plant, as they'll take quite a lot of space. Red orache, too, though its spires are daintier, can look wonderful running through a plot or in the background, but root out ruthlessly any plants that are a muddy colour or are depriving other plants of moisture. (The not dissimilar rhubarb must get a mention. Strictly speaking, you shouldn't let it flower as this weakens the plant, but who can say no to a few of those theatrical crusty brown flower stalks.)

Self-seeding flowers Allowing flowers to self-seed among vegetables is the easiest way to introduce colour into a vegetable garden. Let whatever flourishes have its head, whether it's borage, calendula, evening primrose, heartsease pansies, larkspur, nasturtiums or poppies. I have seen *Verbena bonariensis* looking marvellous growing among red cabbage, and cosmos amid gourds. The art lies in knowing what to pull out, and when, to prevent overcrowding and keep an aesthetic balance between established plants and the invaders.

FAR LEFT: **The globular seedheads of leeks provide some of the most dramatic touches to a kitchen garden.**

CENTRE: **The pods formed by maturing mustard plants have an unexpected geometry.**

BELOW: **Purple-flowering pak choi is reasonably hardy and brings colour into the garden in winter and spring.**

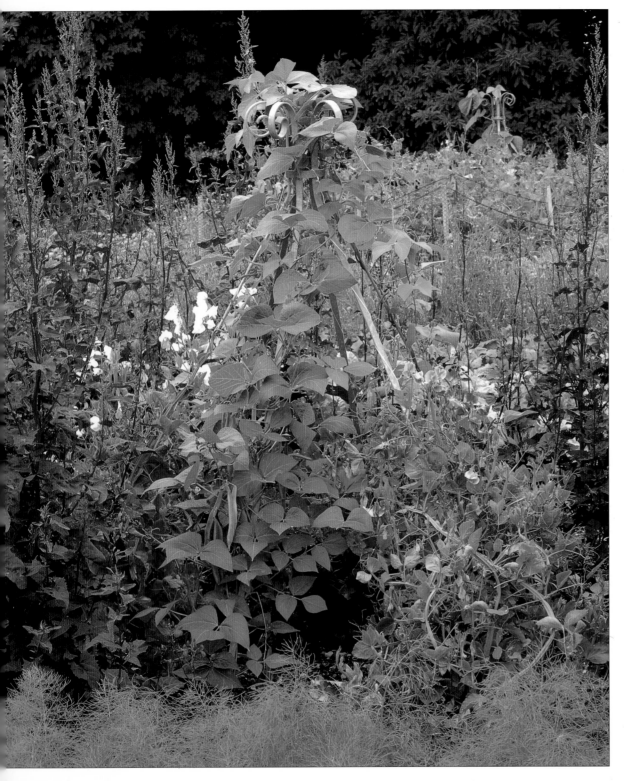

CLIMBERS

Climbers and scramblers tend to be charmers. When did you last see an ugly climbing plant? So any that have the twin virtues of good looks and usefulness merit pride of place in a 'creative' vegetable garden. The choice of climbers depends on the length of the growing season. In regions where summers are cool and short even cucumbers and ordinary climbing beans can be a gamble, whereas long summers and high temperatures mean that the wonderful range of semi-tropical beans, exotic squashes, yams and the yam bean, jicama, can all be grown, often with dramatic results.

Climbing vegetables can be used in many different ways. Arbours, archways, trellises and features that are part of the garden framework can all be adorned with climbers. They can be trained to permanent or temporary free-standing structures, such as obelisks and tepees, or even around a single pillar or post. The less rampant growers can sprawl over steel-wire or wood boundary fences, hurdles or over low fences serving as partitions within the garden. Berried fruits and grapevines can be trained on wires against solid walls and fences, on wires between posts, even along ropes and chains and up pillars.

In a few cases, climbers can be encouraged to ramble into and over existing trees and shrubs. Don't count on them as windbreaks; most climbers are adversely affected by high winds and need a little protection themselves, certainly until they are well established. It is also worth re-emphasizing the need for any

LEFT: **Mundane kitchen gardens are transformed if height is introduced, as here, at Ballymaloe Cookery School, with a tripod of runner beans, sweet peas and red orache.**

ABOVE: **Most climbers grow rapidly, so the scene is constantly changing under their influence. The warmer the climate, the greater the choice of edible climbers.**

supports to be strong and, where necessary, deeply anchored in the ground (see Supports, pp.71–3); mature bean and squash plants can be an enormous weight.

From a practical point of view, climbers and trailers can be divided into those that are truly self-supporting, being well-endowed with tendrils or twining stems (though even these may need a helping hand in the early stages), and those with essentially sprawling habits, which need firm guidance and must be tied to supports. To get the most out of climbers it is worth attaching discreet infills of wire mesh or netting to any framework, and wire mesh (such as pig fencing) to walls. Wandering stems and shoots can then be gently pushed back, encouraged in the right direction, or tied in place. In the case of free-standing structures, train the plants spirally around supports in the early stages of growth, to avoid a bare base.

There are many climbers that deserve a place in a vegetable garden besides those listed below, but sadly for gardeners in cool and temperate climates, many of them are tropical plants. The climbing Malabar spinach, *Basella* is one I wish I could grow outdoors. What lush jungle-like pillars it would make, with its red or green glossy leaves.

CULINARY CLIMBERS

Beans Climbing or pole beans are the most widely grown of the culinary climbers, partly because so many of the varieties have such colourful flowers and also because the twining stems climb so high with such agility. Runner beans, after all, were introduced from the New World to the Old as a decorative plant. The leaves are often not particularly beautiful, but the pods, especially the purple and red-streaked varieties of French bean, can look wonderful. So, of course, can the long slender pods of the semi-tropical 'Yard Long' bean.

It is possible to train beans up unusual supports: sunflowers, for example. The secret, in a coolish climate where beans are slow starters, is to get the sunflowers well established, and when they have reached a height of about 60cm (24in), plant a pot-raised bean at the base of each sunflower. It is also fun to take advantage of the different coloured bean flowers. One year my bamboo and willow trellis sported runner beans with white

RIGHT: **Climbers make excellent use of space. Here a passageway has been made decorative by letting runner beans clamber up sunflower 'Velvet Queen'.**

red, pink and bicoloured flowers along with French beans with deep purple flowers. They looked a picture together. I intend to fan-train several varieties, each with its own string, to climb against the willow fence at the back of my Little Potager (see pp.177–8 for varieties).

The oriental hyacinth or lablab bean (*Dolichos lablab*) is a popular climbing ornamental in warmer regions in the West, and it is a delicious culinary bean. Depending on the variety, the lovely spikes of flowers can be white to deep purple, in the latter case offset by pretty purplish leaves. The sun shining through the red pods is a wonderful sight, as is the combination of purple lablabs romping through pink rambler roses, a great partnership – on a par with purple French beans straying into swathes of *Clematis* 'Jackmanii'.

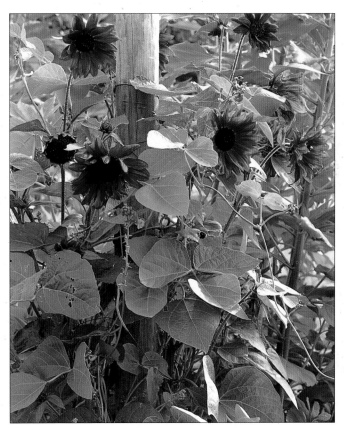

Most beans blend with climbing squashes, sweet peas and any decorative climbers that don't form too dense a canopy. I once saw a Californian garden where the neighbouring lot had been blocked out with a high fence smothered in 'Painted Lady' runner beans, sunflower (*Helianthus maximilianii*) and morning glory, and a riot of yellow, purple and pink was produced.

The 'cucurbit' group There are some superb climbers and sprawlers within this group, including cucumbers and gherkins, melons, watermelons and oriental gourds,

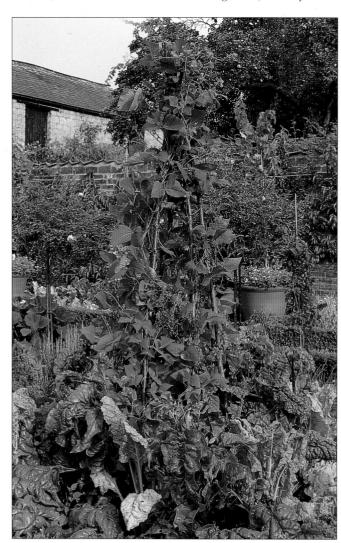

and marrows and pumpkins. They often have large colourful flowers, spectacular fruits, handsome leaves, in some cases, beautiful tendrils, and sometimes soft downy stems. They have to be matched carefully to their supports as some can be very vigorous, so it is best to be guided by their performance in the conditions within your garden. For ordinary arbours, arches, tepees, trellises and garden fences choose the following less vigorous varieties. Ornamental gourds, spaghetti squash, ordinary marrows, the small-fruited 'Little Gem' and 'Rolet', 'Munchkin', with its pretty, miniature pumpkins, and the cream coloured 'Sweet Dumpling' have grown well in my garden, winning additional favour by gripping my willow fencing with little aid. Finer-stemmed plants, such as outdoor cucumbers and watermelons, can be trained up lighter supports, even up strings. To my surprise, cucumbers took kindly to 1–1.2m (3–4ft) high willow hoops, twining to the mid-point then setting off down the other side. In the centre they encountered runner beans, looking for further heights to scale.

LEFT: **Any tall support for climbers makes a natural and practical centrepiece for a kitchen garden bed. Here the runner beans appear to rise out of a lush sea of Swiss chard.**

RIGHT: **The golden hop is a beautiful and fast-growing plant, often used to cover trellises and tall structures to make a living screen, an eye-catching feature or a colourful boundary.**

Many cucurbits can be grown for their 'special effects'. Grow bottle gourds for their shaggy-edged white flowers and large, heart-shaped leaves; 'Tromboncino' summer squash for the dramatic silhouettes of its long thin gourds; bitter gourd for the delicacy of its leaves, its perfumed flowers and alligator-skin fruits; the tiny pear-shaped 'Coloquinte' ornamental gourds (edible when they are young and soft-skinned) for an original, colourful screen.

Hops If ever a plant has inveigled its way into the potager on the most slender culinary grounds, it is the hop, especially the golden form, *Humulus lupulus* 'Aureus'. The flowers of some varieties are used to flavour beer while the young tips are considered a delicacy, but its real value in the potager lies in the speed with which it regenerates itself each spring, covering an arbour or concealing an unsightly feature in a few weeks. For an almost instant focal point, plant a tripod or obelisk at least 2.1m (7ft) tall with a couple of golden hops.

RIGHT: **The simple outlines of the taller varieties of climbing peas can be used to edge the kitchen garden, or to create attractive divisions between sections of a bed.**

Nasturtiums One of the most colourful and accommodating climbers is the tuberous nasturtium (*Tropaeolum tuberosum*), also known as mashua and anu. It tolerates poor soil and light shade, and will scramble up fences or trellises to make a screen studded with dainty orange flowers. Besides the beautifully marked edible tubers which, admittedly, need a long summer to develop, both leaves and flowers are edible. This is true with all the climbing nasturtiums, the ordinary trailing garden ones, as well as canary creeper (*Tropaeolum peregrinum*). Let them meander through beds of brassicas, or allow them to scramble up supports. Any ugly low features will be concealed in no time.

Peas Ordinary garden peas can be considered modest climbers, the tallest reaching to about 1.5m (5ft) high. To make the most of their height, support them with nylon or wire netting, which allows the tendrils to get a grip. Again, varieties with purple flowers are easily the most eye-catching.

MIXING CLIMBING FLOWERS AND SHRUBS WITH VEGETABLES

Climbers are natural mixers: after all, in nature they would be climbing up their neighbours, so provided the soil is moist and fertile enough, some lovely combinations can be planned. Edible plants should really have priority, but climbing annuals such as the 'cup and saucer vine' (*Cobaea scandens*), morning glory, sweet peas and, perennial shrubs like honeysuckle, clematis and rambling roses can easily, and very happily, be integrated into the kitchen garden. There is a huge choice of purely decorative climbing shrubs to supply extra colour and team up with the edible climbers. Narrow it down by selecting at least one fragrant plant for an arbour, by avoiding over-vigorous plants (the large-flowered clematis, for example, are much less rampant than the smaller-flowered ones) and giving priority to plants with a long, decorative season. Many of the climbing roses follow their first flush with prolonged spasmodic flowering. One plant worth considering, because of its vigorous recovery from frost damage in even cold, shady gardens is the Dutchman's pipe (*Aristololochia macrophylla* syn. *durior*). Its heart-shaped leaves quickly make a backdrop or cover an arbour. More tender but wonderfully showy is the twining passion flower, *Passiflora*. Consult specialist catalogues for the many species with edible fruits. For trailing and climbing fruits, see page 129.

LIVING EDGES

For a bold, prominent outline in a decorative vegetable garden, there is nothing to equal a formal dwarf hedge (see pp.63–5), but with informal, less permanent edges a huge range of effects can be achieved, with colours ranging from primary to pastel, and textures from soft to regimented. The choice of plants can be

BELOW: **The red-leaved plantain, with its softly coloured leaves early in the season and the upright, rigid flower spikes later, can be an excellent potager edging plant.**

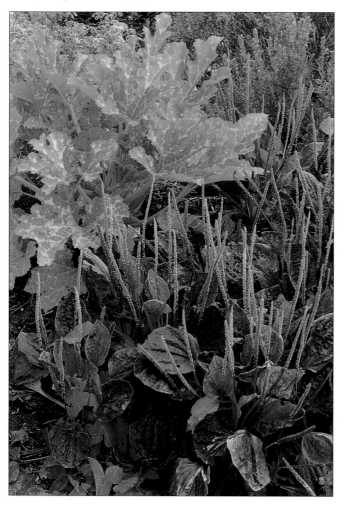

frivolous or restricted to culinary herbs, edible flowers, fruits and vegetables. When choosing plants for informal edging, convention may be thrown to the winds, but candidates should be subjected to a little cross-examination to assess their suitability.

First of all, do they have the right habit for the site? Where a bed is edged with boards or tiles extending well above the soil level, low-growing, sprawling plants such as thymes or alpine strawberries are impractical. Only fairly tall edging plants, such as giant or Chinese chives, would make the right sort of impact. In beds that are more or less level with the path, edging plants along the front should be fairly low growing, so that they don't conceal or shade the plants growing behind them. Taller plants can, however, be used to make a division within the beds, or along the sides or at the back. A band of asparagus can look magnificent behind a bed; so can alfalfa, making a tall evergreen hedge, covered with purple-blue flowers.

Another factor to consider when choosing edging plants is that they should be reasonably easy to keep within bounds. It is extraordinary how quickly an initially eye-catching edge can become tyrannical, taking up more and more space. Lavender can be guilty of this, and at times I have had to discard variegated strawberries, buckler-leaved sorrel, and red-leaved plantain, much as I loved its broad red leaves and flower spikes, all for the crime of engulfing narrow borders. Use vigorous plants like these as an edging for spacious beds or restrict them to corners where they can act as ground cover.

The most important qualification for an edging plant is that it should grow well. There is nothing sadder than a struggling edge. If your parsley is normally bleached with virus or aphid attacks by mid-summer, don't use it. Conversely, if some colourful, low-growing plant looks magnificent in your garden, call it into service in the kitchen plot. Any edge must also be able to hold its own against the sturdier vegetables in the beds, which may threaten to overrun it at various times of the year. If the edging plants are perennials, it is important that they perform well over a long period. If they are annuals, it may be possible to pair them up with good successors or predecessors. A spring-planted edge of curly endive teams up nicely, for example, with a summer planting of 'Salad Bowl' lettuce or rosette pak choi.

Here are a few suggestions for interesting edges, most of which could equally serve as divisions within large beds. (For cultivation of the herbs, edible plants and vegetables, see A–Z Directory, pp.150–199.)

FRIVOLOUS EDGES

These are plants which, although attractive as edging, have no culinary value and could be considered 'frivolous'. Firmly in this category are decorative herbaceous perennials, because they take up considerable space permanently. Lady's mantle (*Alchemilla mollis*), *Cineraria maritima* and catmint (*Nepeta* sp.) are typical of softly coloured plants that flop onto paths. Thrift (*Armeria maritima*) and London pride (*Saxifraga* x *urbium*) make tidier but colourful edges, so do low-growing grasses such as the blue *Festuca glauca*. Annual flowers make wonderful, cheap and cheerful borders around vegetables.

ABOVE: **Many marjorams, such as the golden form here, make compact and colourful edgings. They look good for much of the year, as the flowers and seedheads are generally decorative.**

LEFT: **In spring and summer ordinary garden chives, here teamed with stepover apples, make an effective edging, though they tend to become bedraggled at the end of the season.**

Any of the old favourites that are low-growing will do, such as alyssum, candytuft, lobelia, French marigolds, gazania and nemesia, or try the pale blue, starry-eyed *Laurentia axillaris*. Be bold in using colour, and if there is room, don't be afraid to set the plants in a double row to get a really strong edge.

USEFUL EDGES
Edible flowers Almost all of the many edible flowers are pretty and very decorative (see pp.197–9). Those with the right habit for edging include *Bellis perennis* daisies, pinks (choose old-fashioned, fragrant varieties), and the large

viola family, embracing huge grinning pansies and the tiny heartsease. One year, I alternated black- and white-flowered *Viola cornuta* along one edge of my potager, which created a chequerboard effect. Nasturtiums can make excellent edging, but choose the compact and smaller-leaved varieties.

Herbs A large number of common herbs are colourful in flower. Lavender, with its intoxicating fragrance, is unsurpassable, but it is probably best used as dwarf hedging. Both the green- and gold-leaved forms of feverfew (*Tanacetum parthenium*) produce a mass of white daisy flowers throughout the summer.

Many of the marjorams (*Origanum* sp.) have attractive flowers, the evergreen forms being ideal for winter edges. Winter savory is another herb that flowers quietly in the summer, but remains semi-evergreen in temperate climates. With their tiny but colourful flowers, many of the upright and the more robust creeping thymes can serve as excellent edgers; the shiny broad-leaved thyme is one of the most consistently reliable. A lovely edge is created with white-flowered thymes planted about 30cm (12in) apart. Growing bright red 'Lollo' lettuce in the spaces between the thymes makes a very colourful combination.

91

LEFT: **The creeping thyme *Thymus serpyllum* 'Pink Chintz' makes a soft informal edge and attracts beneficial insects into the garden.**

The chives are a group that can provide neat green edgings over many months before bursting into flower, and some flower twice in the growing season. The giant strain throws up flower spikes 30cm (12in) high; so does Chinese or garlic chives, whose beautiful starry white flowers appear in late summer. Both look dramatic encircling groups of taller vegetables. The nodding onion (*Allium cernuum*), with its white, mauve or pink flowers, can be used in the same way, while the oriental bunching onion can make a sentinel-like edge. With all these, both leaves and flowers can be used in salads or for flavouring. The many decorative but less productive chives available from specialist nurseries also make lovely edges.

Oriental vegetables Excellent edges are found among the oriental vegetables, generally in their prime from late summer to early winter. Some of the best are pak choi, 'shungiku' or chrysanthemum greens, the serrated shiny-leaved mizuna mustard and rosette pak choi, which makes a beautiful, flat symmetrical pattern in its mature stages. Lovely too, though potentially growing over 30cm (12in) are the purple mustards. Not only can all these be grown as single specimens, but bands sown for use as seedling crops make healthy looking, albeit transitory, edges.

Plain green edges For winter edges use evergreens such as the everlasting onion (*Allium perutile*), the jagged-leaved buck's horn plantain, and dainty salad burnet (*Sanguisorba minor*), which has the prettiest globular seedheads in summer. The hardy, glossy-leaved celery 'Parcel' makes a vibrant winter edge; so does scurvy grass (*Cochlearia officinalis* and *C. danica*), though I have to say that I find it unpalatable. The leaves of the root vegetable Hamburg parsley stay green in winter, forming a neat, if sometimes subdued edge.

A superb summer edge is formed by curled parsley, while the taller broad-leaved parsley is best used to divide beds. By chance one year I interplanted the two types in a circle and was surprised at the rich, textured effect that resulted. Curly endive is another good choice for edging as it stays neat and perkily fresh over many weeks. Bands of dill or carrots make a truly delightful, almost feathery border.

Red and green edges For a crunched texture there is nothing that beats the deeply curled 'Lollo' lettuces, using either the red varieties alone or, alternatively, interplanting them with the green to form a very decorative bicoloured edge. Red and green varieties of the loose-leaved 'Salad Bowl' lettuces can be used the same way: they will billow out over the path and create a stunning effect.

In a warm climate, try the same effect with red and green basil. The pretty leaved, low-growing tomato 'Whippersnapper' makes the neatest of summer edges, as do other very compact varieties such as 'Totem', which grows to no more than 45cm (18in) high. For brilliant red, eye-catching margins, use a striking variety of red-leaved beet, such as 'Bull's Blood'.

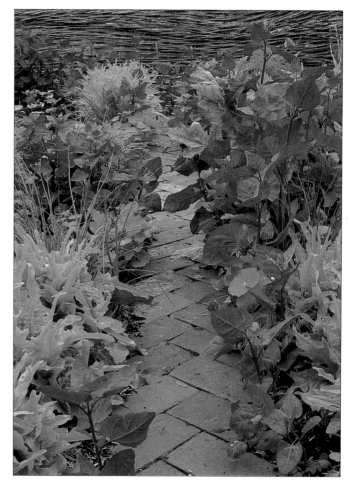

RIGHT: **The 'Catalogna' lettuce edging the central path of my Little Potager has been encroached by self-sown red orache, but they sit happily together.**

GROUND COVER

Ground-cover plants can be very handy in a potager for filling out and filling in. Creeping plants take over the gaps between pavers and steps and soften harsh edges, while larger plants blanket the soil, creating an impression of lushness. Some will even colonize unloved corners and awkward banks. All in all they produce an effect of permanence besides keeping down weeds and being colourful, but there is more. The evergreen and semi-evergreen creeping plants, mainly hardy herbs and low-growing berried fruits, add colour and interest in winter while, in summer, edible flowers and flowering herbs become carpets of colour. Others, mainly herbs again, can be trained into geometric ground-cover features.

TYPES OF GROUND-COVER PLANTS

Ground-cover plants can be loosely divided into those that are naturally creepers, carpeters or sprawlers, and those which, for practical purposes, can be used as ground-cover on account of their bulk or natural vigour.

Perennials Many vegetables, by adding to their girth year by year, come into this category. Typical are the architectural plants that were discussed on pages 81 and 82, such as cardoon, sweet coltsfoot, globe artichokes, rhubarb and the giant herbs lovage and angelica. Seakale is another of these; once established it sits tight on a patch of ground 1 sq m (1.2 sq yd), keeping down any weeds. All of these plants control weeds superbly: they simply block out the light with their large leaves. Although alfalfa, 'Good King Henry' and sorrel are more susceptible to being invaded by weeds, they are all perennials that keep a patch of ground under control and provide useful pickings in the process.

LEFT: **The variegated nasturtium 'Alaska' is a superb foil to the greens of pak choi and lettuce in the Ballymaloe Cookery School garden, southern Ireland.**

RIGHT: **Pert buckler-leaved sorrel is one of the best edges for a winter bed, as it remains green unless subjected to very severe weather.**

ABOVE: **Many tuberous vegetables have extensive foliage, which makes them useful ground-cover plants. Few, however, have leaves as dainty as those of oca.**

Several tuberous vegetables are effectively ground-cover plants and smother anything near them. Potatoes behave like this, and so do Chinese artichokes (*Stachys affinis*), which are invariably mistaken for mint because the leaves and growth habits are so similar. My favourite is oca (*Oxalis tuberosus*), an excellent plant for dull corners, with dainty clover-like leaves that droop with endearing modesty when conditions get too hot or cold, making chequered patterns of light and shade.

Clump-forming and broad-leaved plants
Any plants that naturally make dense clumps double as ground cover. Many herbs perform in this way, including lemon balm, marjoram, mints, sages, tarragon, and the many beautiful varieties of comfrey. Ground cover can also be created by spacing broad-leaved vegetables so that they form a canopy over the soil, with leaves just touching those of their neighbours. Lettuces and endives are typical of vegetables commonly grown this way, but there's no faster way of blanketing the ground than by sowing cut-and-come-again seedlings. For more information see pages 110–13.

Creepers In this group are the creeping herbs, such as thymes and mints, fruits like strawberries, various cranberries, bearberry, and an assortment of creeping members of both the blackberry and raspberry families. Ground cover vegetables tend to be trailers. On a grand scale there are marrows and pumpkins and oriental squashes such as the wax gourd; more modest in habit are gherkins, cucumbers, the iceplant (*Mesembryanthemum crystallinum*), New Zealand spinach and, in

TRAINING A PUMPKIN IN A CIRCLE

Train trailing pumpkins and squashes into compact circles by pinning down the main shoots as they grow, with sticks or pieces of bent wire. It may need to be done daily. Mark the centre of the plant with a long cane as a guide to where to water.

warm climates, peanuts and sweet potato. Most climbing plants will sprawl horizontally if there is nothing for them to cling on to or climb on, making effective and sometimes very beautiful ground cover. The nasturtiums, including the tuberous-rooted nasturtium, also known as mashua and anu, all come into this category. In small gardens, introduce these rampant plants with great care: there is a fine line between welcome ground cover and invasion.

Self-seeders Plants within this group often create excellent ground cover, including chervil, corn salad, cresses, dandelion, salad rocket, winter purslane (*Montia perfoliata*) and, in warm climates, amaranths. In conditions that suit them they will green the ground in no time at all, and they can always be dug in as green manure if they show signs of becoming invasive. Most green manures (see pp.137–8) make excellent ground cover plants, and clovers, fenugreek, mustard, *Phacelia tanacetifolia* and tares all look decorative while growing. Several of the edible wild plants, such as chickweed, wild garlic (*Allium ursinum*), and the various species of *Oxalis* can blanket the ground. Just make sure you keep the upper hand. By their very nature, wild plants are more robust and can become intrusive, smoothering the less sturdy flowers, vegetables and herbs.

Sprawlers Other candidates that are good for use as ground cover are sprawlers and floppy plants, such as bush tomatoes and tomatillo. Peas can be very fetching if given a free rein and allowed to sprawl. They won't be quite as productive as when supported, but the prolific white or pink flowers make a very pretty patch against a background of green leaves and tendrils. I have seen the lablab bean sprawling happily among perennials in a border, its blue-green leaves and purple stems blending well with coloured flowers.

SPECIAL EFFECTS WITH GROUND COVER
Ground-cover plants can be used to create special effects. In a large garden, the more vigorous trailing squashes can romp over great expanses, looking magnificent, but in confined gardens train the shoots round and round into a neat circle. The plants cut quite a figure, but take less space. Pin the shoots down with bent wire or sticks to encourage them to put out extra roots from the stem (see diagram below).

Creeping herbs create delightful effects. The tiny-leaved mint, *Mentha requienii*, which is ideal for flavouring ice-cream, will colonize gravel and steps in the most charming way; sweet woodruff makes a wonderful fringe to paths or shaded edges. Another way to use creeping herbs is as carpets under small fruit trees and ornamental standards. The only proviso is that they can get plenty of sun, but the more robust creeping thymes are ideal: try one of the cultivars of *Thymus serpyllum* of which there are white, pink, magenta or red, or woolly thyme, *T. pseudolanuginosus*, or gold forms such as *T. aureus* or the silver-edged *T. vulgaris* 'Silver Posie' to add a unique sparkle.

When it comes to brightening up the lower levels of the garden, my favourite quartet is iceplant (*Mesembryanthemum crystallinum*), gold purslane, variegated strawberries and 'Alaska' nasturtium. The fleshy iceplant sparkles brilliantly in sunshine, due to tiny sacs on the leaves and stems. Being a tender plant it requires reasonably warm weather to do well, but provided drainage is good, it will tolerate poor soil. Let it romp freely along the edges or against a fence, or give it a section of its own within a bed. Gold purslane, which is a sprawler rather than genuine trailer, has much the same effect: it can illuminate a bed. With both of these plants, keep picking leaves to prevent seeding and prolong their impact. The variegated nasturtium 'Alaska' has the same bright quality, with its creamy-green leaves and clear-coloured flowers, both of which are edible. Naturally a bushy, rather than a trailing nasturtium (although climbing varieties are being developed) but such a prolific self-seeder that it can become overwhelming. For impressive effects, grow it among red-leaved plants such as beets, lettuce, basil or perilla.

The variegated strawberry has no culinary merit, indeed I have never even noticed its berries, but its green and white leaves brighten up dark corners of the garden, with the additional merit of tolerating light shade. Once established it produces runners so freely it may become invasive, so it is important to remove superfluous runners to keep it in place. A wonderful introduction for potager gardeners is the pink-flowered perpetual-fruiting strawberry, particularly the varieties 'Cantata', 'Serenata' and the rampaging 'Pink Panda' and 'Ruby Glow', with flower colours ranging from pale pink to deep red. They all have glossy leaves, they flower in flushes over many months, spread fast and make lively, more or less permanent, ground cover. The fruit, by the way, tastes much better than it looks.

For colourful ground cover consider, also, some of the many flowering plants with edible leaves and/or flowers. Heading a long list are hostas, *Houttuynia cordata*, lungwort (*Pulmonaria*), nasturtiums, the scented-leaved pelargoniums (geraniums), pinks (*Dianthus*), ground-cover roses, various stonecrops and sedums (*Sedum acre, S. album, S. reflexum, S. rosea*) and creeping violets. The peppermint-scented *Pelargonium tomentosum*, with its large soft, velvet leaves, qualifies as one of the most elegant ground-cover plants for a lightly-shaded site. It can be used to flavour barbecued fish.

ABOVE: **Spires of seedling 'Lollo' lettuce manage to escape from the all-engulfing nasturtiums at Ballymaloe Cookery School, southern Ireland.**

RIGHT: **Clipped lemon verbena forms geometric ground-cover hedging in the herb garden at Villandry. It should be pruned regularly to keep it in shape.**

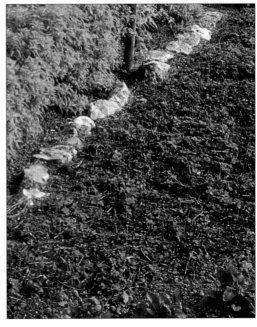

Lastly, herbs can be used to create the special effect best described as 'geometric' ground cover. I first saw this in the herb garden at Château Villandry, where herbs are grown as triangular blocks, the tops trained to 23 or 45cm (9 or 18in) high. Plants used included hedge germander, hyssop, lemon verbena, rosemary, ordinary sage, tricolor sage, a dwarf patch of santolina and winter savory, all edged with a contrasting hedge of clipped box.

TEXTURED EFFECTS

In the normal course of everyday gardening we overlook the diverse textures of even ordinary vegetables, and what they can contribute to the visual qualities of the garden.

PLANTS WITH FORM AND TEXTURE

Crêpe-leaved plants Several brassicas have crêpe and puckered leaves that are remarkably beautiful. There is the much loved savoy cabbage, and the large blistered leaves of purple oriental mustard. The same quality is seen in the strap-like, mellow blue leaves of 'Black' kale, and in a more dramatic form in the symmetrical, ground-hugging rosette pak choi. It is also present in the bubble leaves of the flowering rape 'Bouquet', grown for its flowering shoots, which is perhaps not surprisingly recommended for flower arranging in Japanese seed catalogues.

Crinkly-leaved plants This quality is best exemplified by the curly kales. Their crisp, deeply-curled leaves and sturdy stems transform the winter landscape. Their colours are lovely too: blue-green, deep green and rich crimson in the variety 'Redbor'. Planted closely, the taller varieties have that dense, vegetative look of the rainforest, while the dwarfer forms make a deep-pile carpet over the ground. They look wonderful under a canopy of snow. Although their leaves are less deeply curled, the red-tinged 'Ragged Jack' and the 'Russian' kales, as well as the curly-leaved mustards such as 'Art Green' are also impressive during the winter.

Crinkly leaves are not just confined to brassicas. Think of the celery 'Parcel', with shiny, deep green, crisply curled leaves that remain evergreen in temperatures as low as -10°C (14°F), the curly endives, the red and green 'Lollo' lettuces and curled

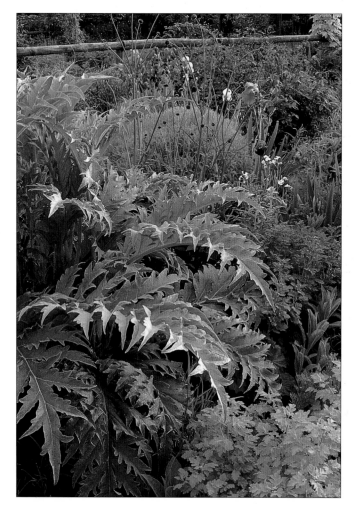

LEFT: **Globe artichoke and cardoon not only have a unique architectural quality but the firm, arching leaves have a texture of their own.**

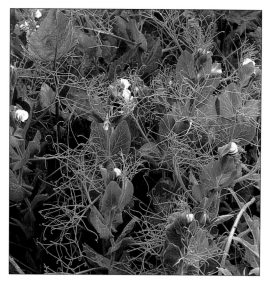

ABOVE: **The wiry stems of semi-leafless peas knit together to make beautiful lace-like patterns. They are best grown in a group to get maximum impact.**

parsley. All these make effective patches if planted in groups but, equally, make strong edges or dividing lines within a bed.

Delicate-leaved plants For a lace-like, fine, spidery texture, there is nothing to beat the semi-leafless peas. In these varieties, the normal leaves are reduced to a mass of tendrils that look uncannily like barbed wire: there's nothing else like them in the vegetable garden. They must be grown in a patch, as the intertwining tendrils keep the plants upright. Quite apart from the peas, what a delicacy those tendrils are, picked young and eaten raw or steamed.

Feathery-leaved plants This category of plants is headed by the fennels, whose light, gossamer leaves give way to the beautiful seedheads described on page 83. Bronze fennel, for me, is one of the most perfect plants for the potager. Its softly coloured foliage allows it to blend with almost any plant in a romantic, misty way. Let it seed where it will, or plant it at random through a plot. Florence fennel, a

FAR LEFT: **Lavender in a mist of fennel may be typical of the traditional cottage garden, but is the sort of planting that adds a romantic dimension to any kitchen garden. It is worth growing lavender for its fragrance alone.**

LEFT: **The glossy, crêped texture of Swiss chard is enhanced by the glowing colour of the leaves and stems. They are superb as single specimens or planted in bold groups, remaining productive over many weeks.**

plant of medium height, needs to be planted in a group in order to make the most of its lovely foliage. Asparagus is one of the taller feathery-leaved plants. Grow it either in a bed on its own, where it will form a very pretty, hedge-like strip, or have a few random plants within a bed or flower border. The red berries on the female plants are a bonus in the autumn. Best of the shorter feathery plants are carrots and dill. Both of these can be sown in patches or in narrow bands, or alternatively intercropped with onions or leeks for a complete contrast of leaf shape. Chervil has a similar light feel. It remains evergreen in moderate winters, so sow it, or allow it to self-seed, among overwintering brassicas, so that it can billow softly around their ugly bare stems.

Glossy-leaved plants Glossiness is a great quality in vegetables, and Swiss chard is the glossiest of them all. A stand of the green- and red-stemmed chards makes a sight that can stop most people in their tracks. Then there is mizuna mustard, with a brilliant gleam to its jagged leaves, whether planted in a patch, as an intercrop or as an edge. The old-fashioned root crop, skirret, is distinguished by the silky sheen to its leaves; celeriac too, has a glossy gleam before the celery fly gets to it.

Mealy-leaved plants Look no further than the grey patina on red cabbage, the hairy leaves and flower buds of borage, and the soft downiness of burdock, the sages, and loveliest of all, the leaves of bottle gourds.

RIGHT: **The contrasting textures of curly kales, red mustard and cardoon blend into a tapestry in my Winter Potager.**

COLOURFUL TOUCHES

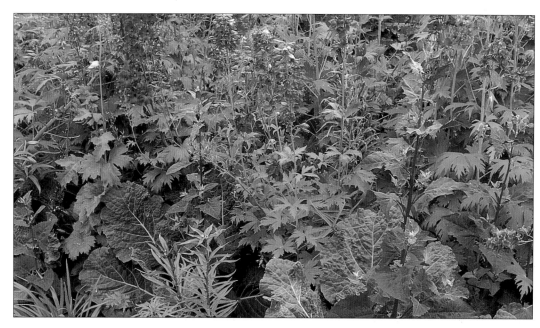

There are essentially two ways to get colour into the vegetable garden. The first is to make use of the many vegetables that are colourful; the second is to incorporate flowers. Purists will use only edible flowers and flowering vegetables, otherwise any flowers that will harmonize with vegetables can be used.

One of the frustrations of trying to grow vegetables in a way that is aesthetically pleasing is that seed catalogues describe only those aspects of a variety that relate to its performance. So it is hard to know if a new variety of courgettes for instance, has deep green leaves, silvery leaves or golden leaves, which might influence your choice. The only solution is to keep your eyes open, and seize any opportunity to visit demonstration grounds and seed company trial grounds open to the public. Then you really can see how varieties differ. The heritage seed specialists, whose valuable work deserves support, often prove to be a useful source of unusual and decorative vegetable varieties (see Suppliers, p.201).

VEGETABLES AND HERBS

As François Carvallo said of planning the potager at Villandry, a true gardener needs the eyes of a painter and decorator. (It is suprising how many fine vegetable gardens are designed by artists.) A good starting point is to group vegetables and herbs, albeit in a rather arbitrary way, into broad bands of colour. From this paintbox you can devise contrasting or harmonizing planting schemes. My own dream, for example, is to make a perfect 'Red Square' in my Winter Potager. Success still eludes me, as some crucial element never quite makes the

desired impact, but in working towards this goal I've had great fun combining purple sage, beets, red-leaved brassicas and winter pansies.

Blue There are very few blue vegetables and herbs, but what lovely shades they are. In some lights brassica leaves seem much closer to blue than green, particularly the Chinese broccoli, calabrese and the violet-curded cauliflowers. The hardy 'January King' types of cabbage and autumn cabbages can be a superb metallic blue. Then there are the crinkly textured, blue-leaved kales and blue tones in the ornamental kales. Leek leaves are often blue to purple, the hardiest varieties being the deepest purple. Soft blue-greys are found in cardoons and globe artichokes, and in the grey- and silver-leaved herbs such as lavender and rue.

Green It is an obvious fact that the majority of vegetables are green, so green is the natural backdrop to colourful planting and can be a constant, calming thread through the garden. Make use of the variations in green. Different varieties of Swiss chard, for example, can range from near yellow to a brilliant deep green.

ABOVE: **It was just a thought to slip the delphiniums in among the ornamental kales and red orache, but how well it worked. Never be afraid to try new combinations. In my experience they almost always succeed.**

BELOW: **Herbs offer many opportunities to introduce colour. Perennial herbs, such as these chives and lovage, are very undemanding and once established, become key elements in the framework of the garden.**

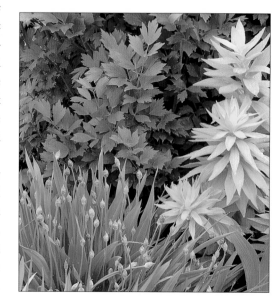

These subtle differences can be used to great effect. (For more details on varietal colours see A–Z Directory, pp.150–199.)

Gold, yellow and cream True golds and yellows are harder to find, except in the golden forms of marjoram, thyme and sage. Gold purslane is the brightest shiny yellow, some Swiss chard varieties have yellow stems and yellow-tinged leaves, while some yellow courgettes have yellow leaves to match. There are beautiful yellow peppers, both sweet and hot, and yellow-fruited tomatoes and aubergines. The most amazing colour I have found in an edible plant is the radiant orange-pink of a quinoa stem, *Chenopodium* 'Andean hybrid'. It didn't fully develop this colour until late in the autumn, but then it was irresistible.

Yellows merge into creams, and here my favourite is the loose-headed Chinese cabbage 'Ruffles', which forms a creamy-yellow centre when mature. Gleams of light come from the variegated forms of alexanders, comfrey, horse radish, mint, sage, strawberry, thymes, and, again, from ornamental cabbages and kales, and the silvery leaves of many courgettes.

Red, purple and pink Some of the most flamboyantly coloured leaves are in the red band. The deepest, pure reds are found in the stems and leaves of red Swiss chard, in several varieties of the red Italian chicory (radicchio), in older varieties of beetroot such as 'Bull's Blood' and 'McGregor's Favourite' and in the bright, tiny, strawberry-like fruits of beetberry or strawberry spinach (*Chenopodium capitatum*). For more purplish-reds, look to the red Brussels sprouts, purple sage, red orache (though its colour varies enormously) and red cabbage, while amaranths display varying shades of blotchy red. For a deeper purple there are the Japanese herb red perilla or shiso, red basil and the dark-leaved chili peppers. Red mitsuba, another Japanese herb, is a soft purple, and bronze fennel is, of course bronze.

The kale family exhibit a host of purple, red, bronze and pink hues. In the ornamental kales they mingle with greens and creams, in the 'Russian' and 'Ragged Jack' kales purples predominate but blend into blue-green, while the curly kale 'Redbor' has near violet coloured stems and, when mature, bronze-red leaves. Purple kohl rabi has purplish-green leaves, reflecting the violet-purple of its bulbous stem. In mid-winter the purple oriental mustards are deeply coloured but, as with many red vegetables, the colours lighten as temperatures rise. As for lettuce, the range of reds widens every

BELOW: **A blaze of colour in a potager bed, with** *Berberis thunbergii* **at the centre, surrounded by a ring of red cabbage, in turn encircled with lavender 'Pink Hidcote', which perfumes the whole garden in mid-summer.**

BELOW: **Leeks are one of the most reliable vegetables for bringing colour to the winter garden. In my Winter Potager their soft, violet-blue colour stands out among neighbouring greens and reds. The hardier the leek, the deeper the purple.**

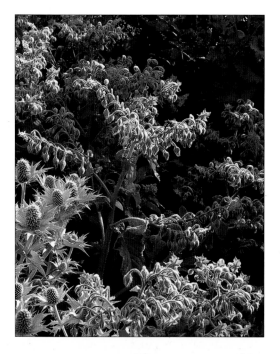

season, from the loveliest bronzes to deep maroon. In this colour range there are also striking reds in the fruits of peppers and tomatoes, and there are purple aubergines, purple peppers, and purple-podded beans and peas.

FLOWERING EDIBLES AND EDIBLE FLOWERS

Herbs There's a long list of herbs that offer attractive flowers along with their other virtues: anise and ordinary hyssop, the bergamots (*Monarda* sp.), chives, clary sage, lavender, marjorams, rosemary and thymes, to name but a

LEFT: **With its misty blue flower and hairy stems, borage is one of the most rewarding edible flowers to work into a vegetable garden, seen here mingling with the spiky flowerheads of *Eryngium*.**

few. Chives, especially the giant forms, make a bold edging or division between beds, often flowering twice in a season. The same is true of the white-flowered Chinese or garlic chives, which is a near-perfect potager plant in my book (see p.191).

Flowers The scope for growing edible flowers in a vegetable garden is unlimited. Among the more colourful perennials are ornamental alliums, tuberous-rooted begonias, the garden forms of *Bellis perennis* daisies, chrysanthemums, daylilies and tiger lilies, erythroniums, fuchsias, hosta, houttuynia, the pinks, *Salvia patens*, members of the viola family and yucca. Popular annuals that can end up on the plate include borage, cornflowers, signet dwarf marigolds and nasturtiums. Add sunflowers to the list, as the seeds are roasted and used to extract oil, and in no time at all the kitchen garden will be a riot of dramatic colour. (For more edible flowers, see pp.197–199.)

Why limit flowers to those with culinary connotations? In the traditional four-square walled gardens sections were often separated by wide borders of herbaceous plants or flowers for the house. It is easily possible to do the same on a more modest scale in the potager. Encircle the whole vegetable plot or individual beds (they need to be a reasonable size or the vegetables will be engulfed) with a wide or narrow band of flowers. Plant clumps at the ends of long narrow beds; use flowers to demarcate sections or as dot plants within a bed. Choose 'your kind of flowers' to create the ambience you feel most at home with. In some gardens only the most lively and vivid oranges, reds and golds – those of dahlias, sunflowers, French

LEFT: **The white flowers of Chinese chives illuminate my Winter Potager in late summer. Relatively slow growing, clumps make excellent edges or corner pieces.**

ABOVE: **Coriander is an annual herb that runs to seed rapidly. Let it, for the delicate, creamy flowerheads and feathery leaves contrast well with bold vegetables.**

RIGHT: **At Sooke Harbour House, Vancouver Island, the flower borders are restricted to edible flowers. Here, Shasta daisies, lilies and pot marigold mingle together.**

and African marigolds, rudbeckias and zinnias – are allowed to mix with vegetables. In others it is all blues, mauves, gentle pinks and white, found in alyssum, catmint, cleome, the Russian sage (*Perovskia atriplicifolia*), blue salvia and the more quietly-coloured cosmos. Some opt unashamedly for uncoordinated gaiety, but whatever the scheme, only include flowers that grow easily in your garden, as you don't want any bother with them. And don't forget to make a place for sweet peas: they are always at home in a potager. (For information about intersowing parsnips and carrots with annual flowers see pp.102–3.)

Vegetables Many vegetables have colourful flowers. The flower buds are the edible part with calabrese, purple-sprouting broccoli and

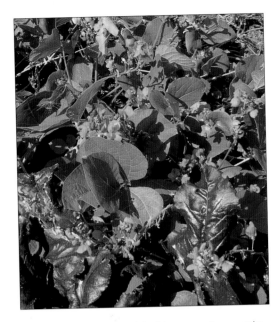

ABOVE: **The dwarf forms of climbing runner beans make a highly coloured patch in my Little Potager, here planted alongside 'Bull's Blood' beetroot.**

BELOW: **It is always worth leaving the occasional chicory plant to seed, as the flowering stems will grow over 1.8m (6ft) high, creating massive spires of blue flowers.**

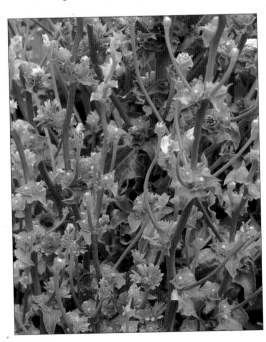

cauliflower. Several oriental greens are grown for their flowering shoots, including choy sum, the yellow-flowered rape, purple pak choi, the flowers of which contrast with the slender purple stems, and the sturdier white-flowered Chinese broccoli.

In the squash family, flowers may be more sparse but pumpkins, marrows and oriental gourds compensate with showy and, incidentally, edible flowers. Okra has got eye-catching yellow flowers, which is not unexpected in a member of the hibiscus family, and flowerheads of amaranths, sweet corn, quinoa and other grains can be stunning shades.

Brightly coloured climbing peas and beans were discussed earlier, on pages 87 and 89, but there are many colourful dwarf forms that are definitely worth growing. Grow asparagus peas for dainty orange-brown flowers, azuki beans (in a warm climate) for yellow flowers, broad beans for their white, purplish and in several heritage varieties, crimson flowers, dwarf runner beans in a dense mass for a blaze of orange-red, and purple-podded French beans for a purple patch. I've more than once sacrificed broad beans for a vase of their flowers. Subtly coloured potato flowers have met the same fate, but at least the tubers stand to

RIGHT: **This is the colourful result of allowing different plants to self-seed. Nasturtiums clamber around the stems of red orache, and parsley seedheads peer through the nasturtium leaves.**

gain by removing the flowers. (For other vegetables with worthwhile flowers in their later stages, including leeks and radish, see pp.83–5.)

INTERMINGLING ANNUALS

For many years now I have taken carrot seed, mixed it with the seed of several different annual flowers, and sown the mixture together in a patch in the spring. For most of the summer all you see is the colourful annuals, but the carrots develop quietly among them, carrot fly

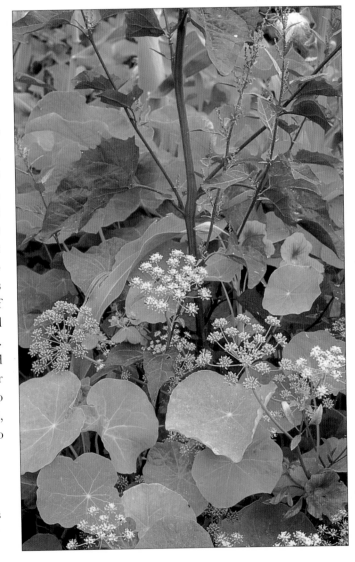

apparently thrown off scent by the flowering entourage. The secret is to choose annuals with fairly feathery leaves so the carrots are not overwhelmed. I have successfully used blue flax (*Linum usitatissimum*), cornflower, godetia, larkspur, love-in-a-mist, nemesia, scabious and some of the lightweight everlasting flowers such as *Rhodanthe*. Others that would be just as suitable are *Chrysanthemum carinatum*, *Cosmos* 'Sonata' and pheasant's eye (*Adonis annua*). Last year I tried it with parsnips, and rather to my surprise, it worked: I thought they would have needed more space, but the colourful summer patch of cornflower nurtured healthy parsnips for winter use. As for the ratio of annual to vegetable seed, I have never made accurate trials but suggest a roughly 50:50 mix, using up to four annuals in the flower half. I measure out the seeds in a teaspoon, and mix them in a cup

BELOW: **Violas and pansies are colourful over many months, and have edible flowers. Here violas are framed with salad rocket.**

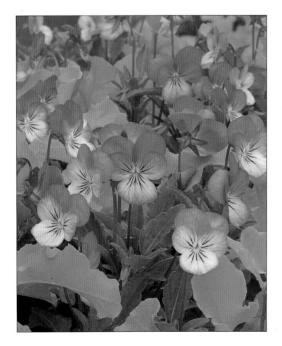

RIGHT: **Spring bulbs, here *Tulipa* 'Apricot Beauty' and *Narcissus* 'Pipit' flower among overwintered chicories in the spring.**

before sowing. Sow by any of the methods used for cut-and-come-again patches, see pages 110–13.

MIXING BULBS WITH EDIBLES

Ornamental bulbs can easily be matched with vegetables. To my surprise, one spring a clump of grape hyacinths sprung up in my garden alongside an overwintered cardoon. The clear blue hyacinth flowers and blue-grey cardoon leaves looked lovely together, so now the cardoon in the centre of my Winter Potager is surrounded with *Muscari* 'New Creation', and globe artichokes, which have the same soft grey leaves, are interplanted with drifts of *Muscari* 'Blue Spike', guaranteeing a brilliant blue carpet every spring.

Strawberries, either fruiting or variegated-leaved forms, can be under-planted with tulips, or tulips can be slipped in between red chicory plants (ideally the hardy variety, 'Treviso') in the autumn. Indeed any spring-flowering bulbs can be liberally planted in a winter potager. Their flowering will make a colourful bridge between the tailing off of overwintered vegetables at the end of the spring and the first summer plantings. Herbs, too, can be underplanted with bulbs: creeping thymes with autumn crocus work particularly well. Flowering bulbs are an excellent choice

for fruit borders, too. At Cranborne Manor, in Dorset, south England, morello cherries are underplanted with bluebells and crocuses, and apples with forget-me-nots.

Another approach is to plant vegetables around bulbs, an art Rosemary Verey has perfected at Barnsley House, Gloucestershire, south-west England, with tulips and lettuce. The tulips are planted in early autumn, and lettuce, sown indoors in late winter, is planted out among the tulips when they peep through in spring. They make a lovely show together.

VEGETABLES IN THE FLOWER BEDS
If flowers can be grown in vegetable beds, the reverse is also true. Beautiful perennial herbs and vegetables such as asparagus, bronze fennel, cardoons, globe artichokes, rhubarb and seakale can win a place on merit in any herbaceous border. Climbing vegetables growing up elegant structures can look natural in flower beds, either in the background or as prominent features. The many vegetables with colourful leaves or distinctive foliage (see pp.96–9) can be woven into flower beds to great effect, as long as the soil is fertile enough and there is enough moisture to sustain them. Spreading plants such as courgettes and pumpkins are best planted singly, but otherwise plant vegetables in irregular shaped drifts. Amaranths, aubergines, red-leaved beetroot, fennels, leeks, lettuce, orache, ornamental kales, peppers, red cabbage, sweet corn, Swiss chard, tomatoes, and many herbs can all enhance a flower bed. Vegetables and herbs can also be grown as edges in the ornamental garden. Try interplanting mahogany-flowered French marigolds and curled parsley for the best of both worlds.

BELOW: **At Sooke Harbour House, Vancouver Island, the seascape is framed with seeding fennel and daylilies, while globe artichokes, ornamental kales, pot marigolds and nasturtiums, all with culinary use, fill in the picture.**

INTERCROPPING

It is the mixing, matching and intermingling of vegetables that makes the creative potager so different from the traditional vegetable garden, with its rectangular beds, more often than not planted in unyielding rows. Intercropping, in all its guises, is the cornerstone of this successful mingling. Simple, dramatic patterns are made by intercropping contrasting plants – red with green, tall with short, austere with lush. The more complicated, but deeply satisfying 'tapestry' effects come from skilfully interweaving strands of contrasting or complementary plants into a background carpet. Occasionally, the visualized effects fail to materialize: pests or disease outbreaks, the weather, unpredictable performance (most commonly caused by one vegetable taking over another), or mistimed planting may be to blame. Yet even in less than perfect combinations there is always an element of beauty, along with the satisfaction of using space as intensively as possible.

Intercropping is when two or more crops are grown together within the same area. Rows of one may alternate with rows of another, or plants of different crops may alternate within a row. Often fast- and slow-growing crops are paired: the fast-growing one is cleared before the slower one needs the space. In undercropping, a low-growing or trailing crop is planted between or beneath a tall crop.

THE PATTERNS

All kinds of patterns can be drawn with the intercropper's pen. On the whole, the simpler they are, the more striking the effect will be. In a formal setting their impact is heightened dramatically when they are confined within a crisp frame of clipped hedging or herbs.

The pattern is often determined by the shape of the bed. One approach to square and rectangular beds is to plant in concentric squares around a central clump or plant, for example, a globe artichoke, surrounded by a broad band of chard, finished with an edge of lettuce. If the bed is against a wall, place an eye-catching group or plant in the centre at the back, then surround its exposed sides with up to three bands of different plants. A circular bed can be planted in several rings around a central pivot, while concentric semicircles fit naturally in the

RIGHT: **The contrasting colours of interweaving bands of 'Lollo' lettuce and curly endive make a striking pattern.**

BELOW: **Leeks are an ideal crop for interplanting, and when a low-growing subject such as lettuce is used, the contrasting heights are an extra, decorative element.**

frame of a half-circular bed. Outlying beds of irregular shapes can be turned into a patch-work with alternating red and green plants.

Another function of intercropping is that it can be used for pencilling outlines. Boundaries between and around beds, and the lines delin-eating patterns, for example the pie-shaped sections in a circle, can be highlighted with brightly coloured or upright plants that stand out from their neighbours. Lines of leeks and onions can zigzag dramatically through a gar-den; pairs of crossing zigzags will make a series

of diamonds, perfect for interplanting with a dwarfer crop. Use slender lines of seedlings to etch delicate patterns in and around newly planted brassicas, while wider bands of plants can capture the feel of a gentle stream: picture drifts of parsley or dill, even dwarf peas, mean-dering between banks of rounded cabbage.

PRACTICALITIES

To make intercropping work there must be a natural contrast between the various elements, whether in colour, height or texture, and they must also have complementary, rather than competitive growth habits. Lettuce will be spoilt if planted too close to floppy plants such as spinach; Italian chicory, on the other hand, tolerates a little overhanging. Pretty effects can result from impromptu inter-mingling, such as nasturtiums and trailing marrows wandering through potatoes.

Getting the perfect picture may mean juggling with spacing and timing. It will often make sense to adopt wider spacing than normal for the intercrop-ping plants, to allow both parties elbow room. A carpeted effect, however, depends on strictly even spacing so that mature plants will blanket the ground. F_1 hybrid varieties (see p.200), with their uniform growth, can help to ensure an even look. As

LEFT: **Patterns with intercropping: in the foreground mizuna and red 'Oak Leaf' lettuce, and behind, endive and red 'Lollo' lettuce.**

for timing, there is bound to be an element of guesswork: germination and growth rates are variable at the best of times, even between dif-ferent varieties of the same vegetable. Between different vegetables they can vary enormously. Use all available information to co-ordinate your plantings (see Planning for Succession chart, p.149), but keep detailed records of your own. They will ultimately be the most useful data on sowing times and successful combina-tions under your conditions, enabling you to re-create happy partnerships another year. Guidelines to intercropping:

• Avoid untidy and sprawling plants such as potatoes, bush tomatoes, and broad beans other than trailers, which can be 'channelled' down rows or between other plants.

• Where it is feasible, use plants rather than sowing seed, as this eliminates a great deal of unpredictability. A line of onions, for example, is much easier to establish using sets or young plants rather than seed. On the whole, plant the slowest-growing or longest-lasting plants before the faster-growing crops. This makes it easier to judge the amount of space to leave for the companion crop.

• If it is necessary to leave gaps for future planting, mark them clearly with sticks. Spots for sweet corn may have to be 'reserved' until the risk of frost is past, but young inter-cropping plants can be set out beforehand, or seedlings sown, in what will eventually be the spaces between the corn plants.

• Work out complex patterns on the ground before you start planting, outlining them with sand if necessary. Make sure you have enough plants to fulfill your plans, and a few spares in case things don't turn out as planned.

• When planting a shaped area, start at the narrowest point, for example, the top of a semicircle or the tip of a triangle.

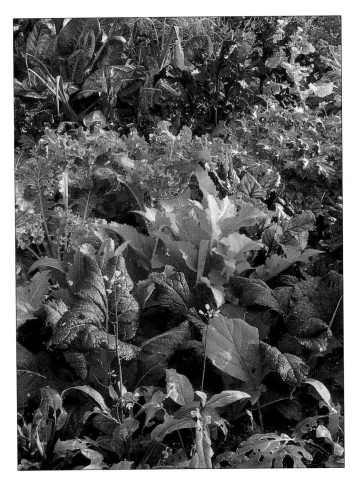

ABOVE: **One of my favourite intercropping combinations can be seen here with purple pak choi (in the foreground), 'Green-in-the-Snow' and 'Art Green' mustards, mizuna greens and 'Bull's Blood' beet.**

OPTIONS FOR INTERCROPPING

The choices for intercropping are very wide and if you have an adventurous streak, don't hesitate to try out new combinations. The suggestions that follow are based on my own tried and trusted favourites, along with others I have either seen or heard about. They are grouped according to the main elements of contrast, which are colour, height and texture. (For details on sowing times and spacing see A–Z Directory, pp.150–199).

CONTRASTING COLOURS

Different coloured varieties of the same vegetable The most natural and even effects come from intercropping of this sort, for example:

• lettuce – red and green forms of 'Salad Bowl' and 'Lollo', red and green varieties of cos, headed and cutting lettuce;

• kales – blue/green, red and the blue or 'Black' kales;

• perilla (shiso), mitsuba and basil – red and green forms;

• summer purslane – yellow and green forms;

• chard – green-, yellow- and red-leaved forms;

• fennel – bronze and green (allow the two of them to self-seed together).

Vegetables with deep red leaves Striking vegetables of this colour intercrop very effectively with dark, light green and blue-green vegetables. The following are some suggestions:

• red-leaved beet and the hardy red chicory 'Treviso' with blanching celery, loose-headed Chinese cabbage, endive, leeks, lettuce, mizuna greens, pak choi and parsley;

• red lettuce with virtually any vegetable, but particularly cabbages, carrots, leeks and onions. Loose-headed forms such as 'Lollo' and 'Salad Bowl' retain their colour and form over many weeks.

Other combinations The following groups of plants work well together:

• golden purslane with red and green lettuce;

• red cabbage edged with grey-leaved plants, such as artemisia, the yellow-green *Helichrysum* 'Limelight', *Helichrysum petiolare*, lavender, or any blue flowers, such as nepeta and salvia;

• red sorrel and green basil;

• 'Black' kales with red lettuce;

• red orache and 'Catalogna' lettuce;

• interplanted white alyssum and thyme on either side of a band of strawberries;

• red perilla and flowering buckwheat;

• nasturtiums among Florence fennel;

• red chicory with Florence fennel;

• light green 'Santo' cabbage between rows of dark-leaved spinach;

• purple Brussels sprouts and canary creeper (*Tropaeolum peregrinum*).

CONTRASTING HEIGHTS

Asparagus The very light shade cast by the feathery asparagus fern allows underplanting and undersowing with seedling crops and salads; or parsley can be sown and left to self-seed.

BELOW: **Onions can be successfully intercropped with lettuce. It is best to plant sets or module-raised plants, as seedlings risk being swamped before they get established.**

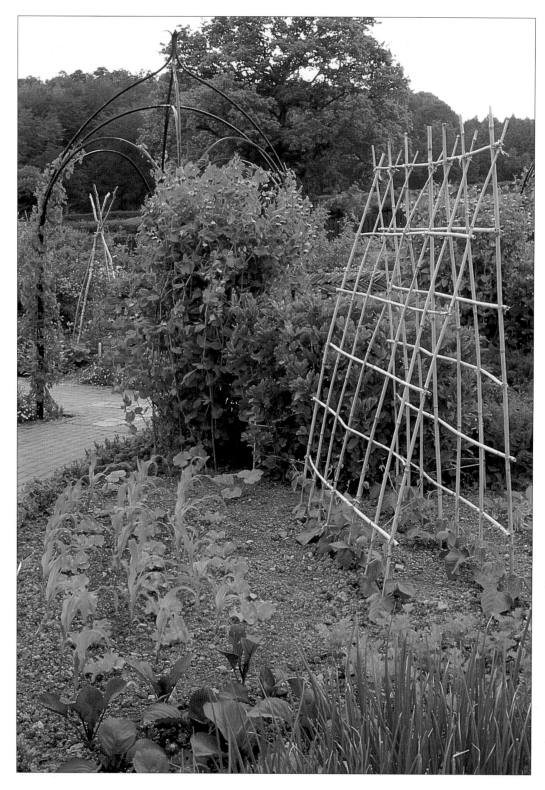

Brassicas The tall-stemmed brassicas, such as Brussels sprouts and tall kales can be intercropped with all the plants listed under *Leeks*, though winter cabbage intercropping would require very wide spacing. Trailing marrows, gherkins and nasturtiums can run between rows of brassicas. The plants with a bushier habit, such as calabrese, cauliflower, kohl rabi and Chinese cabbage are best intercropped in the earlier stages only. Use fast-growing salads or seedling crops, then pull them out as the main crops mature.

Dwarf peas Tall peas generally cast too much shade for intercropping, but rows of dwarf peas can be intercropped with a wide range of salads, spinach beet and dwarf beans. Peas can also be sown in criss-crossing bands (*see* Leeks).

Leeks Being compact, tall, long-standing and a pretty blue-green colour, leeks are one of the best vegetables for intercropping. Garlic, green onions and shallots are good substitutes over

LEFT: **Sweet corn lends itself to intercropping with many different vegetables. In the potager at Rosemoor, Devon, south-west England, lettuce is being used.**

BELOW: **Winter leeks and red 'Salad Bowl' lettuce make an excellent contrast of form and colour in my Little Potager. The slower-maturing leeks were planted first.**

shorter periods. Onions can be multi-sown (see p.143) to give greater impact; garlic can be left to flower. All can be intercropped on a row basis, interspersed in groups between other plants, or planted in an 'X' across a bed, allowing for intercrops in the arms of the cross. The following work well with leeks:

- lettuce – all types, including red and green 'Salad Bowl', jagged-leaved 'Catalogna' and curly-leaved 'Lollo';
- summer salad plants, such as endive, 'Sugar Loaf' and red Italian chicory;
- winter salads, such as hardy lettuces, winter purslane, 'Grumolo' and red 'Treviso' chicory, corn salad, lamb's lettuce and chervil;
- summer or winter cabbage, purple mustard, pak choi and 'Ragged Jack' kale;
- carrots, chrysanthemum greens and New Zealand spinach;
- bands of seedlings and radishes (see Effects with CCA Seedlings, p.112);
- Swiss chards, especially red-leaved types.

Standards Make the most of the height and bare stems of standards. François Carvallo commented on 'the marvellous grace' with which the vegetables hold their own with the standard roses at Villandry. The many types of fruit, ornamental trees, shrubs and herbs, which can be grown on 1–1.2m (3–4ft) stems give vegetables plenty of clearance. Summer bedding plants, such as fuchsia, heliotrope, lantana, pelargoniums and streptosolen, grown as standards, can be woven into vegetable beds to great effect. A bold example from Haskell's Nursery in the US was red-flowered fuchsia 'Gartenmeister Bonstedt' underplanted with black- and white-fruited aubergines.

Sweet corn As the slender leaves block out relatively little light, sweet corn can be grown fairly close together and undercropped, or further apart and intercropped. To ensure cross-pollination, plants should be grouped in a block. There is a wide choice of intercrops:

- any summer or winter salad plants and seedling crops;
- courgettes and dwarf French beans;
- gherkins and cucumbers, and trailing marrows;
- amaranths, beetroot, spinach and chrysanthemum greens;
- crops that can remain after the sweet corn is harvested, such as hardy celery, mizuna, parsley;
- annual flower mixes (for details of varieties, see pp.102–3);
- climbing beans (that can clamber up the sweet corn if it is well enough anchored).

CONTRASTING TEXTURES

While contrasting or harmonizing textures are a feature of almost all intercropping, a few partnerships work on textures alone, for example Chinese cabbage with carrots, parsley with chard or leeks, and curly endive with cutting lettuce.

Most plants with attractive textures (see pp.96–7) are shown off best when planted in groups, to form circles, squares, triangles or river-like drifts – whatever is appropriate to the design of the plot. The secret is to plant them so they completely cover the ground when fully grown. A compact, crowded look reinforces their dramatic qualities: a blanket of iceplant has far more sparkle than a single plant, and the play of light and shade across expanses of dill or fennel is very striking. These textured blocks can be bounded by a contrasting edge, such as a low hedge, herbs, flowers or simply a neat rim of lettuce, beetroot, parsley, purslane or rosette pak choi. Conversely a carpet of crinkled lettuce, endive, iceplant, glossy-leaved mizuna or shining beet can be offset by stern rows of leeks or onion, or a sumptuous boundary of kales or chard. Some of the best textured effects are achieved with seedling crops.

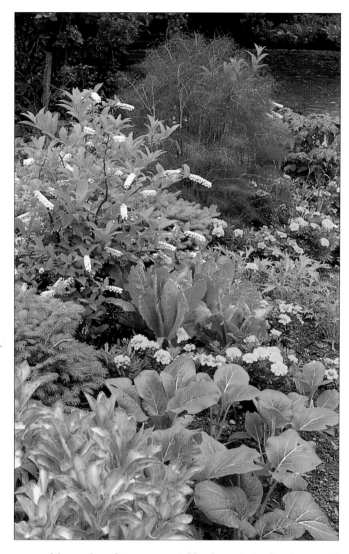

RIGHT: **Intercropping not only makes optimum use of space but can be very colourful. Here, French marigolds weave their way between vegetables.**

SEEDLING PATCHES

One of the quickest, easiest and most effective ways of introducing colour into a vegetable garden is to sow seedling crops. They can form bold and beautifully textured patches, or picturesque details with threads of gold, green or red weaving their way through taller vegetables.

Seedlings have the potential to be boldly dramatic, but the quiet day by day drama of their growth and development is intriguing to watch. Take seedling red mustards, sown in spring in concentric semicircles separated and outlined by rings of onion sets, as I did in my Little Potager several years ago. The first sign of germination is the faintest trace of purple showing just above ground level, yet within a few weeks they will be transformed into vibrant purple bands standing out clearly against the bright green shoots of the sprouting onion sets.

Seedling crops are any fast-germinating edibles that can be sown fairly thickly, then cut at the seedling stage, when they are about 5–10cm (2–4in) high, depending on the plant. Many will then re-sprout to give two or even three more cuttings, earning them the handy label of 'cut-and-come-again' (CCA) crops. These seedlings are usually much more nutritious than older leaves and have a wonderfully fresh, often sweet taste. Their youthful vigour is reflected in the glossy freshness of their appearance: a perky young patch of pak choi leaves, for example, is a beautiful sight.

While the majority of CCA seedlings are grown as short-term crops, some can be left in the ground and will grow larger, remaining productive over many months (see p.113). Perpetual spinach and 'Sugar Loaf' chicory are two examples. In terms of both space and time, there can be few more productive ways of gardening than growing CCA seedlings.

SUITABLE CROPS

A wide range of vegetables can be used as CCA seedlings, many having the extra dimension of colour or texture that makes them potentially decorative. Among lettuces, the 'Salad Bowl' types and the old-fashioned 'cutting' lettuces are perfect for seedling crops, the red-leaved varieties making for superb colour contrasts. Many other salad crops can be used: chicories, corn salad, cresses, which form moss-like strips or patches within a few days of sowing, curly endive, gold and green summer purslane, winter purslane, radish and salad rocket. Many brassicas qualify: kales, mustards, (especially the deeply curled and red-tinted ones) and most of the oriental greens, such as mibuna and rosette pak choi. An exception is Chinese cabbage, as it tends to be rather rough in the seedling stage. Candidates in the spinach family include amaranths, orache and spinach. Among herbs are chervil, coriander and dill.

Various seed mixtures are sold for CCA seedlings. The European salad mix, known variously as *mesclun*, *misticanza* or 'Saladini' may include as many as 12 plants, developing at different rates over several months. 'Oriental saladini' is a selection of six, oriental brassicas. Mixes of chicories, kales, mustards and spicily flavoured seedlings are also available. All the vegetables are productive, easy to use and, because of their diversity, look pretty when growing.

LEFT: **Drills of lettuce seedlings are hightly productive and look very pretty, especially when sown on the diagonal across the corner of a bed.**

ABOVE: **This 'spicy greens' seedling mixture can be cut several times. It should be sown in parallel drills, which will merge into a carpeting patch in a very short time.**

SOWING AND GROWING

Whatever method is used, the soil needs to be reasonably fertile and weed-free, or germinating weeds will smother the sown seedlings. (For instructions on how to prepare a seedbed, see p.141.) If a weed problem is likely, allow the first flush of weeds to germinate and hoe them off before sowing. As a rough guide, sow seeds 1cm (½in) apart to give them enough space to develop steadily without overcrowding.

On the whole, seedling crops do best in the cooler months of the year: there is a tendency for them to run to seed faster in the heat, so spring and autumn sowings are usually the most successful. As they are grown at high density, they must be kept well watered. Cut the seedlings as soon as they reach a useful size,

cutting just above the seed leaves or the lowest pair of leaves. Remove any loose leaves that fall on the patch, as they sometimes rot and discolour the seedlings beneath. Don't hesitate to clear away seedlings as soon as they look straggly, become coarse or start to interfere with anything they are intercropping. With a few exceptions, theirs is a short, sweet life, but a flagging patch can sometimes be revived with a feed of liquid fertilizer.

Broadcasting Scatter the seed evenly on the surface of the soil, then cover by raking first in one direction, then at right angles. Alternatively cover the seed with a 5mm–1cm (¼–½in) layer of sifted soil or potting compost. Broadcasting is a quick method, but subsequent weeding is tricky in a densely sown patch.

Miniature circles Neat 'dabs' of seeds can be sown like punctuation marks between plants. For a tiny circle, press out an imprint with, for example, the lid of a large jar, scatter seed within its markings, then rake or sieve soil over them. I first saw this done with rounds of radish between sweet corn: the radish were not pulled for use, but left to flower among the corn.

Single drills Seed is sown into a narrow drill, which can be anything from 1 to 5cm (½ to 2in) deep. In wet conditions, line the

RIGHT: **Mixtures of red and green lettuce varieties are widely available, and make a colourful splash when grown as cut-and-come-again seedlings.**

drill with potting compost to help germination; in dry conditions water the bottom of the drill thoroughly, sow the seed, and cover it with dry soil. This 'dust mulch' slows down evaporation and keeps the seed moist until it germinates. Use single drills where a fine line, rather than a broad band, of seedlings is wanted.

Wide drills A 10cm- (4in-) wide onion hoe is ideal for making shallow, wide drills, which can be solitary or in a parallel series, each as close

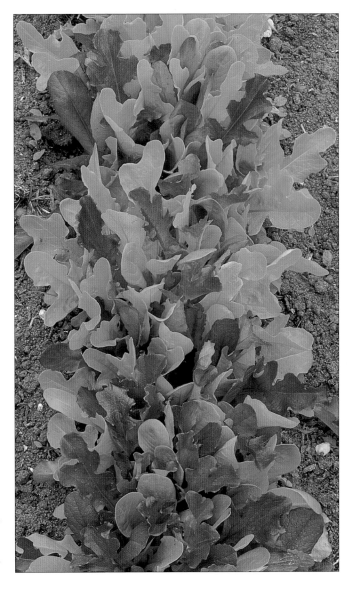

to its neighbour as possible. Scatter the seeds evenly then cover with soil. In the early stages the individual drills of seedlings stand out clearly, but later seedlings spill over into the space between the rows making dense patches.

EFFECTS WITH CCA SEEDLINGS

All sorts of patterns can be carved out with seedlings. A single straight drill or band of seedlings strikes a resonant chord between parallel rows of greens or leeks. Where plants such as leeks are grown in a square formation, a grid of seedlings can be sown among them. Try sowing red seedlings in one direction, green in the other, for a cheery grid effect. Whenever winter brassicas are planted, seedlings can be sown around them in squares, circles or wavy lines. I have enclosed a kale within a diamond of red 'Friulana' lettuce seedlings to good effect.

One advantage of this sort of intercropping is that the seedlings carpet the ground until the space is needed by the maturing plants they surround. Another useful practice is to sow seedlings on the soil above potatoes when they are first planted. They will be cleared long before the potato leaves poke through.

Growing seedlings in patches creates all sorts of opportunities. For a stripy, angled look in the early stages, sow drills diagonally across rectangular or triangular beds. Intensify the striped effect by aligning rows in different directions in adjoining beds or patches. Make full use of different coloured seedlings to get a patchwork look. For example, sow alternate sections of a quartered square, dovetailed triangles, or segments of a circle with red and green lettuce or yellow and green purslane. A simple series of squares down the length of a bed can also be beautiful.

LEFT: Bands of lettuce seedlings sown in a double triangle around a slow-growing cauliflower utilize the ground in the plant's early stages and make a pretty pattern.

BELOW: In this example of creating effects with seedlings, a red cabbage is encircled with a wide band of 'Frisby' lettuce, which responds well to CCA treatment.

CUT-AND-COME-AGAIN (CCA) SEEDLING TABLE

	Germination	Cuts	Life span	When to sow	Attractive
Corn salad	3	2–3	3+	❄	*
Curly endive	2	2–3	3–4	✿	*
Curly kale	3	2–3	6–8+	❄	
Dill	2	2	2–3	✿	*
Garden cress	1	2–5	1–2	❄	*
Lettuce, cutting	2	2–3	3–4	✿	*
Mibuna greens	2	2	3+	❄	*
Mizuna greens	1	4	4+	❄	*
Orache	2	3	3	✿	*
Oriental saladini	1	3–4	2–5	❄	
Pak choi	1	2–4	2–4	❄	*
Radish	1	2	1–2	✿	*
Red mustard	1	2	2–3	✿	
Salad rocket	1	3–5	2–3	❄	*
Spinach	2	3–4	2–5	✿	
Spinach, perpetual	2	3–4	6	✿	*
'Sugar Loaf' chicory	2	2–3	3–4	✿	*
Summer purslane	2	2–3	2	○	
Texsel greens	2	2	2–3	❄	
Winter purslane	3	2–3	2–3	❄	*

Use the chart to create patterns with seedlings and to plan intercropping.

KEY

▢ **Germination time**
Average time before the seedling appears above ground.
1 less than a week; 2 2–3 weeks; 3 3 weeks

✂ **Cuts**
Average number of cuts from one sowing.

🕐 **Life span**
Average time in months of useful cropping.

When to sow
✿ can sow throughout the growing season
❄ best sown in cool conditions
○ requires warm conditions

* attractive in flowering or seeding phase

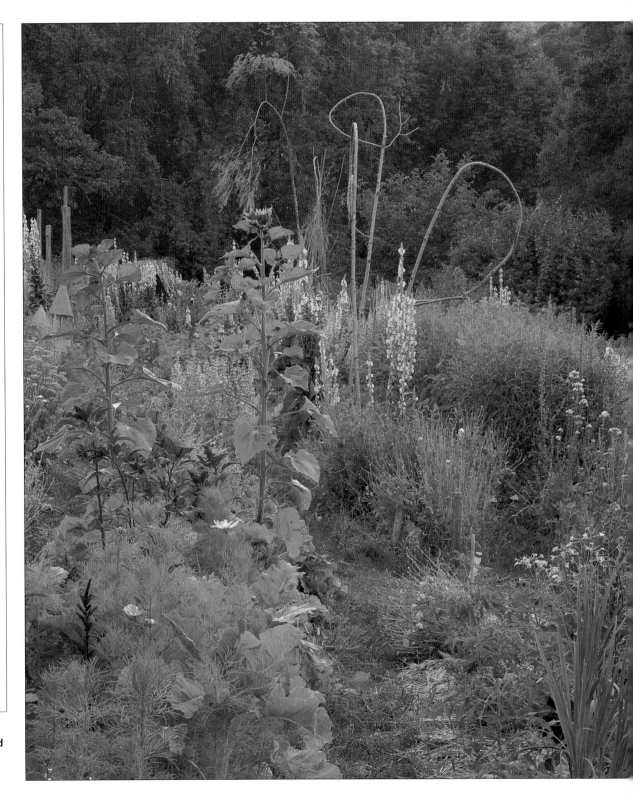

RIGHT: **Nature is profligate, and most of the poppies, red orache, verbascums and sunflowers here have grown from 'volunteer' seedlings with a spectacular result.**

FRUIT AS A DECORATIVE FEATURE

THERE IS ALWAYS A PLACE for fruit in a kitchen garden. Not only is it productive, but almost all fruit is decorative at blossom time and when fruiting: think of the texture and colour of grapes, peaches or red currants. Often, too, fruit trees have beautiful leaves or stems and radiant autumn colour. Fruit ages gracefully, giving a garden an air of permanence, which is why it plays such a memorable role in the best known potagers. Villandry has its cloistered alleyways of vines and stately, distaff pears as sentinels at the gateways of each square. At Barnsley House, Gloucestershire, south-west England,

the silhouettes of the goblet apples and pears stay in the visitor's memory. This chapter looks at how fruit can be used to show off, and complement, the vegetables and herbs in the kitchen garden, with the emphasis on what is appropriate in small and medium-sized gardens.

LEFT: **Apple trees underplanted with bulbs in the orchard at Cranborne Manor, Dorset, guarantee a spectacular spring display.**

ABOVE: **The fruit on espaliered trees is of exceptional quality, benefitting from full exposure to the warmth of the sun.**

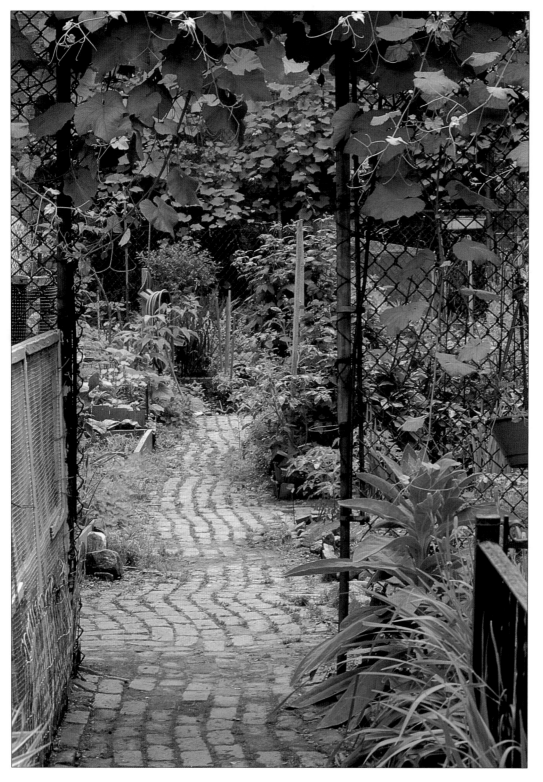

USING FRUIT CREATIVELY

In the classic European walled kitchen garden apples, apricots, cherries, currants, figs, gooseberries, grapevines, peaches, pears and plums were elegantly trained against the high brick walls, usually in the 'restricted' forms of fans, espaliers and cordons. The walls protected the plants from wind and frost, and fruit ripened well in their reflected heat, looking magnificent. If you are lucky enough to have a high wall around your garden, then make as much use of it as you can for growing fruit.

The modern kitchen garden is more likely to be bounded by wooden fencing and trellises. Though these offer less warmth, fruit can be trained against them in formal, traditional ways to make a delightful enclosure for vegetables. Post-and-wire supports may look bare when first erected, but are soon covered, and are often a good way of dividing a vegetable garden into sections or of screening it from the rest of the garden. Bush fruits such as gooseberries and currants can be grown around the perimeter as an informal hedge, provided the more rampant varieties are avoided.

Trailing berried fruits are more informal, but can be put to good use sprawling over boundary fences or on supports of various kinds. The thorniest blackberries are fearsome, but there are plenty of gentler, pretty-leaved varieties. Beautiful features can be made by training natural climbers such as blackberries, blackberry hybrids, vines and kiwis on arches, obelisks or pergolas. Apples and pears, grown

LEFT: **Grapevines are among the most beautiful of climbing plants, and are easily trained over arches or trellises, as seen here in a New York Community Garden.**

116

as extended cordons, can be trained upwards and overhead to clothe an arch or, most magical of all, to form a tunnel of fruit.

It is very tempting to mingle ornamental climbers with fruit: clematis and roses can look wonderful clambering up old apple or pear trees. With trained fruit, however, space is more limited, and there is the risk of ripening fruit being shaded from the sun. One solution is to space out fruit along a trellis, planting ornamentals between them. Combining ornamentals with trailing berries is easier and for this, light-weight climbers, such as Canary creeper (*Tropaeolum canariense*), are best. With

BELOW RIGHT: **Standard gooseberries fit neatly into a potager, whether in the vegetable beds, along a pathway or as a focal point in a key position.**

BELOW: **A specimen fruit tree makes a natural focal point in a kitchen garden. An apple trained into a classical goblet shape, as here, is an attractive feature year round.**

RIGHT: **Apples grown as cordons can be trained against a wall, or to posts and wires as a boundary, or to form a dramatic living screen or partition within a garden.**

clematis, choose the less vigorous types, which are pruned back each spring, such as *Clematis texensis*. Try the double-flowered magenta *C. viticella* 'Purpurea Plena Elegans' to contrast with light green foliage, and 'John Huxtable' or 'Comtesse de Bouchaud', both pale-coloured Jackmanii types, to contrast with darker leaves, say those of trailing berries. For best results, prune the clematis back hard in spring in the first two or three years, to within 30cm (12in) of the ground. This encourages the production of plenty of stems. In subsequent years, prune them 'semi-hard' or back to the level of the lowest branch of a supporting tree or rail of a fence.

SHAPELY AND COLOURFUL TREES

Many fruit trees are intrinsically beautiful and make eloquent centrepieces and focal points. Suitable examples include the purple-leaved filbert *Corylus maxima* 'Purpurea', medlars, the small weeping mulberry *Morus alba* 'Pendula', quince, with its large, wide-eyed blossoms, gnarled old apples and pears, and crab apples. Of the crabs 'Crittenden', 'Dartmouth', 'John Downie' and 'Montreal' are some of the varieties blessed with lovely blossom, as well as edible fruit. In warm climates, there are the glossy-leaved, evergreen citrus fruits, such as lemons, limes, loquat and oranges, along with bananas, the nut-bearing species of *Macadamia*, persimmons, pomegranates and many more. The evergreen huckleberry (*Vaccinium ovatum*) has beautiful, smoky-red shoots in spring. It is just a question of choosing whatever suits the climate and scale of the garden.

Think of autumn colour, too, when it comes to choosing fruit. Several vines (see pp.127–8) and trailing berries have beautiful autumn colour, as do high- and low-bush blueberries (*Vaccinium corymbosum* and *V. angustifolium*) and the high-bush cranberry (*Viburnum trilobum*). Asian pear, chestnuts, medlar, persimmon and pomegranate are among tree fruits that are colourful in autumn, while the hazelnuts have decorative catkins in winter.

In skilful hands, apples and pears can be trained into highly ornamental forms – flat-topped 'tables', 'crowns', goblets, and weeping trees, but these are best undertaken with expert help. In essence, the outline of the required form is constructed with a framework of canes and, as the tree grows, the leading shoots and

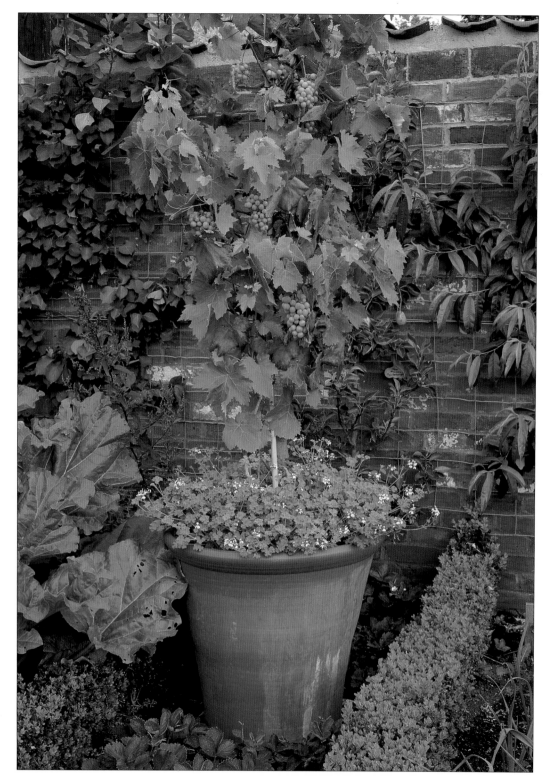

RIGHT: **Grapevines grow very successfully in pots. This one stands in a box-edged bed against a wall in summer, but is moved back into a conservatory during the winter.**

FRUIT AS A DECORATIVE FEATURE

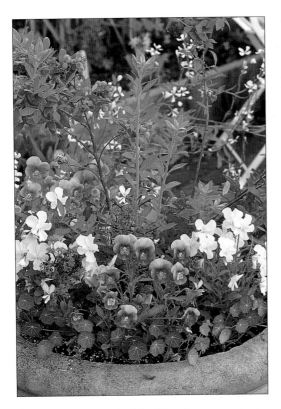

ABOVE: **The decorative high-bush blueberry grows best in acid conditions. Growing it in a pot allows its soil requirements to be met more easily (see pp.32–3).**

selected sideshoots are tied to the framework. A few specialist nurserymen sell trained trees, and will advise on training.

For a vertical form there are the columnar tree fruits (see pp.132–3), while naturally bushy fruits, such as gooseberries and red currants, can be grown as standards on a leg to give them height and elegance. They look their best when lining paths, in the centre of a bed, or accenting key points in the overall design.

FRUIT IN CONTAINERS

Fruit grown in pots can make very handsome specimens, and there are several practical benefits. The soil can be tailored to the needs of the crop (alkaline for peaches, acid for blueberries),

tender fruits can be moved under cover when necessary, it is easy to keep an eye on watering and pollination, and pots can be moved into prominent positions when the plants are at their most theatrical.

Ideal for pot growing are the genetic dwarf nectarines, such as 'Nectarella', and peach varieties, such as 'Bonanza', 'Garden Annie', 'Garden Lady', introduced in the 80s. The columnar apples and pears can be grown in large pots. A generally suitable size and dimension for containers is about 25l (6.25gal) with a diameter of about 45cm (18in). Some of the prettiest effects can be obtained by training vines into standards, goblets, or a flat-topped, umbrella-shape, using a framework of canes or wires.

There is a long tradition of growing strawberries in pottery strawberry pots, ideally large pots at least 45cm (18in) high or in wooden barrels, with 5cm (2in) diameter holes drilled in the sides about 15cm (6in) apart. Plant the strawberries in early spring or late summer layer by layer as the containers are filled with potting compost. Both standard varieties and more delicate alpine varieties look wonderful tumbling out of pots. It is quite practical to move them around the garden, to show them off when they are in flower, or to shade them from full sun in the summer months.

RIGHT: **Tree fruits, such as this apple tree, can be grown in pots to restrict growth and encourage fruiting.**

INTEGRATING FRUIT INTO THE GARDEN

Fruit can also be integrated into the kitchen or flower garden as edging and ground cover. For a knee-high edge, use the horizontal 'stepover' apples and pears (see pp.125–7). For low edges, use compact runnerless strawberries, the most suitable being the alpine strawberries, *Fragaria vesca* 'Semperflorens'. There are red, white and yellow forms, all easily raised from seed, but best replaced every two or three years or they deteriorate. Second choice would be some of

ABOVE: **A row of stepover apples no more than 45cm (18in) high with double-flowered strawberries growing alongside makes a neat edge or boundary.**

the perpetual or remontant strawberries, most of which have few runners and so remain compact. They have several flushes of fruit a year, but are best replaced after one or two seasons.

There are several low-growing berried plants, generally from northern latitudes and requiring acid soils, which make attractive ground cover. In suitable conditions it is worth cultivating them on banks and in spare corners around the potager. A list of suitable plants includes the Arctic raspberry (*Rubus arcticus* ssp. *arcticus*), with its pretty purple flowers in spring, common bearberry (*Arctostaphylos uva-ursi*), the creeping raspberry (*Rubus calycinoides*), which

RIGHT: **The bright flowered Arctic raspberry forms dense mats of bright green leaves with attractive autumn tints.**

FAR RIGHT: **The white strawberry, with its well deserved reputation for flavour, is both a neat and undemanding edging plant for potagers.**

has minute yellow fruits, cranberry (*Vaccinium oxycoccos*), cowberry or lingonberry (*V. vitis-idaea*) and dewberry (*Rubus caesius*). For the flamboyant pink-flowered strawberries, see Special Effects with Ground Cover, page 95.

Fruit, flowers and herbs can often share beds and borders. Tree fruits growing against a wall or fence can be underplanted with spring-flowering bulbs, spring or summer bedding plants, and even perennials. Acid-loving fruits, such as blueberries, can blend into borders of azaleas, while red currants can be planted in a shrubbery. Bushy herbs can flounce around the

feet of fruit trees – lavender under olives and sages beneath quince are combinations I've encountered – while creeping thymes can nestle around the base of any standard tree.

SELECTING FRUIT

The choice of what fruit to grow, where, and how is influenced by climate, soil and the size of the garden. As with vegetables, fruit must thrive if it is to be productive and beautiful. It makes sense to concentrate on what grows well in your area rather than coaxing along borderline fruits, however tempting they may be. If your garden is in a frost pocket, opt for late-flowering varieties. As for soil, most fruits have much the same requirements as vegetables – well-drained, deep, fertile, slightly acid, and a reasonable supply of moisture throughout the growing period. Because fruit may be in the ground for many years, a good start is essential. If soil conditions are poor, delay planting until fertility and, in particular, any inadequate drainage have been improved (see Soil Fertility, pp.136–40). In very small gardens the choice is inevitably restricted, but dwarfer, compact varieties are continually being introduced. Fortunately, tree fruits such as apples and pears can be kept small and beautiful by growing them as cordons and espaliers, perfect forms for the potager.

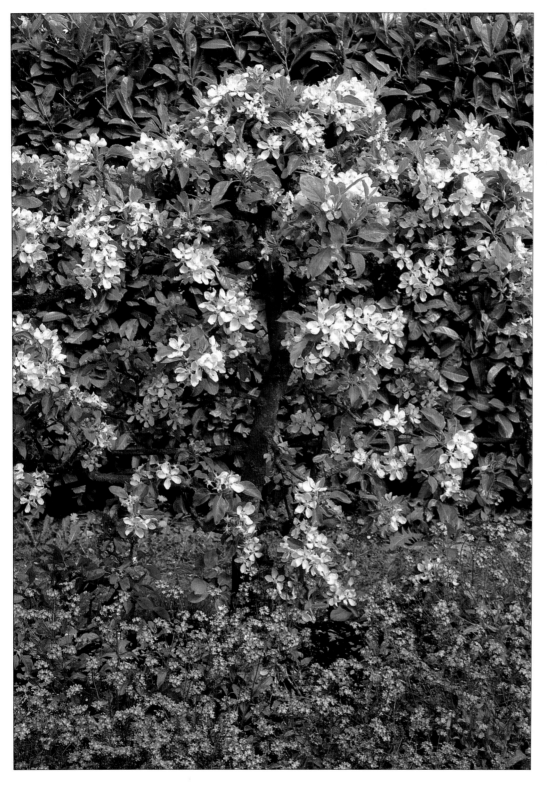

FRUIT AS A FRAMEWORK

TRAINED FRUIT ON BOUNDARIES

The first step in growing fruit against a wall, fence or trellis is to put up horizontal, parallel wires so the branches and young growths can be trained into position. The wires need to be taut, strong (use about 14-gauge soft galvanized wire) and at least 5cm (2in) clear of the wall. Attach them to vine eyes, hammered or screwed in, and keep them taut with straining bolts at either end. The lowest wire can be 38cm (15in) above the ground. For most purposes, space the wires about 30cm (12in) apart up the wall, although they will need to be about 15cm (6in) apart for fan-trained fruit. Where espaliers are being grown, put the wires up after planting, gearing the spacing to the tiers of the branches. If ornamental climbers are to be added (see p.89), use pig netting, or weave vertical wires between the horizontal wires to make roughly 23cm (9in) squares.

In the absence of walls, fences or trellis, fruit can be trained on wires stretched between posts. Use metal posts or pressure-treated softwood posts, which need a life expectancy of at least 20 years. End posts should be strutted and need to be very strong, about 12 x 12cm (5 x 5in) in diameter, with intermediate posts of 7.5–10cm (3–4in) every 4m (13ft) or so.

The list of fruits that can be grown against supports – and so used to provide a framework – is very long. Hardy tree fruits include apples, cherries, damsons, gages, medlar, pears, plums and quince. Slightly less hardy fruits, which in

LEFT: **Spring flowers are the perfect bedfellows for fruit: here forget-me-nots complement apple blossom at Cranborne Manor, Dorset, south-west England.**

ABOVE: **The simplest way to create a diamond lattice apple boundary is by planting oblique cordons alternately facing left and right.**

coolish climates benefit from being trained against walls and solid fences, include apricots, Asian pears, figs, nectarines and peaches, while in warm climates this applies to loquat, persimmon, and various citrus. Then there are the soft fruits, such as gooseberries, red currants, white currants and, last but not least, the climbing and trailing fruits such as grapevines, kiwi and the extensive tribe of blackberries, hybrid berries and other related berries.

For practical purposes, walls and supports need to be at least 1.8m (6ft) high, and ideally higher for trailing berries, two-tiered espaliers and soft fruit cordons and fans. Apple, pear and plum cordons, multi-layered espaliers and fan-trained stone fruits really need walls or fences that are 2.1–2.5m (7–8ft) high with wires 30cm (12in) apart. Not all fruit varieties are suitable for training in restricted forms. With apples and pears, for example, spur-fruiting

varieties are more suitable than tip bearers. Seek advice from specialist nurserymen. See also Further Reading, page 201.

The aspect of the wall affects the fruits that can be grown on it. In the northern hemisphere use walls with a south, south-east or south-west orientation for the sun-loving, less hardy fruits such as apricots, nectarines and peaches, along with apples, grapes, pears and plums. Most of these fruits can also be grown on a west-facing wall. Use the north-facing, sunless walls for growing blackberries, gooseberries, morello cherries, some pears, culinary plums and red currants. All these, as well as apples, pears and plums, can be grown on east-facing walls. The reverse applies in the southern hemisphere.

Practicalities Tree fruits can only be grown successfully against walls or other surfaces in restricted, two-dimensional forms if their natural vigour is curtailed. This is achieved in the

LEFT: **A latticed effect can also be obtained by double grafting on either side of the rootstock so the branches form a wide 'V', overlapping in a diamond pattern.**

BELOW: **Where fruit is trained against wires, a system of strong supports with tensioning wires is essential.**

RIGHT: **The acid-fruited morello cherry is frequently trained as a fan against walls, or as here, against a wooden shed. It will tolerate a partially shaded situation.**

first instance, by selecting and planting fruits grafted onto dwarfing rootstocks (see Glossary, p.200), and subsequently by severe pruning. It is standard practice to graft most tree fruits, including apples, cherries, citrus, nectarines, peaches, pears and plums, onto rootstocks of related species which, among other factors, influence the eventual size of the tree. Cordons, espaliers and fans are generally, but not invariably, grafted onto semi-dwarfing or the more dwarfing of the available rootstocks. An incidental benefit of this is that dwarfing rootstocks bring trees into bearing sooner – in some cases in the year following planting – as opposed to three or four years later with more vigorous rootstocks. Fruiting, in its turn, further restricts the tree's vigour and size.

Once the basic framework of the tree has been established by winter pruning in the first year or two after planting, the trees are kept in shape almost entirely with summer pruning. This quick and easy job encourages the production of fruit, and limits surplus growth, and essentially consists of cutting back the side-shoots that have developed during the current season (see Cordons, p.124).

Trees that are grown in restricted forms bear heavily for their size, but inevitably produce less fruit than large free-standing trees. The quality of the fruit, however, is exceptional, and this is largely because the branches are fully exposed to the sunshine.

Selecting and planting Fruit is a long-term investment, and it is essential to start with top-quality plants, preferably bought from a specialist nurserymen. Most people buy two to three year old trees with the basic framework

already trained. An alternative, if you are able to do the training yourself, is to buy one year old 'feathered maidens' – young trees with the first handful of lateral shoots ('feathers') developing on the stem. The feathers become the fruiting spurs or branches. For training cordons, the more feathers the better.

Trees can be bought 'bare-rooted' or in containers. Bare-rooted trees, lifted straight from the ground, must be planted while dormant in the autumn or spring, though never in cold or wet soil. Container-grown trees can be planted at any time of the year, but need to be watered carefully until they are established. Beware of plants with pot-bound roots: they never grow well.

Prepare the soil by digging deeply and working in a generous amount of well-rotted manure or compost. The ground at the base of a wall or fence tends to get very dry, so plant at least 25cm (10in) away, leaning the tree back towards the wall. Before planting, trim back any protruding tap-roots. After planting, put a cane into the ground alongside the stem and at the same angle. Tie the tender young stems to the cane, rather than to the wire, to prevent chafing. In the later stages of training, canes can be tied to the wires at appropriate angles. Use a half-hitch on the wire and a loop around the cane so it doesn't slip.

Apples, pears, plums and sweet cherries are rarely self-fertile, and only fruit well if cross-pollinated by another variety growing nearby. In these cases, it is necessary to plant two or more varieties, choosing compatible varieties that flower at roughly the same time (for further information, consult the supplier, or see Further Reading, p.201).

TRAINED FRUIT FORMS

Cordons The basic cordon is a single stem with fruiting spurs emanating along its length. Its compactness makes it one of the most useful forms of trained fruit, especially for small vegetable gardens. Cordons can be grown vertically, at an oblique angle (usually at 45 degrees to the ground), or even horizontally. Oblique and horizontal cordons are particularly useful against low walls or fences. Cordons have many merits: they can be closely spaced, are easily managed, they make neat patterns, and cross-pollination problems are resolved by slipping in one plant of the required pollinator. The basic single stem can be augmented to give two, three or more parallel stems creating, respectively, double (or U-cordons), triple cordons or multiple cordons. For training and pruning, each branch is treated as a single cordon. (For training and pruning apple and pear cordons, see diagrams below.)

Fruits that lend themselves to being grown as cordons are apples, red and white currants, gooseberries, the self-fertile kiwi, pears and quinces. Stone fruit such as cherries and plums can be grown as cordons and may look good in their early years, but considerable skill is required to keep them under control later.

Apples and pears fruit best, and are easiest to train as oblique cordons. They can also be trained as vertical cordons to cover arches and tunnels or as free-standing trees (see Using Fruit Creatively, p.116). Cordon apples can be grafted onto very dwarfing rootstocks if the soil is highly fertile; otherwise it is better to use semi-dwarfing rootstocks. Pears are grafted onto the standard quince rootstocks. Cordon apples and pears are normally spaced about 75cm (30in) apart – though occasionally they are squeezed in closer.

The simplest way to make a neat, lattice pattern of criss-crossing stems is to plant cordons obliquely, alternately angled to the left and to the right. This makes a lovely screen, but requires a lot of trees (see p.122). It can also be done, with half the number of trees, by training double cordons in a 'V'-shape, or with a double graft on either side of the rootstock.

While plums that are grafted onto dwarfing 'Pixie' rootstock can be planted as oblique cordons spaced about 1m (3ft) apart, their vigour necessitates pruning several times in the summer, and they are better grown as fans. Red currants, white currants and gooseberries grow equally well as vertical or oblique cordons. Space single cordons 30–35cm (12–14in) apart, adopting the wider spacing on poorer soils. For double or triple cordons, space the plants two and three times further apart respectively as they require considerably more room.

Once the basic framework is established, cordons are kept within bounds mainly by summer pruning. Timing is the key: pruning too early encourages growth instead of restricting it. With apples, the current season's shoots should be pruned when pencil thick and starting to darken and harden at the base. Shoots on the main stem are then pruned back to three leaves above the basal leaf cluster, while shoots on existing spurs are cut back to leave one leaf. For information on pruning other fruits, see Further Reading, page 201.

HOW TO TRAIN A CORDON

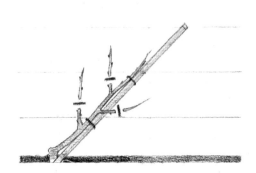

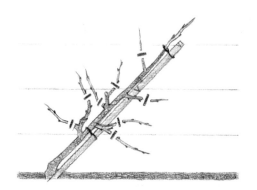

1 Plant a one-year maiden tree at 45 degrees in winter while it is dormant. Prune back the sideshoots (laterals) to four buds. The main shoot (leader) is left unpruned until it is 15cm (6in) above the wire.

2 In early winter next year, prune sideshoots on the main stem to four buds and sideshoot sub-laterals to one bud. When long enough (see diagram 1) cut the leader to within two buds of the old wood in late spring.

3 Subsequently control growth with summer pruning. Cut sideshoots to three leaves beyond the basal leaf cluster, and sub-laterals to one leaf. Cut the leader back to within two buds of the old wood.

ABOVE: **Apples and pears trained as espaliers make an elegant boundary, especially when touching branches are grafted together to form a seamless screen.**

BELOW: **Apricots require warmth in summer for the fruits to ripen, so thrive when grown against a sunny stone or brick wall. They are suitable for fan training.**

SPLICE GRAFTING

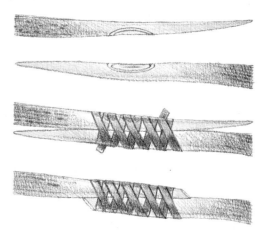

In late winter, choose pencil-thick stems and make shallow 5cm- (2in-) long, facing cuts, 15cm (6in) from the tips. Bind them together with plastic tape. Eventually cut off the old stems just beyond the join.

Espaliers and stepovers An espalier is a tree or bush in which pairs of branches, like outstretched arms, are trained horizontally from the main stem. At its simplest (exemplified by the knee-high 'stepover' apples and pears), there is just one tier of branches, but espaliers can be formed with two, three or more tiers, spaced 38–45cm (15–18in) apart. With their elegant symmetry, espaliers are one of the most dramatic, two-dimensional forms for trained fruit. They look good against walls, but they also make beautiful free-standing screens trained on post-and-wire fences. When the outstretched branches of neighbouring trees eventually touch, they can be grafted together with a simple splice graft (see diagram above) to make a continuous screen. They are very productive because, without a leading shoot, all the plant's energy is diverted into producing fruit, rather than new growth.

A very pretty effect, which also encourages fruiting, can be created by gently arching the top 'arms' of an espalier. In a more elaborate technique the branches can be trained outwards, then upwards, and eventually even down again, to form 'windows' or enclosed circles. These too, can be completed by grafting branches where they meet with a splice graft. Alternatively, the branch ends can simply be tied together, though this is less satisfactory as

HOW TO TRAIN A STEPOVER APPLE

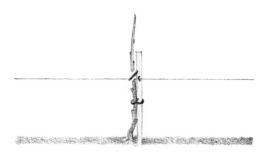

1 In autumn or winter plant a one-year dormant tree grafted on the dwarfing M27 rootstock. After planting, cut the main shoot to 30cm (12in) above ground and tie it to a post in a figure of eight.

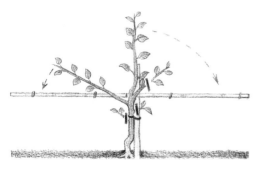

2 Let three shoots develop. In late summer, bend the two strongest gently to the wire. Tie them to a bamboo cane attached to the wire. Prune the third shoot to one bud; rub off any buds on the main stem.

3 Next spring prune the arms to 60cm (24in) from the main stem. In late summer prune laterals on the arms to three leaves above the basal leaf cluster, and sub-laterals to one leaf.

there is bound to be a certain amount of chafing. Training is done during the summer months when the shoots are still supple.

Apples and pears (including Asian pears) are the most popular espalier tree fruits. Apples are normally grafted onto a dwarfing rootstock spaced 3–3.8m (10–12ft) apart, or onto a semi-dwarfing rootstock spaced up to 3.8–4.5m (12–15ft) apart. Pears, grafted onto a quince rootstock, are spaced about 4.2m (14ft) apart. Mulberries, loquat and some citrus fruits can also be grown as espaliers.

It takes several years to train multi-tiered espaliers, as they are built up a tier at a time, a year for each tier. To save time they are usually bought with one or two tiers already trained. Further tiers can be developed from the central leader if required. Training a 'stepover', from a one-year grafted maiden can be done over two seasons (see diagrams left).

The key to training espalier tree fruits is to remember that shoots naturally grow more vigorously vertically than horizontally. So, shoots that are to become the horizontal arms of the espalier are initially trained to canes attached to the training wires at a 45 degree angle in a V-shape; in autumn they are carefully lowered to a horizontal position. (This is unnecessary if training a one-year maiden as a stepover.) The same principle can be applied where an espalier is growing unevenly: the more vigorous branch can be slowed down by retying it at an angle closer to the horizontal. The training of cordons and espaliers may occasionally be thwarted when bare stems are

produced without fruit buds, or by a lack of shoots where they are required. 'Nicking' a dormant bud, which is making a V-shaped cut just through the bark 1cm (½in) below the bud, encourages fruit bud formation, while 'notching' in the same way above a bud encourages shoot formation. This must be done in spring.

Compared with the grandeur of a mature, multi-tiered espalier, the single-tiered stepover is a modest affair. Yet a row of stepovers planted 1.5m (5ft) apart looks very picturesque when lining a path, or edging borders or beds. Apple stepovers are generally grafted onto the very dwarfing M27 rootstock and pears onto Quince C. For support, each plant needs to be tied to a short post, put in the ground before planting, and trained to a single horizontal wire, which is stapled to the posts at a height of 30–45cm (12–18in), depending on the height of the stepover. Once established, stepovers are pruned in summer in the same way as cordons.

LEFT: **The single-layer espaliers known as 'stepovers' require the minimum of pruning. They make an unobtrusive edge and are suitable for small gardens.**

red currants, white currants and gooseberries shouldn't be grown as stepovers, but the arms would have to be at least 38cm (15in) off the ground to prevent the fruit being soiled.

Vines on the boundary The grapevine, with its knotted stems, beautiful leaves and handsome fruit, demands a place in the decorative kitchen garden. In cool climates the choice of outdoor varieties is restricted, and a sheltered, sunny aspect is essential for fruit to mature. But wine and grapes apart, there are several varieties worth growing for their decorative value alone. Grapes can be bought as one- or two-year-old canes and are normally planted 1.5m (5ft) apart.

The grapevine is a natural climber with curling tendrils. Left untrammelled, some varieties will climb high into trees or clamber over the boundary wall, but if good quality fruit is required, or they are being grown against walls, fences or free-standing post-and-wire supports, they must be trained.

A vine can be trained into almost any form – cordon, espalier, fan, pole or standard – by a host of methods. All depend on the fact that grapes develop on laterals on the current year's wood. Whatever the final form, the first few years should be spent developing the framework, without allowing the vine to fruit. From then on the vine is pruned back to its basic framework of permanent branches each winter.

For a kitchen garden wall or fence, a double or multi-stemmed cordon is one of the neatest and most productive forms, making maximum use of the height of any surface. Allow at least 1m (3ft) between each vertical shoot or 'rod' to accommodate the summer growth. Prune them on the 'rod and spur' system (see p.200).

The following are decorative varieties: *Vitis cognetiae* has very large leaves with spectacular autumn colour, but rarely any fruits. *V. labrusca* (a group known as the 'strawberry vines' and including 'Fox Grape' and 'Concord') has decorative foliage and variously coloured, edible grapes. The leaves of *V. vinifera* 'Brandt' (also known as 'Brant') turn from green to a beautiful red in autumn and it has small black edible grapes. *V. v.* 'Californica' is purely ornamental

If the spur systems become too long and large, shorten them by occasionally cutting back into older wood. Stepovers can also be trained with a single arm coming out on one side if there is insufficient space for two arms. Although I have never seen it done, there is no reason why

HOW TO TRAIN A MULTI-STEMMED CORDON VINE

1 Plant a one year vine in the dormant season. Cut the main stem back to three buds. To form the horizontal framework tie two 2.1m (7ft) canes at 45 degrees to the wire. Train the two strongest stems to them.

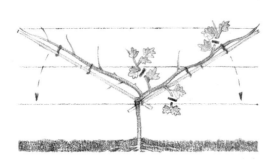

2 In summer nip shoots on the main stems to one leaf. When the stems have made good growth untie them in late summer, lower and tie them to a horizontal wire. When dormant, prune the tips to 1.8m (6ft).

3 Shoots develop along the branches in summer. To make the vertical framework, select four shoots 1m (3ft) apart. Tie them upright to the wires. Prune other shoots and sideshoots to one or two leaves.

with grey leaves and crimson autumn foliage. *V. v.* 'Incana' (also known as 'Pinot Meunier', 'Miller's Burgundy', 'Dusty Miller', 'Wrotham Pinot') has mealy, soft purple foliage, and black grapes for eating and wine. *V. v.* 'Purpurea' (also known as 'Purple Vine', 'Teinturier Grape') has deep purple leaves all summer but inedible blue grapes. (For training grapevines on arches and other supports, see pp.130–1.)

The Chinese gooseberry or kiwi, *Actinidia chinensis*, is another beautiful but rampant fruiting vine that can be incorporated into a large kitchen garden. Its drawbacks, besides its over-vigorous nature, are the susceptibility of the young growths to frost, and the need to plant at least one male to every seven female plants to ensure pollination. It fruits in the same way as the grapevine and, broadly speaking, can be trained and pruned in the same way, except that in winter, shoots are pruned less severely, to about 10cm (4in) from the stem.

The related *Actinidia arguta* 'Issai' is a more practical proposition for a modest-sized kitchen garden wall, fence or trellis. The fruits are much smaller, but it is hardier and less rampant. It is self-fertile, although it fruits better if cross-pollinated with, for instance, the self-fertile *A. polygama*, another species with small, but edible fruits. Like a grapevine, it can be trained as a single or multi-stemmed cordon: allow about 45cm (18in) between each upright stem.

Fan training An expertly trained fan tree, the branches radiating web-like over a high wall, is a wonderful sight. To do it well requires skill, patience and time. The starting point is a tree with two low strong branches on either side of the main stem. These are trained outwards at an angle close to the horizontal and the central leader is removed, so the network of fanning shoots all spring from these two low branches. Fans are usually bought as partially trained two to three year old trees (for training and pruning fans, see Further Reading, p.201). Fans take a lot of space: most tree fruits need to be 4–6m (13–20ft) apart, though sour cherries require 5–8m (16–25ft) between each plant. Soft fruit fans need to be 1.8m (6ft) or so apart.

Suitable fruits include apples, pears and Asian pears, the black mulberry, stone fruits such as apricots, cherries, damsons, gages, nectarines, peaches and plums, while for soft fruit gooseberries, red currants and white currants are best. In expert hands, trailing vines can be trained as fans, while the less vigorous trailing berries are easily trained into a basic fan shape.

WAYS OF TRAINING TRAILING BERRIES

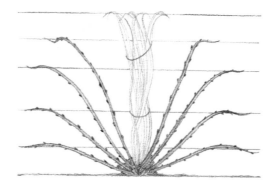

In summer, bunch new young canes in the centre, tying them loosely to the wires between the fruiting canes. In late summer, cut off the old canes at ground level and tie in the young canes in a fan shape.

The wave system (left) and spiral (right) suit varieties with long, vigorous canes. Use wire, plastic or raffia twists to tie the canes in position, trying to keep an even distance between them.

CLIMBERS AND TRAILERS ON THE BOUNDARY

Trailing berried fruits With their vigorous canes, trailing berries provide a fast means of covering fences and other supports, but their rampant nature needs to be kept in check. Most of them are less fussy about soil and situation than tree and bush fruits, which means that they can be grown in less well-drained or shadier sites in the garden, although fruit quality will be better in lusher conditions. They need space, and should be planted 1.8–4.5m (6–15ft) apart, depending on variety.

The group is made up of: a) hybrid berries with blackberry parentage, such as loganberry and tayberry; b) cultivated blackberries (there are many varieties); c) other hybrids, such as youngberry and silvanberry; d) a few distinct species, such as Japanese wineberry. In most cases, the colourful berries gleam prominently when fruiting, some also have pretty foliage (Oregon thornless or parsley-leaved blackberry is a notable example), while others have beautiful stems. The mealy grey stems of the American black raspberry and the reddish stems of the Japanese wineberry are at their best in autumn. For extra colour, the less vigorous clematis (see p.117) can be planted against the end posts to trail along the horizontal supports among the berry canes. Train them on parallel wires 30cm (12in) apart, pruning back each spring to prevent unruliness.

If the more vigorous and thorny varieties are banished to outlying boundaries of the garden they can be allowed to romp freely. Within the confines of a garden, however, they need to be trained. They can be tied onto strong trellis work or rigid wire or plastic netting; but if grown against walls, fences or on free-standing supports they must be attached to horizontal wires. They can also be trained along ropes or chains. Raspberries, which have long, upright canes, look best tied to wires in a single row. This makes an effective screen. The tops of long canes can be bent down to the top wire, to give a hooping effect.

The trailing berries all fruit on the canes produced in the previous season. This makes pruning straightforward: in winter the old, fruited canes are cut out at the base, and the current season's canes tied in, presenting an opportunity for creating some elegant patterns. In summer old and new canes jostle for space, and unless they are segregated, there is chaos. The simplest method is to train old canes to one side and new canes, as they grow, to the other. For a prettier effect, fan the fruiting canes evenly to either side, guiding the new canes up the centre initially, then fanning them out lower down in winter. Long canes can be woven between the wires in a wave-like pattern; or the longest cane on each side can be coiled into a spiral (see diagram, p.128).

RIGHT: **Besides its pretty flowers and fruits, the American black raspberry has mealy grey stems all year round.**

RIGHT: **Japanese wineberry** *Rubus phoenicolasius* **has soft pink bristles on its stems and decorative leaves. It is a moderately vigorous, easily trained vine.**

FAR RIGHT: **The high-bush blueberry is a shrubby plant, easily worked into flower borders in areas with acid soil.**

USING FRUIT FOR ORNAMENTAL HIGHLIGHTS

Fruit can be so much more than a productive embellishment for boundary walls and screens. It can be an ornamental feature in its own right, probably at its most dramatic trained on arches, tunnels and pillars. It goes without saying that arches, indeed any structures that are used to support fruit, must be substantial and well anchored, but with pretty blossom in the spring, green leafiness in summer, fruit in autumn, bare branches in winter – what more could you ask of a garden feature?

ARCHES

Apples and pears can be trained as cordons up a simple metal or wooden arch, either tied to the pillar itself or to wire supports. When the trees meet overhead, they can either overlap or be splice-grafted together to make a continuous line (see diagram, p.125). The naturally fastigiate Ballerina apples train well over an arch, but seek specialist advice on varieties and appropriate rootstocks for the arch in mind: high and wide span arches will require more vigorous varieties than small arches. A lovely feature can be made with a pair of crossed arches spanning the intersection of two paths (see also Focal Points and Features, p.67).

Trailing and climbing fruit can be tailored to arches, arbours and any tall structures but will need some form of trellis-work, wires or rigid netting to which they can be tied for support. One of the most effective examples of a

LEFT: **The beds in this circular potager are elegantly linked with arches, this one planted with a fast-growing hop providing a leafy canopy every summer.**

ABOVE: **Vistas created with apples trained over arches: in the foreground crossing arches span a path intersection, leading down steps to the apple tunnel.**

RIGHT: **Apples planted 1m (3ft) apart and trained over metal arches make a tunnel entrance to the vegetable garden at Cranborne Manor, Dorset, south-west England.**

on arches. They are fairly rampant climbers and will need frequent pruning to keep them within bounds.

TUNNELS AND WALKWAYS

A fruit tunnel epitomizes the romantic kitchen garden, but in order to accommodate it the garden needs to be fairly large. A small-scale, tunnel-like vista can be created with a series of free-standing arches, spaced about 1m (3ft) apart. In a true tunnel the arches are linked, sometimes with a series of intermediary arches parallel to the pathway, but more usually with horizontal bars of metal, wood, or other rigid material. This allows apples and pears to be trained as espaliers, as well as cordons. Cordon tree fruits, and climbing and trailing fruits can

trellised archway of climbing berries I've seen is in the Royal Horticultural Society model fruit garden at Wisley, Surrey, south England. Constructed of wooden lattice-work in 12 x 7.5cm (5 x 3in) squares, it is about 2.5m (8ft) high and 1.2m (4ft) long. One side is planted with tummelberry and Oregon thornless blackberry, the other with tayberry and thornless boysenberry. Every winter, five or six canes from each plant are trained upwards, in neat parallel lines spaced about 15cm (6in) apart, covering the framework from top to toe.

Vigorous climbing fruits such as kiwi, grapevines and, in suitably warm climates, edible varieties of passion fruit such as *Passiflora edulis* var. *edulis* and var. *flavicarpa* can be trained

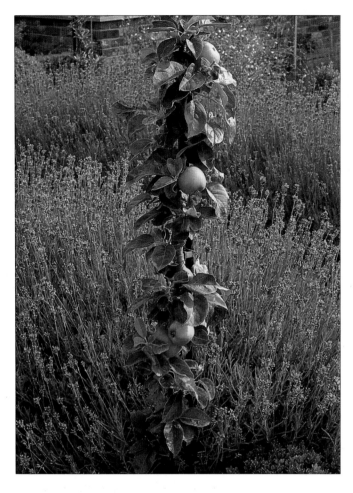

LEFT: **The columnar Ballerina apples, here rising from a bed of lavender, make a striking silhouette in a vegetable bed.**

be imaginatively worked into a tunnel. I have seen Japanese wineberry stems being trained in three ways, in two directions alongside the path, and then on an arch over the path. With care, ornamental climbers can be interplanted in a fruit tunnel, but choose the less vigorous types that can be pruned back yearly, to avoid shading ripening fruit.

COLUMNAR EFFECTS

Only a handful of fruit trees grow naturally in a columnar form, but the Canadian discovery in the 60s of a genetically columnar apple led to the Ballerina series. In these rod-like trees the fruit develops from spurs on the main stem, so only the minimum winter pruning is required. They reach their maximum height of about 3.8m (12ft) in ten years or so, but if they start to look too tall their height can be controlled by cutting back the leading shoot and leaving just a couple of buds of the current year's growth. This is probably best done in winter. Several new shoots will develop as a result. Remove all but the straightest, treat it as the leader, and prune it back hard in its turn in the following years in winter. The trees are grafted on fairly vigorous rootstocks and don't normally require staking. Their drawback is that only a few varieties are available (my favourite is the crimson-flowered crab apple 'Maypole') and they have less disease resistance than some modern varieties of apple.

The trade name Minarette has been given to a range of apples, pears and plums, grafted onto dwarfing rootstocks and trained as vertical cordons. Their eventual height depends on the rootstock used. They need to be supported with 2.1m (7ft) stakes, and require very careful pruning – especially the stone fruits – to keep a compact, neat shape. Apple Minarettes do not

HOW TO TRAIN A STANDARD RED CURRANT

1 Plant a one year rooted cutting in the dormant season. Select the strongest, upward shoot to train as leader and tie it to a 1.2m (4ft) cane for a 1m (3ft) stem. Cut off all other shoots close to the stem.

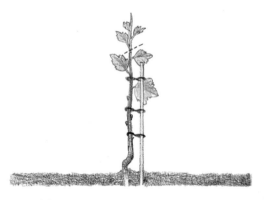

2 The following summer, leave the leader unpruned and tie it to the cane. Rub off any buds low on the stem. In winter cut the leader to 30cm (12in) above the cane. (If it is too short, leave unpruned for a year.)

3 Several shoots will develop the next summer. In winter shape the head. Select four or five shoots forming an open goblet shape, cut them to 15cm (6in) to an outward facing bud. Remove awkward branches.

have the tidy look of Ballerinas, but at the time of writing there is a much wider choice of variety. All these columnar forms require fertile soil and must be kept well watered, especially during their formative years. Consult the suppliers for detailed advice on cultivation.

If you are prepared to undertake a fair amount of tying and pruning, climbing fruits can be trained quite effectively on a single, free-standing pillar or post. The canes of berried fruits, and even raspberries, can be more or less 'gathered' around a post, with the new shoots tied in as they develop. They are bushier at the base so eventually form a pyramid-like silhouette. Choose the less vigorous and thornless

varieties of blackberry, and less rampant berries like tayberry (a raspberry x blackberry cross), or American black raspberry (*Rubus occidentalis*). The main stems of a grapevine or kiwi can be trained against a substantial post some 2.5–3m (8–10ft) high to make a leafy pillar in summer. To ensure the kiwis fruit successfully, plant a male and a female plant either side of the post. The self-fertile kiwi (see p.128) can be grown as a single cordon on upright poles, with the plants spaced about 1m (3ft) apart.

On a smaller scale, bush fruits such as gooseberries and red currants can be grown as standards on a slender 1–1.2m (3–4ft) stem (see also pp.68–9). Standard gooseberries are often seen in potagers, but as they are weak-stemmed and have to be budded or grafted onto a stronger rootstock, they are usually purchased already trained. They are normally pruned tightly into a ball-like head, but can also be trained over an umbrella-shaped frame to give a weeping effect.

Red currants, with their prettily dropping clusters of flowers, followed by bright berries, are perhaps better value in a potager than gooseberries. Being strong-stemmed they can be grown on

ABOVE: **A line of standard apples marshalled between trim rows of boxwood on either side of a pathway make an original feature in a potager in Seattle, western USA.**

their own roots, which makes them relatively easy to train. See diagrams opposite for the initial stages. From then on it is trained in the same way as a normal red currant bush (see Further Reading, p.201). Starting with a cutting, it is possible to achieve a pleasing, goblet-shaped standard 1.2–1.5m (4–5ft) high within three or four years. With skill, red currants too can be trained into a weeping form. White currants are unsuitable for training as standards.

Vines lend themselves to being trained as a bare-stemmed standard, on whatever height stem is required. If pruned back each winter to just a crown-like cluster of buds on the top of the stem, the new growths will hang down like a weeping curtain.

Various tree fruits can be encouraged into a weeping form by the technique known as 'festooning', in which young branches are weighted, tied or pegged down to encourage downward growth. This, incidentally, stimulates fruit bud formation. It is most commonly done with apples, cherries, medlars and plums.

LEFT: **The kiwi is a vigorous climber and easily trained over archways and trellis, or as here, over the front door of Sooke Harbour House, Vancouver Island.**

133

POTAGER MANAGEMENT

A VEGETABLE GARDEN WHERE there is an emphasis on ornamental qualities makes more demands on its owner than an ordinary kitchen garden. Every vegetable has to look its best and play a part in the overall picture, but there may also be an emotional tug-of-war between what is practical and what is aesthetically pleasing. I can hardly bear, each spring, to pull up the last leeks and spoil the stripe they make across the bed. Of course, they should be cleared so the ground can be prepared for summer planting, but if just a couple are left, think how lovely those seedheads will look in a few months. Where appearance matters so much to you, there has to be a little bending of the rules.

There can be no such give and take on quality. If the garden is to look beautiful, the vegetables must be grown to the highest standards. My 'Golden Guidelines' for potager management can be summarized as 'muck, mulch, raise good plants, keep order!' This chapter looks at how to apply these guidelines and to achieve a happy compromise between beauty and productivity.

LEFT: **The willow sculpture scarecrow in the garden at Ballymaloe Cookery School epitomizes the fun of gardening.**

ABOVE: **Borage and pot marigolds are the cheeriest of self-seeding edible flowers, but must be kept under control.**

SOIL FERTILITY

Fertile soil is the most important element in growing healthy vegetables, and the key to creating fertile soil is to work in as much bulky organic matter as possible. Organic matter is anything of animal or vegetable origin, such as manure, compost, rotted straw and seaweed. Its role in improving soil fertility is complex. Essentially, it provides food for earthworms (their preference is for animal manures), and the worms feed on the organic material, converting it into humus from which plant foods are released. Earthworm activity has other beneficial effects, the most important being the creation of a soil structure that both retains moisture and is well drained. In addition, the worm casts made by some types of worm are full of plant foods and useful micro-organisms. And finally, when the worms die, their decayed bodies are a rich source of nitrogen.

There are many approaches to manuring, but standard practice is to dig the ground in autumn, working bulky manure into the soil at the same time. On heavy soil, an excellent strategy is to ridge up the beds in early winter, then to cover them with manure. With narrow beds it is easy to spade the outer edges over the middle to make a ridge. The soil in the ridge will drain well and is more exposed to frost, which helps break up clods of soil, while the layer of manure, which can be anything from 7.5 to 10cm (3 to 4in) thick protects the soil from the destructive effect of heavy winter rain. By the spring, earthworms will have worked in much of the manure. With light soils, which

RIGHT: **Maintaining a high state of soil fertility is vital if vegetables are to flourish. Winter manuring is feasible where there are no overwintering crops in the ground.**

ABOVE: **On heavy soils it is advisable to cover the soil with a thick layer of manure in the autumn, which earthworms will work in, improving fertility and drainage.**

ABOVE: **Homemade compost not only helps to maintain the soil's fertility, but is invaluable for mulching between plants to keep down weeds and conserve moisture.**

have a more fragile structure, it is better to cover the surface with manure in the autumn but to postpone digging until the spring.

In an intensively cultivated, decorative vegetable garden, especially one where winter crops follow the summer crops with little or no break at all, there are fewer opportunities to manure a large stretch of ground in one go. In these cases, dig in fairly well-rotted manure or compost wherever a plant is removed and another is planted, and keep the ground well mulched with organic matter at all times.

To keep soil fertility high, try to work in some organic matter every year. In gardens where the level of fertility is low, extra feeding will probably be necessary in the early stages. As an organic gardener, I mainly use seaweed-based fertilizers or liquid comfrey feed, watered or sprayed on plants that seem to be below par.

Good soil structure, which is at the heart of soil fertility, is easily destroyed by treading on the soil, especially when it is very wet or very dry. Designing the garden beds so they can be cultivated comfortably from the paths is the best way to prevent this happening.

GREEN MANURING

Green manuring, the practice of growing a crop which is dug in to improve soil fertility, can be used very effectively in an intensively worked, potager-type vegetable garden. Even very small patches of ground, just a square metre (1.2 sq yd) or so, can be sown with a green manure. As it happens, many green manure crops are very pretty plants, especially when flowering. For optimum benefit they should be turned in before they flower, but since the flowers often attract beneficial insects (see p.144), it is easy to justify leaving a few clumps to flower colourfully.

There are two obvious slots for annual green manures in decorative vegetable gardens. Early in the season a fast-growing green manure can be sown in a winter potager, to be dug in before the main winter crops are planted in early to mid-summer. This has the added advantage of making the soil much more moisture retentive. Useful and pretty green manures for this purpose are fenugreek

RIGHT: *Phacelia tanacetifolia* is an excellent green manure; not only does it add nutrients and humus to the soil when dug in, but it looks beautiful when growing.

(*Trigonella foenum-graecum*), with its clover-like leaves, *Phacelia tanacetifolia*, which has lovely blue flowers and ferny foliage, and buckwheat (*Fagopyrum esculentum*) with its dainty white flowers. These last two attract beneficial insects.

The other use for green manure is at the end of the season. Hardy green manures can be sown from early autumn to early winter, after a summer crop is cleared, and dug in the next spring before sowing and planting begin. They keep the ground covered, thereby protecting the soil, and also prevent nitrogen from being washed out of the soil during winter rains, by taking it up in autumn and releasing it when they are dug in. Nice looking green manures for this type of use are crimson clover (*Trifolium*

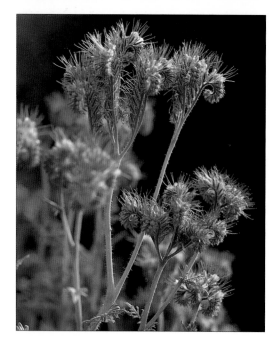

ABOVE: **Crimson clover can be an overwintering or summer green manure. For maximum benefit it should be turned in before it flowers ... but there's a case for bending the rules!**

LEFT: **The flowers of *Phacelia tanacetifolia* are a striking blue and supply nectar to various beneficial insects, so there is every reason to grow them in the decorative vegetable garden.**

incarnatum), field or winter beans (*Vicia faba*), grazing rye (*Secale cereale*) and winter tares (*Vicia sativa*). Before they are dug in, the foliage can often be cut and used for mulching. Russian comfrey (*Symphytum* x *uplandicum*) is a perennial 'manuring' plant with beautiful flowers. Its leaves, which are rich in nutrients, can be used for mulching or to make a liquid feed. The most productive cultivar is 'Bocking 14', which

spreads less than some of the more common forms, although all types can be grown in a garden for their decorative value and general usefulness.

MULCHING

Mulching, which is the practice of keeping the soil covered with organic material, plastic film and, in hot climates, even stones, is an excellent technique for a crowded kitchen garden. It conserves the moisture in the soil, keeps down weeds, and where an organic mulch is used, it improves soil fertility.

The best time to mulch the soil is after planting. In dry areas, water well after planting, then mulch with at least 2.5cm (1in) of organic matter (see p.136). A thicker mulch can be used if the plant is of a reasonable size and will not be swamped by it. Where seeds have been sown *in situ*, perhaps for a cut-and-come-again (CCA) crop, wait until the seedlings are through and standing proud of the soil before mulching. Remember that mulching maintains the status quo, keeping warm soil warm, and cool soil cool, so never mulch waterlogged or cold soils until they have dried out or warmed up. In the long term, however, working organic matter into the soil is the best way of remedying poor drainage, which is the most likely cause of cold and wet soils.

A wide range of materials can be used for mulching. They should be fairly loose structured or they are awkward to apply. Some of the most popular options include composted municipal waste, garden compost, leaf mould, manures, stinging nettles, well-rotted straw, wilted comfrey leaves, any peat substitutes, and in the USA, salt hay.

Mulching with any of these materials, as long as they are laid 2.5–5cm (¾–2in) thick, is the best way to keep down weeds in a potager. Any weeds that do germinate are easily pulled out. Plastic film mulches can also be used, but are unsightly, so restrict their use to large plants, such as courgettes and marrows, which soon conceal them under their leaves.

With plants that are naturally spreading or grow close to the ground, typically lettuce, cabbage and spinach, weeds can very largely be controlled by planting at equidistant spacing in both directions. The mature plants then blanket the ground and deprive weed seedlings of the light they need in order to germinate. All that is needed is a little hand-weeding in the early stages. This method will not work as

ABOVE: Plastic mulches are far from aesthetic but are useful for conserving soil moisture and suppressing weeds. Once plants are established, the plastic is hidden.

effectively with narrow-leaved plants such as onions. The combination of mulching and equidistant spacing is highly recommended to control weeds. Don't forget, though, that many of the common weeds are edible: dandelions, chickweed, field penny cress, fat hen (lamb's quarters) to name a few.

ABOVE: Composted bark is a suitable material for mulching in vegetable beds, being easily handled and a pleasant colour. Work around plants soon after planting.

WATERING

It is stating the obvious to say that plants need moisture: they can't absorb nutrients from dry soil. Most vegetables, especially green leafy vegetables and fast-growing cut-and-come-again seedlings require a lot of water, far more than annual flowers. Water requirements are highest when plants are grown densely, as is often the case in a decorative vegetable plot. Yet a garden laid out in patterns, or with beds of varying sizes and shapes is undeniably more awkward to water, especially with hoses, than a conventional vegetable garden. This means that in a potager watering often has to be done by hand. The best alternative is porous seephose or perforated polythene tubing, which is flexible enough to be laid on the ground between plants. It is attached to a tap or hose.

It is important to make watering effective. Occasional, heavy watering, wetting the soil to 5–7.5cm (2–3in), is far more beneficial than frequently sprinkling the soil, which encourages roots to stay near the surface, rather than going down deep in search of water.

LEFT: Growing plants such as 'Sugar Loaf' chicory at equidistant spacing creates a dense patch of green, which blankets the soil and prevents weed seeds germinating.

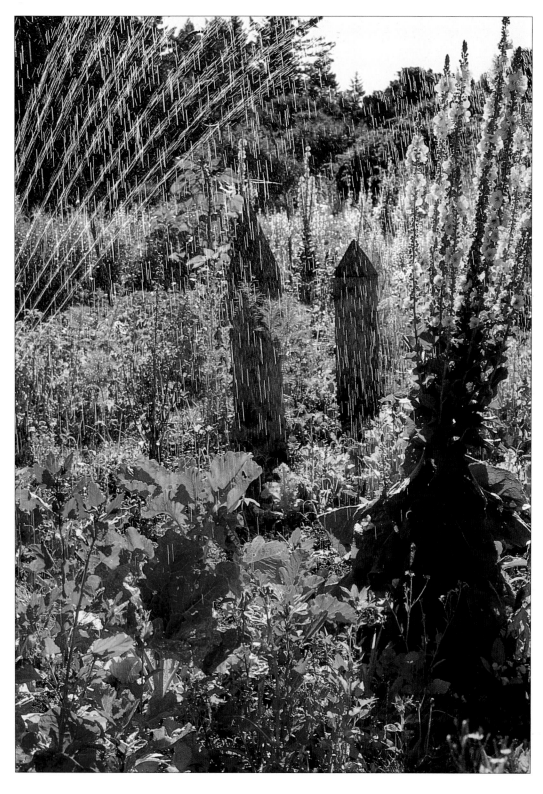

If water is scarce, limit watering to the critical stages. Seedlings and young plants need gentle watering until they are well established; fruiting crops, such as peas and beans, need water when they start to flower; leafy vegetables like salads and brassicas need water most about 10–20 days before they mature. A single, very heavy watering at these stages makes the best use of water. Mulch immediately after watering to prevent loss through evaporation.

LEFT: **Overhead watering is best done in the evening to minimize loss of water through evaporation.**

BELOW: **Laying porous seephose between plants is one of the most efficient and flexible ways of watering, used here to establish globe artichoke offsets.**

RAISING GOOD QUALITY PLANTS

Most vegetables can be raised from seed quickly and easily, and there are various methods for doing this, as explained below. The choice of method will depend on the plant in question, the season and the site.

DIRECT SOWING

Cut-and-come-again (CCA) seedlings are sown direct in the ground and left unthinned (see Seedling Patches, pp.110–13). The seed of many other vegetables is sown in the ground, and then thinned in stages to the final spacing required. This quick method is best reserved for good sowing conditions when the soil is friable and moist, and for vegetables, such as root vegetables, which don't transplant well. There is, however, always an element of chance, with seeds failing to germinate as a result of the soil drying out or becoming waterlogged, or from pest attacks or disease in the vulnerable early stages of growth.

SOWING IN DRILLS

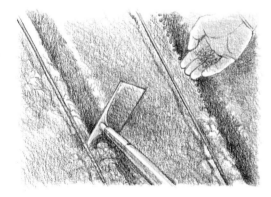

The standard method of sowing outdoors is in a shallow drill made with the blade of a hoe. Seed is spread evenly along the drill and covered with a thin layer of soil after sowing.

ABOVE: **Raising plants in modules with no competition from neighbouring seedlings enables them to develop a sturdy root system, guaranteeing rapid growth.**

SOWING IN SEEDBEDS

To save space in the main vegetable garden, vegetable seed can be sown fairly closely in a separate seedbed, from which the young plants will later be lifted and transplanted into their permanent positions. This is a common method of raising leeks, brassicas and salad plants. The disadvantage is that the roots are inevitably damaged when the plants are lifted, and this causes a setback (or check) after transplanting.

A seedbed is prepared by raking backwards and forwards over soil that has been dug, until the surface is smooth, and free of stones and lumps of soil. It must be free of perennial weeds, as it will be difficult to weed without disturbing the seedlings. The seedbed should be in an open unshaded position.

RAISING PLANTS 'INDOORS'

This is a term for sowing plants in protected, usually warmer conditions, perhaps in a greenhouse, a heated propagator, or on a windowsill. Although most commonly used to start off tender plants, which cannot be planted out until the risk of frost is past, it can be used for many hardy vegetables to give them a good start.

Sowing in broad, flat drills is a useful method for creating bands of colour and patterns in a decorative vegetable garden, and is recommended for CCA seedlings (see pp.110–13).

141

RIGHT: **An old-fashioned cold-frame blends nicely into a kitchen garden, and is useful for raising seedlings and hardening-off plants grown under cover.**

The standard method is to sow seed in a small seedtray or pot, then to prick out the seedlings into larger seedtrays, spacing them about 2.5–7.5cm (³⁄₄–3in) apart, depending on the plant. Before being planted outside, they are hardened-off gradually to acclimatize them to lower growing temperatures, over a two- to three-week period. Start by increasing the ventilation, then put them in a cold-frame or sheltered position outdoors for longer periods each day, either covering them or bringing them back indoors at night if cold weather threatens. Separating the closely-grown plants raised in seedtrays tends to damage the delicate root hairs, and they suffer a degree of 'shock' when transplanted. This is avoided by raising plants in modules.

A module is any container in which a single seed can be sown, and the young plant grown on until it is ready for planting out. The most common types of modules are moulded plastic or polystyrene seedtrays divided into individual cells (the plants raised in them are often known as 'plugs'), or small clay or plastic pots, normally of 2.5–7.5cm (³⁄₄–3in) diameter. Standard seedtrays can be divided into cells with interlocking plastic or cardboard dividers.

The container is filled with good-quality potting compost which should be firmed gently before the seed is sown. An alternative system is to make small cubes or 'blocks', which is done by compressing special blocking compost with a blocking tool, the compost and tool being available from specialist suppliers. Whatever the method, pre-mix the compost beforehand so it is thoroughly moist. Push in the seeds, covering them firmly but gently with compost. Small seeds need to be just covered and larger seeds need to be about 1cm (¹⁄₂in) deep. It is

SOWING IN MODULES

Sow one or two seeds in each cell, thinning to the strongest after germination if necessary. Small seeds can be picked up on the tip of a bodkin.

Module-raised plants suffer the minimum check when planted, and can be kept in modules for several weeks if conditions are unsuitable for planting.

easy to pick up large seeds, such as cucumbers and beetroot, between the fingers but this is trickier with small seeds. One method is to put them onto a piece of paper and push them off singly. Another is to use a piece of broken glass, a darning needle or bodkin: if the tip is moistened it will pick up even the very small seeds, which drop off on making contact with the compost. Whatever the method, gently press the seeds in and cover them lightly with compost.

If there is a risk of seed germination being low, sow several seeds per cell initially. After they have germinated, nip off surplus seedlings at the base leaving just the strongest one. In some cases cells are purposely 'multi-sown' to save both time and space, with up to six seeds per cell, for planting out as one unit. This can be done with Chinese chives, leeks and onions. Seedlings sown in modules must be hardened-off in the normal way.

Modules have advantages over other ways of sowing, and are particularly suitable for raising potager plants. The reasons are as follows:
• The seedling (unless intentionally multi-sown) has no competition from other seedlings, so grows fast and develops into a strong plant with a compact root system. There is virtually no root disturbance when it is transplanted, so it grows away rapidly.
• Plants can be kept in the modules, giving them extra feed if necessary, until conditions are right for planting. In standard seedtrays the young plants start to deteriorate if planting has to be delayed. Extra plants can be raised and kept at the ready, either to replace damaged plants or for a follow-on crop.
• A range of plants can be raised in a single modular tray, provided they have the same cultural requirements. A 20-cell tray, for example, could theoretically be sown with 20 different lettuces or six different brassicas.

KEEPING ORDER

While the charm of a formal potager lies in the clarity of its patterns, in an informal potager there is a fine line between the natural look of 'sweet disorder' and messy chaos. In both styles, potentially disruptive elements have to be kept in check. The worst culprits are floppy vegetables, gaps and rampaging self-seeders.

The vegetables with the most potential for looking untidy are fairly low-growing, slightly sprawling plants, such as dwarf beans, dwarf peas (rather than the climbers, which are grown on supports) and bush tomatoes (rather than cordon tomatoes, which are staked individually, and can look very elegant, especially if grown up soft steel spiral supports).

Subtle support is the best solution to this problem. Push some small twiggy branches in the soil among sprawling plants in the early stages or curtail their later wanderings with a mini-fence of short criss-crossed bamboo canes,

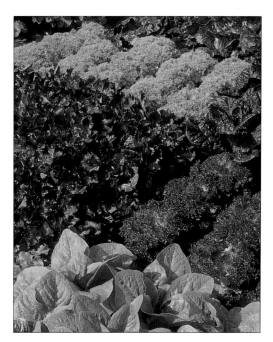

or low overlapping hoops of dogwood, young willow or any other supple material.

Gaps are caused by pest or disease attacks and, naturally enough, by harvesting vegetables. Damage to the appearance of the potager can be limited by growing plenty of cut-and-come-again vegetables such as loose-headed lettuces, spinach and CCA seedlings, which have a 'presence' in the ground over long periods. Where patterns are involved, harvest in as balanced a way as possible. At Villandry they pick evenly from each of the four beds in any square planted with the same crop.

As for filling gaps caused by plant failure, always have a few spare plants in modules or pots. If necessary, pot one or two into large pots, up to 10–12cm (4–5in) in diameter. They can be used to replace fairly mature plants, should the need arise. Plan the succession of planting carefully (see pp.148–9) to avoid leaving extensive gaps when a crop is cleared. Have your next crop ready for planting, or sow fast-germinating CCA seedlings in the space.

Controlling self-seeding plants is a matter of will-power. Borage, nasturtiums, red orache, the peony-flowered poppy 'Pink Chiffon', even calendula are just a few of the self-seeders that are lovely at times, but then outstay their welcome. Borage becomes a bully, the poppies turn an ugly crumpled brown after flowering and crush smaller plants, and nasturtiums take over. This is the point when the plants must be uprooted, but leave just a couple of them, in as inconspicuous a position as possible, so that they may re-seed the following year. For more information see Drama from Seedheads and Flowering Vegetables, pages 83–5.

LEFT: **Creating a tapestry of well-grown, contrasting salad vegetables is a source of deep satisfaction. Always have a few spare plants ready to replace any casualties.**

CONTROLLING PESTS AND DISEASES

Healthy plants are beautiful plants, so plants attacked by pests and disease are, by definition, unsightly. But what can be done to control pests and diseases in a decorative vegetable garden? Undoubtedly the first line of defence is growing plants well. Strong plants growing in fertile soil with adequate moisture and space is always the best insurance against attack. Beware of overcrowding: fungus diseases in particular spread rapidly in stagnant conditions. Where plants are grown too close together, they will compete for water and nutrients. Slugs always seem to start on the weakest plants.

Growing flowers and herbs among or near vegetables can be beneficial. Open, flat flowers such as baby blue eyes (*Nemophila*), *Convolvulus*, fennel, poached egg plant (*Limnanthes*) and pot marigold (*Calendula*) attract short-tongued, aphid-eating beneficial insects such as hoverflies, while French marigolds help to deter whitefly. Growing different vegetables together also acts as a deterrent: pests love monocultures. I've found that sowing annual flowers and carrots mixed together puts off carrot fly.

A sound preventative measure is to rotate the crops. Growing related groups of vegetables in different beds each year over a three- to five-year cycle prevents the soil pests and diseases, which attack each group, building up to damaging proportions. The main groups, from the rotation point of view, are alliums (onion and leek family), brassicas (cabbage family),

LEFT: **The colourful quilt of pot marigolds in the garden at Ballymaloe Cookery School, southern Ireland, is a source of edible flowers and attracts beneficial insects.**

legumes (pea and bean family) and the *Solanacae* (potato and tomato family). It is certainly worth trying to plan your garden so that a bed will mainly grow legumes one year, brassicas the next, onions the next and so on. The order doesn't matter much – the point is to ring the changes. Fit salads and miscellaneous vegetables into the main groups. One four-year sequence I use in the small beds in my Little Potager is peas, cabbages, salads, courgettes. In very small gardens it is hard to operate an effective rotation system, as soil pests and diseases have some mobility and can migrate into an adjacent bed, but at least avoid growing plants from the same group in the same ground in consecutive seasons.

As an organic gardener, I restrict spraying to the few chemicals, such as derris, pyrethrum and insecticidal soap, which have no damaging long-term effects. Otherwise I rely on picking off or squashing pests such as slugs, caterpillars, snails and green, black and mealy aphids by hand. I also grow the most vulnerable plants – carrots and brassicas in my case – under fine insect-proof nets laid carefully over low metal hoops and pinned down at ground level. These keep out flying pests such as flea beetle, root flies, butterflies and moths, but it is hard to make them look beautiful. A compromise is to protect vegetables in their early stages, when attacks are the most damaging, and remove the nets once the plants are well established.

Birds are a problem in many gardens, and here the remedy can add rather than detract from the scene. Handsome scarecrows are fun, and the Asiatic split-cane cages, which can be put over individual plants, are beautiful and functional. Where the whole vegetable garden has to be enclosed in a free-standing wire or net cage, grow climbing flowers, gourds or beans against it (see Climbers, pp.86–9).

LEFT: One of the practical benefits of the cottage garden tradition of interplanting vegetables, herbs and flowers is that pests are confused and tend to cause less damage than in a conventional, monocropping situation.

BELOW: The main task of this New York birdscarer was to attract attention, inform and amuse passers-by. He was wearing an 'Aids Awareness' T-shirt when I encountered him in the famous Liz Christy Community Garden, in Manhattan.

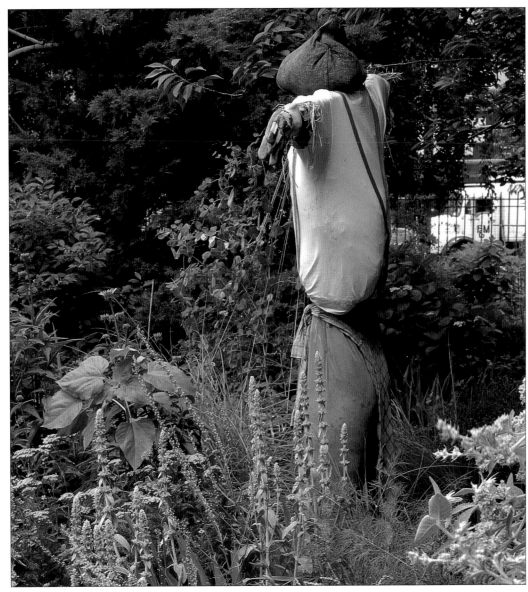

PLANT PROTECTION

Most kitchen gardens in temperate climates make some use of greenhouses, low polythene tunnels, walk-in polytunnels, cloches or cold-frames. They are useful for raising plants, to grow the more tender vegetables, and for very early season and winter crops. Sadly their practicality is rarely matched by their beauty and modern equipment, in particular, with its reliance on plastic materials, tends to strike a discordant note in a potager setting.

It is a different story with reproduction and period garden equipment. The dome-shaped glass bell jars and the leaded lantern cloches associated with nineteenth-century market gardens and private gardens are handsome objects. The originals can still be put to practical use, if you can find and afford them. If you want to use modern cloches, it is worth hunting for the more stylish ones.

As for garden frames, the concrete-sided models and modern metal and glass types are rather utilitarian-looking unless exceptionally well designed, but wooden and brick-sided frames, whether free-standing or lean-to types against a wall or fence are more mellow. Similarly, timber-framed greenhouses blend more easily into the garden than the harsher lines of a metal-framed structure. The ugly ducklings of the kitchen garden are walk-in polytunnels (hoop houses), which are made from plastic film anchored over a framework of arching steel-tube hoops. Yet they are practical, a fraction of the cost of greenhouses and

RIGHT: **Make a greenhouse into a beautiful feature by grouping pots around it, as here with *Lonicera nitida* 'Baggesen's Gold' standard topiaries.**

have the great merit of being easily moved to a new position. This prevents soil-sickness from developing, as occurs in greenhouse soil in which tomatoes are grown year after year.

The answer to this aesthetic dilemma is to disguise structures that are an eyesore, and to make a feature of any that are reasonably handsome. For example, try grouping elegant pots and containers around the greenhouse entrance, or erecting an arch over the doorway. With a permanent greenhouse, the arch could be planted with perennial ornamental climbers, grapevines or berried fruit; otherwise grow climbing beans and squashes, perhaps mixed with annual flowers such as sweet peas (see Climbers, p.89).

Unattractive garden features can also be screened off with tall cane supports or trellis-work (see Supports, pp.71–3) or planted with edible, and/or ornamental annual climbers. If the screen is placed to run parallel to a green-house, the shade it provides will be beneficial in summer. I always disguise my outsize polytun-nel by planting sunflowers alongside it down the entire length. They are spaced a little closer than usual, 12cm (5in) apart, so competition keeps them relatively compact.

There are no reasons why a creative approach to planting should not be adopted inside greenhouses and polytunnels. When I visited the Centre for Alternative Technology in mid Wales, I was inspired by what I saw in an irregularly shaped, large polythene-covered struc-ture. There were no conventional rectangular borders or beds but instead they were all shapes and sizes, some raised, some at ground level, and all prettily edged with tiles, bricks and stones. The overall impression was of healthy crops and colour, in part due to the flowers growing among the veg-etables, both for decoration and to attract beneficial insects. There was intercropping too: in one log-edged bed sweet corn, undercropped with 'Salad Bowl' lettuce, intermingled with self-sown Welsh poppies and fox-gloves. I have seen a polythene structure squeezed onto a ter-raced slope in Wales, with the bank inside planted with flowers and herbs, and the vegetables grown in shapely patterned beds.

FORCING POTS

The traditional, lidded clay pots that are used for forcing and blanching rhubarb and seakale are lovely objects to have in a decorative vegetable garden – functional and ornamental. In practice, they are only in use for a matter of weeks in spring, covering the plants as the shoots break through from dor-mancy. When they have fulfilled their role they can be left among the maturing plants or nonchalantly grouped in a corner. Get hand-thrown pots, or genuine old pots if you can. Sometimes old chimney pots, large drainage pipes and bits of masonry are called into service for blanching. In China, miniature chimney-like pots, each fitted with a tiny lid, are used for blanching Chinese chives.

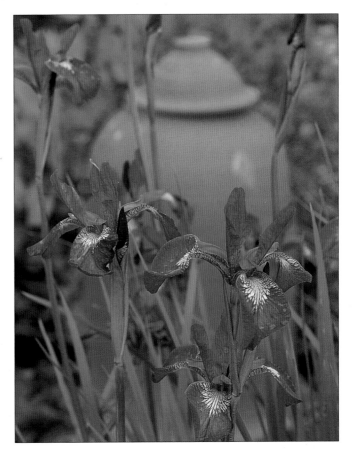

PLANNING FOR SUCCESSION

A decorative vegetable garden looks best when it is burgeoning with plants. The challenge lies in keeping it fully productive over as many months as possible, planning for at least two, perhaps even three crops in each bed during the year. In practice, climate governs the options. When are the last spring frosts and the first winter frosts likely to be? Is winter mild enough to grow hardy brassicas and overwintering green manures? Is summer long enough and hot enough for the semi-tropical beans and squashes? These critical elements underpin the planting plans.

There are essentially two ways to keep the pot boiling: either sow or plant the next crop as soon as the previous crop is cleared, or operate a relay system by intercropping the next crop among the previous crop. The winter greens, for example, can be intercropped among the spring lettuces or shallots, which will be cleared by early to mid-summer.

The best way to set about planning for succession is to decide what the main crop will be in each bed, then to see whether a quick-maturing crop can be fitted in beforehand, or if it can be followed with a summer or autumn crop, or perhaps an overwintering crop. To illustrate this, here are some examples from my Little Potager, in which the segments of the central circle are lettered A–H. The blank potager plan for the current year, in keeping with the rotation plan, indicates that the main crop in Bed A is brassicas, in Beds B and E legumes . . . and so on.

For Bed A, I choose red cabbage, always a potager success with me. The plants are sown the previous autumn and planted out in early to mid-spring. As they normally stand into early autumn, the most practical follow-on crops are autumn-sown overwintering broad beans, or a late-sown green manure such as rye grass or field beans.

In bed B, the main legume will be spring-sown semi-leafless peas. There is no time to sow anything beforehand, but they will be cleared by mid-summer, leaving several choices for a follow-on crop including red chicory, leeks, lettuce or oriental greens. The other legume plot, however, is reserved for the frost-tender dwarf runner beans or French beans, which cannot be planted or sown until the risk of frost is over in early summer. Here there is time for a preliminary crop of cut-and-come-again seedlings, or radishes. Or it can be planted with early lettuce, which can be intercropped in its later stages with the young bean plants. The beans are unlikely to finish cropping until mid-autumn, so when they are lifted I will just spread the ground with manure for winter.

A 'ground occupancy' chart is a very useful visual aid for planning. Plot vegetables against months, blocking in the periods when the vegetables are normally in the ground (see the table opposite for the main vegetable crops). If you want to make accurate plans for your own conditions, make a personal chart of your favourite crops, ideally based on your garden records. Have a separate entry for alternative sowings and plantings as with, for example, spring, summer and autumn cabbage, or alternative growing methods, such as headed or cut-and-come-again lettuce. The table will give an 'at-a-glance' view of how different crops can be dovetailed together. Useful supplementary information would be lists of crops that mature in less than eight weeks, in less than twelve weeks, that overwinter outside or would benefit from protection in winter.

ABOVE: **Although the standard module tray is very convenient to use, any seedtray can be partitioned into individual cells with strips of plastic, wood or cardboard.**

It is also useful to know how long it takes a plant to mature (see the planning chart opposite for the average number of weeks from sowing to maturity for the most widely grown vegetables). Figures comparing different varieties are sometimes quoted in seed catalogues. Use these figures in planning, but do bear in mind that performance on the ground can be very different from the 'average'. Any plan must be treated with a degree of flexibility. Some seasons, a crop matures faster than in others and occasionally there is a failure. It is usually possible to fill the breach with plants reserved in containers or a quick sowing of CCA seedlings. I always keep a few plants of green-leaved Swiss chard handy for this purpose; even when kept in modules for several months, they get established quickly, without bolting as one might expect. If your beds are edged with annual plants, don't forget to plan for their succession too. An edge of parsley, for example, can be cleared in late summer and replanted with winter pansies, or it can follow winter pansies when they are cleared in early summer.

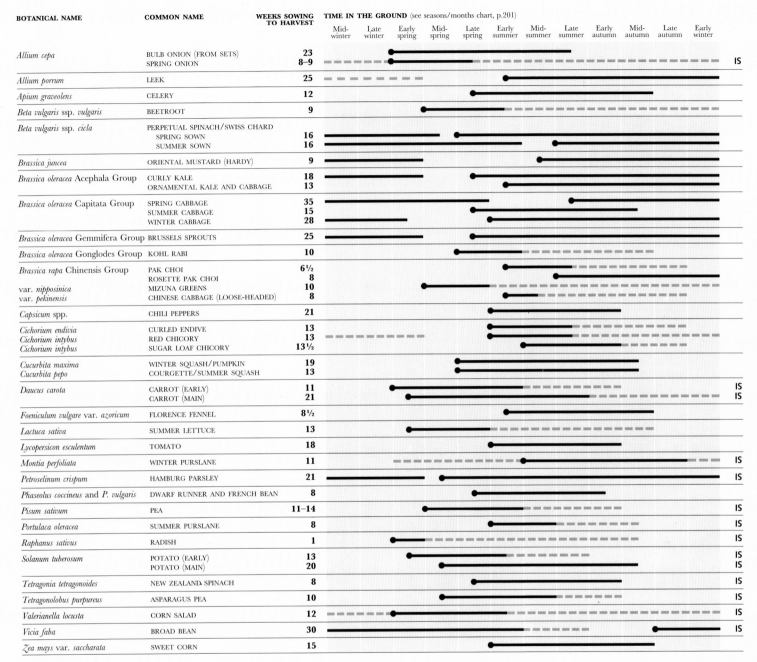

BOTANICAL NAME	COMMON NAME	WEEKS SOWING TO HARVEST
Allium cepa	BULB ONION (FROM SETS)	23
	SPRING ONION	8–9
Allium porrum	LEEK	25
Apium graveolens	CELERY	12
Beta vulgaris ssp. *vulgaris*	BEETROOT	9
Beta vulgaris ssp. *cicla*	PERPETUAL SPINACH/SWISS CHARD	
	SPRING SOWN	16
	SUMMER SOWN	16
Brassica juncea	ORIENTAL MUSTARD (HARDY)	9
Brassica oleracea Acephala Group	CURLY KALE	18
	ORNAMENTAL KALE AND CABBAGE	13
Brassica oleracea Capitata Group	SPRING CABBAGE	35
	SUMMER CABBAGE	15
	WINTER CABBAGE	28
Brassica oleracea Gemmifera Group	BRUSSELS SPROUTS	25
Brassica oleracea Gonglodes Group	KOHL RABI	10
Brassica rapa Chinensis Group	PAK CHOI	6½
	ROSETTE PAK CHOI	8
var. *nipposinica*	MIZUNA GREENS	10
var. *pekinensis*	CHINESE CABBAGE (LOOSE-HEADED)	8
Capsicum spp.	CHILI PEPPERS	21
Cichorium endivia	CURLED ENDIVE	13
Cichorium intybus	RED CHICORY	13
Cichorium intybus	SUGAR LOAF CHICORY	13½
Cucurbita maxima	WINTER SQUASH/PUMPKIN	19
Cucurbita pepo	COURGETTE/SUMMER SQUASH	13
Daucus carota	CARROT (EARLY)	11
	CARROT (MAIN)	21
Foeniculum vulgare var. *azoricum*	FLORENCE FENNEL	8½
Lactuca sativa	SUMMER LETTUCE	13
Lycopersicon esculentum	TOMATO	18
Montia perfoliata	WINTER PURSLANE	11
Petroselinum crispum	HAMBURG PARSLEY	21
Phaseolus coccineus and *P. vulgaris*	DWARF RUNNER AND FRENCH BEAN	8
Pisum sativum	PEA	11–14
Portulaca oleracea	SUMMER PURSLANE	8
Raphanus sativus	RADISH	1
Solanum tuberosum	POTATO (EARLY)	13
	POTATO (MAIN)	20
Tetragonia tetragonoides	NEW ZEALAND SPINACH	8
Tetragonolobus purpureus	ASPARAGUS PEA	10
Valerianella locusta	CORN SALAD	12
Vicia faba	BROAD BEAN	30
Zea mays var. *saccharata*	SWEET CORN	15

TIME IN THE GROUND (see seasons/months chart, p.201)

Mid-winter · Late winter · Early spring · Mid-spring · Late spring · Early summer · Mid-summer · Late summer · Early autumn · Mid-autumn · Late autumn · Early winter

KEY

Average number of weeks from sowing to harvest is based on good growing conditions.

— Average time in the ground assuming plants are raised in modules and planted wherever feasible (see Cut-And-Come-Again (CCA) Seedling Table, p.113).

- - - Cropping extended by successional sowing (see p.200).

IS Cases where the crop is sown *in situ*.

● First sowing or planting.

General note: *The table is based on cropping in my garden in the UK (US Zone 8). In warmer areas tender vegetables can be sown in situ, or planted earlier, and harvested later. In cooler areas the season will be shorter. Only the main plantings of the more important vegetables are included here. For minor crops and perennials see A–Z Directory. In practice, there is enormous variability in one season.*

A–Z
DIRECTORY

ALMOST ANY PLANT CAN LOOK GOOD if it is growing well, but some are inherently more beautiful than others. This section concentrates on vegetables, herbs and edible flowers with decorative qualities, and suggests ways they can be used in all types of garden. While their ornamental potential is obvious in some cases, in others it is less so. Texsel greens (see p.154), for example, is normally unlikely to attract a second glance, but it will fill a space with glossy, healthy leaves in a remarkably quick time.

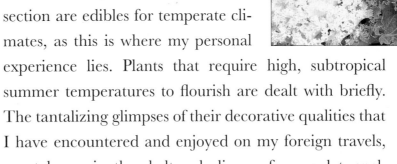

Most of the plants included in this section are edibles for temperate climates, as this is where my personal experience lies. Plants that require high, subtropical summer temperatures to flourish are dealt with briefly. The tantalizing glimpses of their decorative qualities that I have encountered and enjoyed on my foreign travels, or at home in the sheltered climes of my polytunnel, make me envy those gardeners in warm climates.

LEFT: **The bluish-red tint of the hardy 'January King' cabbage is a source of rich colour in the winter potager.**

ABOVE: **Kale 'Osaka White' is one of many highly ornamental kales that are used to create spectacular autumn displays.**

FINDING NEW PLANTS AND NEW VARIETIES

Finding decorative varieties of established and novelty vegetables is a challenge, as there is a surprising amount of coming and going in the world of edible seeds. Long-established, often colourful favourites may be withdrawn from mainstream sources but reappear in specialist and heirloom seed catalogues. Interesting new varieties, introduced with a great fanfare one season, can mysteriously disappear by the next.

Mail-order seed catalogues are generally the best source of the more unusual varieties, though they rarely describe their appearance in any detail. Always make allowance for some exaggeration in the accounts of the plants' performance, too. Some seed companies have open-days on their trial grounds and there is no better way to compare, for example, all the varieties of red lettuce, than seeing them grow side by side under identical conditions. While old varieties have romantic appeal, wonderful names and often great attributes (such as 'Bull's Blood' beetroot (see pp.173–4), with its scarlet leaves), the modern F_1 hybrids have a vigour and uniformity that can make a spectacular contribution to a decorative vegetable garden.

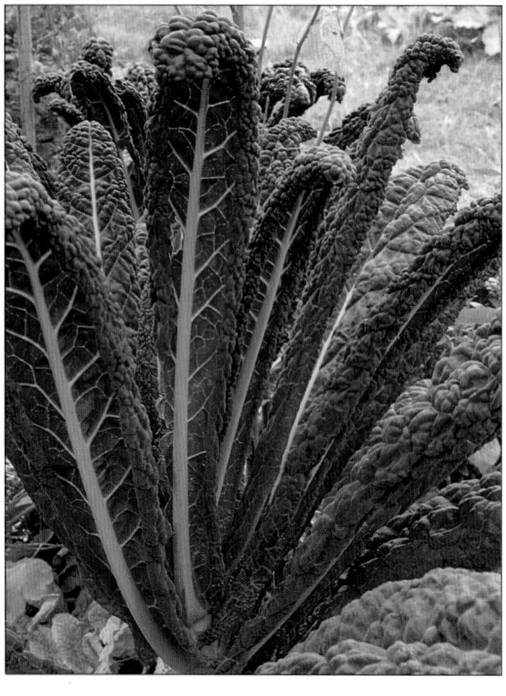

Varieties named here are ones that are noted for their decorative qualities. Where none is mentioned, assume that any variety will perform equally well.

GROWING CONDITIONS

With vegetables, probably more than any other group of plants, good cultivation is the key to making them both look their best and be truly productive. See Chapter 5, pages 136–140 for general advice on creating the optimum soil and growing conditions.

It is assumed here that plants will be raised individually in modules or some kind of small pot, so that top-quality plants are produced for planting out. The only exceptions are cut-and-come-again (see Seedling Patches, pp.110–13) *in situ* sowings for seedling crops, and those root crops that are best sown direct in the ground. Unless otherwise stated, assume a vegetable requires full sun, good fertile soil and plenty of moisture throughout its growing period.

It is difficult to forecast a plant's height or spread, as these can vary from season to season, and with seed quality and the growing conditions. The dimensions given are the average size of a plant at maturity based on my experience, but treat them with reserve and amend them in the light of your own experience.

LEFT: **The handsome 'Black' kale was, until recently, little known and appreciated outside Italy.**

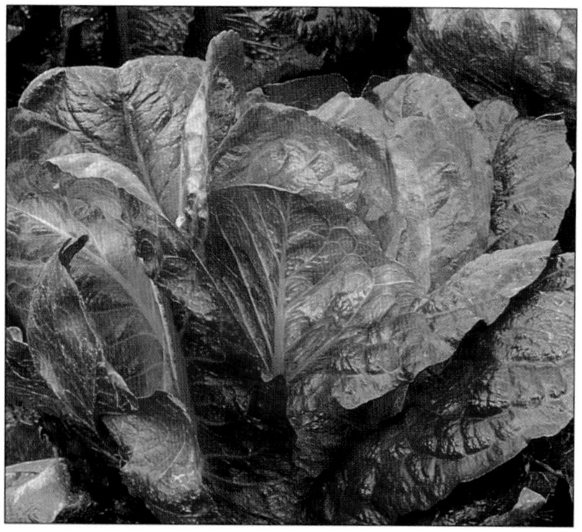

RIGHT: **Almost every type of lettuce occurs in red and green forms: the old red Cos lettuce 'Rouge d'Hiver' looks dramatic interplanted with its green counterpart.**

Anyone serious about creating a 'picture' with their vegetables should try to keep their own records. This will make it easier to repeat the successes and avoid repeating the failures.

The potential spread of a plant is a useful guide to spacing. Plants with a 30cm (12in) spread can be planted 30cm (12in) apart, but in many cases they will do well and create more of a visual impact if planted a little closer.

KEY TO SYMBOLS USED IN THE A–Z DIRECTORY

↕	Average height of plant at maturity
↔	Average spread of plant at maturity
T	Tender; plants that are killed by frost and damaged by low temperatures
HH	Half-hardy; plants that can survive only limited cold or very light frost, unless in a sheltered site
H	Hardy; plants that can survive temperatures of -5°C (23°F); those plants described as 'exceptionally hardy' can survive lower temperatures than this
(cut symbol)	Cut-and-come-again
(shade symbol)	Tolerates light or moderate shade

Note on measurements: measurements are given in metric with imperial conversions in brackets. Where these are not exact, they are accurate enough for practical gardening purposes.

TABLE OF COMMON AND BOTANICAL NAMES

Alfalfa (Lucerne) *Medicago sativa* — p.189
Alkanet *Anchusa azurea* — p.199
Amaranth *Amaranthus* — p.162
Angelica *Angelica archangelica* — p.192
Angled luffa *Luffa acutangula* — p.185
Anise hyssop *Agastache foeniculum* (syn. *A. anathiodora*) — p.197
Asparagus *Asparagus officinalis* — p.186
Asparagus pea (*Tetragonoides purpureus*) — p.179
Aubergine (Eggplant) *Solanum melongena* — p.182
Basil *Ocimum basilicum* — p.194
Beetberry *Chenopodium foliosum* — p.164
Beetroot *Beta vulgaris* spp. *rubra* — p.173
Bergamot (Bee balm) *Monarda didyma* — p.199
Bitter gourd, Karella (Bitter melon) *Momordica charantia* — p.185
Borage *Borago officinalis* — p.197
Bottle gourd, Calabash gourd *Lagenaria siceraria* — p.185
Broad bean (Fava bean) *Vicia faba* — p.179
Bronze fennel *Foeniculum vulgare* 'Purpureum' — p.192
Brussels sprouts *Brassica oleracea* (Gemnifera group) — p.158
Buckler-leaved sorrel *Rumex scutatus* — p.190
Buck's horn plantain *Plantago coronopus* — p.170
Cabbage *Brassica oleracea* (Capitata group) — p.157
Cardoon *Cynara cardunculus* — p.187
Carnation (Garden or clove pinks, sweet william) *Dianthus* spp. — p.199
Carrot *Daucus carota* — p.174
Cauliflower *Brassica oleracea* (Botrytis group) — p.156
Chayote (Christophine) *Sechium edule* — p.185
Chervil *Anthriscus cerefolium* — p.193
Chicory (red and green and 'Treviso' types) *Cichorium intybus* — pp.165–6
Chili pepper *Capsicum annuum* (Longum group), *C. frutescens* — p.180
Chinese broccoli (Chinese kale) *Brassica oleracea* var. *alboglabra* — p.159
Chinese cabbage *Brassica rapa* (Pekinensis group) — p.159
Chinese chives (Garlic chives) *Allium tuberosum* — p.191
Chinese violet cress *Orychophragmus violaceus* — p.170
Chrysanthemum greens (Shungiku, Garland Chrysanthemum) *Chrysanthemum coronarium* — p.165
Clary sage *Salvia sclarea* — p.199
Common chive *Allium schoenoprasum* — p.191
Common fennel *Foeniculum vulgare* — p.192
Common hyssop *Hyssopus officinalis* — p.193
Common myrtle *Myrtus communis* — p.194
Common rosemary *Rosmarinus officinalis* — p.196
Common sage (Garden sage) *Salvia officinalis* — p.196
Common sorrel (Broad-leaved) *Rumex acetosa* — p.190
Corn salad (Lamb's lettuce, Mache) *Valerianella locusta* — p.171
Cucumber *Cucumis sativus* — p.183

Cultivated celery *Apium graveolens* var. *dulce* — p.162
Currant tomato *Lycopersicon pimpinellifolium* — p.181
Daisy (English daisy) *Bellis perennis* — p.197
Dill *Anethum graveolens* — p.192
Daubenton perennial kale *Brassica oleracea* (Acephala group) — p.186
Daylily *Hemerocallis* spp. — p.199
Endive *Cichorium endivia* — p.165
Everlasting onion *Allium cepa* 'Perutile' — p.186
Florist's chrysanthemum *Dendrantheuma × grandiflora* (syn. *D. × morifolium*) — p.199
Florence fennel *Foeniculum vulgare* var. *dulce* — p.174
Flowering rape hybrid 'Bouquet' *Brassica rapa* var. *oleifera* — p.160
French bean (Snap bean) *Phaseolus vulgaris* — p.178
Garden cress (Peppercress) *Lepidum sativum* — p.169
Giant chive *Allium schoenoprasum.* var. *sibiricum* — p.191
Globe artichoke *Cynara scolymus* — pp.187–8
Good King Henry *Chenopodium bonus-henricus* — p.187
Grain amaranth *Amaranthus hypochondriacus* — p.180
Ground cherry *Physalis pruinosa* (syn. *P. pubescens*) — pp.181–2
Hamburg parsley *Petroselinum crispum* var. *tuberosum* — p.175
Hollyhock *Althaea rosea* — p.199
Houttuynia *Houttuynia cordata* — p.199
Iceplant *Mesembryanthemum crystallinum* — p.169
Jerusalem artichoke (Sunchoke) *Helianthus tuberosus* — p.188
Kale *Brassica oleracea* (Acephala group) — p.155
Kohl rabi *Brassica oleracea* (Gonglodes group) — p.158
Korila *Cylanthera pedata* — p.185
Lablab bean (Hyacinth bean) *Dolichos lablab* — p.177
Lavender *Lavandula* spp. — p.199
Leafy amaranth *Amaranthus giganticus* — p.162
Leek *Allium porrum* — p.173
Lemon verbena *Aloysia triphylla* (syn. *Lippia citriodora*) — p.191
Lettuce *Lactuca sativa* — pp.167–8
Lovage *Levisticum officinale* — p.193
Malabar gourd (Chilacayote) *Cucurbita ficifolia* — p.184
Mallow *Malva* spp. — pp.188–9
Marjoram *Origanum* spp. — p.195
Marrow (American summer squash, courgette) *Curcurbita pepo* — pp.184–5
Mibuna greens *Brassica rapa* var. *nipposinica* — p.160
Mint *Mentha* spp. — p.193
Mizuna greens *Brassica rapa* var. *nipposinica* — p.160
Mustard *Brassica juncea* — p.154
Nasturtium *Tropaeolum majus* — p.198
New Zealand spinach *Tetragonia tetragonoides* — p.171
Nodding onion *Allium cernuum* — p.186
Oca *Oxalis tuberosa* — p.189
Onion *Allium cepa* — p.172
Oriental bunching onion *Allium fistulosum* — p.172
Oriental greens *Brassica rapa* spp. — p.158
Oriental saladini (various) — p.161
Pak choi *Brassica rapa* (Chinensis group) — p.159
Parsley *Petroselinum crispum* — pp.195–6
Parsnip *Pastinaca sativa* — pp.174–5

Pea *Pisum sativa* — p.178
Perilla (Shiso) *Perilla frutescens* — p.195
Potato *Solanum tuberosum* — p.176
Pot marigold (Calendula) *Calendula officinalis* — p.198
Purple-flowered pak choi *Brassica rapa* var. *purpurea* — p.161
Quinoa *Chenopodium quinoa* — p.180
Radish *Raphanus sativus* — p.175
Red orache (Mountain spinach) *Atriplex hortensis* — p.163
Rhubarb *Rheum × cultorum* — pp.189–90
Rock hyssop *Hyssopus officinalis* ssp. *aristatus* — p.193
Rose *Rosa* spp. — p.199
Rosette pak choi *Brassica rapa* var. *rosularis* — p.161
Runner bean *Phaseolus coccineus* — p.177
Salad rocket (Rucola) *Eruca sativa* — p.167
Salsify (Oyster plant) *Tragopogon porrifolius* — p.176
Scorzonera *Scorzonera hispanica* — p.175
Seakale *Crambe maritima* — p.187
Scented-leaved geranium *Pelargonium* spp. — p.199
Signet marigold (Gem series) *Tagetes tenuifolia (signata)* — p.199
Society garlic *Tulbaghia violacea* — p.199
Spinach *Spinacia oleracea* — p.171
Strawberry spinach *Chenopodium capitatum* — p.164
Summer purslane *Portulaca oleracea* — p.170
Sunflower *Helianthus annuus* — p.198
Sweet cicely *Myrrhis odorata* — p.193
Sweet corn (Corn) *Zea mays* — p.182
Sweet potato *Ipomoea batatas* — p.188
Sweet melon *Cucumis melo* ssp. *melo* — p.183
Sweet woodruff *Galium odoratum* — p.199
Swiss chard (Seakale beet), perpetual spinach *Beta vulgaris* spp. *cicla* — p.163
Tarentina myrtle *Myrtus communis* ssp. *tarentina* — p.194
Taro (Dasheen) *Colocasia esculenta* — p.187
Tetragonolobus purpureus — p.179
Texsel greens *Brassica carinata* — p.154
Thyme *Thymus* spp. — p.196
Tomatillo *Physalis ixocarpa* — pp.181–2
Tomato *Lycopersicon esculentum* — p.181
Tree onion (Egyptian onion) *Allium cepa* (Proliferum group) — p.186
Tree spinach *Chenopodium giganteum* 'Magentaspreen' — p.164
Tuberous-rooted begonia *Begonia × tuberhydrida* — p.199
Tuberous-rooted nasturtium (Mashua, Anu) *Tropaeolum tuberosum* — p.190
Viola *Viola* spp. — pp.198–9
Watermelon *Citrullus lanatus* — p.183
Welsh onion (Ciboule) *Allium fistulosum* — p.186
Wild, cutting or leaf celery *Apium graveolens* — p.162
Winter purslane (Miner's lettuce) *Montia perfoliata* (syn. *Claytonia perfoliata*) — p.169
Winter savory *Satureja montana* — p.196
Winter squash, pumpkin *Cucurbita maxima* — pp.184–5
Winter squash, pumpkin *Curcurbita moshata* — pp.184–5
Winter squash, pumpkin *Curcurbita pepo* — pp.184–5
Yacon *Polymnia sonchifolia* — p.189
Yucca *Yucca* spp. — p.199

Texsel greens

Mustard 'Green in the Snow'

Purple mustard 'Red Giant'

BRASSICAS

The popular image of brassicas is of boring 'greens' rather than candidates for the decorative vegetable garden. They are unfairly maligned, for they include kales with their wonderfully textured leaves, and the beautifully shaped rosette pak choi and mibuna greens. There's a richness of colour too: every shade of green from the lightest to near black, the sultry blue of the 'Black' kale, the purples of oriental mustards and red cabbage, and the multicoloured rainbows of the ornamental cabbages and thick, strong kales. (The 'cabbage-like' brassicas are often referred to broadly as 'Crucifers', though technically brassicas are a botanical group within Cruciferae.*)*

TEXSEL GREENS *Brassica carinata*
This fast-growing, nutritious and tasty vegetable of African origin was introduced to the West in the 60s. One of the daintier brassicas, it has small shiny leaves with a healthy look. It grows best in cooler months and can be cut from 7.5cm (3in) to

30cm (12in) high. It can be grown as a CCA crop or thinned to 10cm (4in) for slightly larger plants. Use it to intercrop large winter greens or to fill a gap.
↕ 25cm (10in) ↔ 15cm (6in) H ⊖

MUSTARDS *Brassica juncea*
The word 'robust' accurately describes the typical mustard. The plants are strong and sturdy, their flavour ranges from hot to very spicy, and several of them have outstanding hardiness. The majority are green-leaved, but the leaves themselves can be broad, serrated or deeply curled with kale-like rigidity. Some of the oriental broad-leaved types form a nugget-like heart, used for pickling, and even the stems of these types have an exceptional flavour. In some varieties the leaves are a rich purple, while others are essentially green with a strong purple tinge.

On the whole the mustards are happiest when grown in cool weather. They have a tendency to run to seed in the heat, though some curly-leaved American varieties, such as 'Fordhook Fancy' and 'Giant Southern Curled', are relatively heat tolerant. Sow in mid- to late summer, and plant them 30–45cm (12–18in) apart, the wider spacing

for the larger varieties. In temperate climates they are ideal autumn and winter vegetables, or use them to follow an early summer crop, such as lettuce or peas. They generally look best planted in bold groups. For a dramatic effect interplant green and red varieties, and edge the beds with winter pansies.

The mustards can also be sown thickly as CCA crops. Visually this works best with the red and curly mustards. These types can be sown in spring and early summer for a quick crop, as well as in mid- to late summer. The red mustards germinate very fast, so are excellent for intercropping. I have sown them in spring in three semicircular bands, separated by single rings of onion sets. The upright green blades of the onions made a neat foil to the broad-leaved purple seedlings. Curly- and red-leaved mustards look handsome in large containers, but ensure that they are kept very well watered.
↕ 30–45cm (12–18in) ↔ 30–45cm (12–18in) H ⊖
Recommended green varieties
'Amsoi' Large; broad-leaved; excellent flavour
'Art Green' Medium height; very curly-leaved; adapted to heat and cold
'Green in the Snow' Medium height; serrated leaves which can look scraggy; very hardy
'Green Wave' Medium height; light green frilled leaves
Recommended red varieties
'Osaka Purple' Medium height; greenish leaves with a purple tint
'Red Giant' Large; deep purple leaves, slightly coarse

'Black' kale

Curly kale 'F₁ Winterbor'

KALES *Brassica oleracea* ACEPHALA GROUP

The kales and collards, as some forms of kale are known in the United States, are a large and variable group. They are mostly rugged, hardy vegetables often proving the mainstay of a kitchen garden in winter. While the fairly coarse leaves can be harvested throughout winter, many forms also produce tender, delicately flavoured shoots in spring, perfectly timed to fill the notorious 'vegetable gap'. The kales with decorative or feathery leaves, those with a crêpe-like texture, and those with reddish pigments (which so often seem linked with hardiness) are among our most beautiful vegetables. The many varieties of ornamental kales display combinations of all these features.

'BLACK' KALE (PALM CABBAGE)

It is not surprising that this eye-catching kale, with its elegant tuft of long, narrow, metallic-blue, ostrich feather leaves, has acquired a host of descriptive names: palm cabbage (*chou palmier*), black cabbage or kale (*cavolo nero*), black palm cabbage, Tuscan kale, feathery kale (*cavolo a penna*) and, in California, dinosaur kale are a few of them. The spiritual home of kale is Tuscany in Italy, where it has been grown for centuries and used to make a filling winter soup. Two forms are known: an early maturing variety with narrow, very crinkly leaves, and a later form, somewhat hardier, with broader but plainer leaves. The leaves, to quote Vilmorin's classic *The Vegetable Garden* of 1885, 'grow straight and stiff at first, but afterwards become curved outwards at the ends, giving the plant a very elegant appearance'.

The standard practice in Italy is to sow every year in spring, setting the plants out in summer spaced 35–40cm (14–16in) apart. The leaves are harvested progressively during the winter. According to Vilmorin, however, it is a short-lived perennial, and will continue growing for up to three years before reaching its maximum height of about 2m (6½ft) and flowering. Grown this way, it is a wonderful plant to weave into a flower border, either singly or in groups.

As an annual vegetable, it makes a striking 'dot plant' in the centre of a bed, at the ends or at the corners. Alternatively, group plants together. I've intercropped them in the early stages with red lettuce and red Italian chicory: the soft blue and dull reds make a lovely contrast. For a colourful autumn scene surround them with ornamental kales. The latter will succumb to bad winter weather but the black kale looks wonderful under a blanket of snow.
↕ 60cm–2m (24in–6½ft) ↔ 45–60cm (18–24in) **H**

CURLY KALE (BORECOLE)

There should be the word 'crunkled' to describe the crisp convoluted texture of the curly kales. Both the tall forms and the compact dwarf forms have a mysterious rainforest density, especially if viewed from above. The traditional curly kales are deep green to blue-green in colour, but the variety 'Redbor' is a violet-stemmed, bronze-red kale.

For a very pretty, close-knit ground-cover effect, sow them in spring as CCA seedlings, either in patches or in narrow bands, letting them weave between tall, established vegetables, or using them to outline patterns. They are much slower growing than most CCA crops, but stay looking neat over many months. Seedlings can be cut when 5–7.5cm (2–3in) high. If you prefer taller plants, 23cm (9in) or so high, set module-grown plants or thin seedlings 15cm (6in) apart. Individual leaves can be picked from these 'mini-vegetables' after about 18 weeks, leaving them to re-sprout. They'll often give a green showing right through winter into the spring.
Dwarf: ↕ and ↔ 30–38cm (12–15in) Tall: ↕ and ↔ 60cm–1m (24in–3ft) **H** ⊝

Recommended varieties
'F₁ Shobor' Medium height; a vigorous, modern variety; deep green
'F₁ Winterbor' Tall; blue-green; exceptionally hardy
'Vates Dwarf Blue' Dwarf; a very pretty old variety; blue-green in colour
'Western Autumn' Medium height; compact and deeply curled; green

ORNAMENTAL KALES AND CABBAGES

These flamboyantly variegated kales and cabbages are the glamour queens of the kitchen garden. They are edible in small quantities in salads but are mainly used as a garnish. At their best in autumn, their colours intensify once night temperatures fall below 15°C (59°F). There are many colour combinations, some contrasting, others more subtly blended, but among the most common are green with cream, and purplish-blue with crimson or pink. As for the shapes of the leaves and plants, the modern varieties fall into three main types with variants.

The round-leaved forms that closely resemble common cabbage are fairly low-growing and flat in habit; they are the least hardy. The fringed-type are characterized by dense rosettes of deeply ruffled leaves; they are dwarf to medium in height, and generally hardier than the round-leaved ones, though they will not survive severe frost. Quite distinct are the taller feathered kales, with deeply serrated leaves; these are the hardiest of them all.

At the time of writing there are several series of similar varieties available, often having matching pairs. These can be very useful in the potager, for example, for creating edges of alternate colours.

Ornamental kale Osaka Series

Kale 'Ragged Jack'

Cauliflower 'Romanesco'

The red forms can normally be distinguished at the seedling stage by the pinkish hue to their stems.

On the whole, the ornamental kales look their most dramatic when planted in groups, whether in vegetable or flower beds. This is especially true of the very uniform, low-growing hybrids. The more highly coloured kales look stunning edged with grey-leaved plants such as *Artemisia*, or variegated mint or thyme. The taller feather types make effective dot plants: interplanting with curly endive is a great way to disguise their bare stems. The more dwarf types are the most suitable for containers.

Sow in late spring and early summer in modules or 10cm (4in) pots. Plant out in summer with the lowest leaves just above ground level. Space them 30–40cm (12–16in) apart, depending on the cultivar.

Recommended varieties

Osaka Series and **'Pink Beauty'** Low-growing and round-leaved

Chidori and **Wave Series** and **'Prima Donna'** Medium sized, typical fringed varieties

Coral, Peacock and **Feather Series** Hardier and taller, deeply serrated leaves, the Feather Series is the tallest

↕ 30–60cm (12–24in) ↔ 30–45cm (12–18in) **H**

NB Although technically distinct, the ornamental kales and cabbages are grouped together here, and referred to as kales, as this is the standard practice in seed catalogues at the time of writing.

RUSSIAN KALE

This old-fashioned kale has a mild flavour and pretty, blue-green, toothed-edged leaves which take on purple-red hues in cold weather. 'Ragged Jack' is a somewhat similar old variety, which grows to 30cm (12in) or so. Siberian kale (strictly speaking not a kale but in the rape family) is a very hardy, vigorous plant with frilly blue-green leaves growing to about 35cm (14in) tall.

Sow in late spring in a prominent position and let it grow to its full height. Alternatively, sow it *in situ* in spring, early summer or autumn as a dainty CCA plant in a low-growing patch, in narrow bands or in a single drill. Either leave the plants unthinned to pick as tender seedlings or thin to 25–38cm (10–15in) apart for small plants. It can be picked over many months and self-seeds readily.

↕ 70cm (27in) ↔ 50cm (20in) **H** ⊖

CAULIFLOWER *Brassica oleracea* BOTRYTIS GROUP

I never used to consider cauliflower suitable for the decorative vegetable garden. The summer and autumn types are tricky to grow, while the spring heading ones occupy a lot of space for the best part of a year. Then one bitterly cold, winter day, an overwintering spring heading cauliflower caught my

eye: magnificent, statuesque, with white veins prominent on the blue-green leaves. Ever since then, a small bed in my Winter Potager is set aside for them each year. As they are slow growing, there is plenty of scope for intersowing around them.

Sow spring heading cauliflowers in late spring and plant out in mid-summer 70cm (27in) apart. I use either the white-curded 'Walcheren Winter' varieties or the purple-headed 'Purple Cape'.

If you have space, fertile soil, adequate moisture and coolish summers it is tempting to grow those autumn cauliflowers with exceptionally beautiful curds, such as 'Romanesco' with its lime green, pinnacle-shaped head, and the purple-headed varieties like 'Violet Queen'. Sow these in late spring, and them plant in early summer 60cm (24in) apart.

The 'Nine Star Perennial' perennial broccoli is a distinct form of cauliflower deserving a place towards the back of a low-maintenance potager. The large branching plant is a splendid sight in spring, bedecked with miniature white or greenish curds of 2.5–5cm (¾–2in) diameter. It needs fertile conditions and is not truly perennial, deteriorating after three years or so. Sow in spring and plant out in summer, allowing it a 1m (3ft) square. Cut off all flowering shoots to conserve its vigour.

Overwintering cauliflower ↕ 60cm (24in) ↔ 70cm (27in) **H**; Summer cauliflower ↕ 45cm (18in) ↔ 60cm (24in) **HH**; Perennial broccoli ↕ 1m (3ft) ↔ 1m (3ft) **H**

Savoy cabbage

Cabbage 'Tronchuda'

CABBAGE *Brassica oleracea* CAPITATA GROUP
I am always surprised at how beautiful cabbages are, especially when their everyday greens, blues and reds are touched by soft evening light. They have a quality that is difficult to define. Their very ordinariness and solidity makes them excellent decorative vegetables. With their compact heads, firm leaves and steady, predictable growth you know where you are. Moreover, the size of the head can be controlled by spacing: plant them closely for small heads, far apart for large ones.

It is easy to intercrop them in the early stages, for example with lettuce, to make neat chequer-board patterns. Grown closely at even spacing they always make a strong solid patch, contrasting well with taller vegetables, soft-leaved plants such as fennel and dill, and even with flowers.

RED CABBAGE
The leaves of young red cabbages are a soft blue-grey highlighted with deep purple veins, but as the plants mature, the colour becomes a deeper blue-red, overlaid with a sheen of grey. Visitors to my potagers often ask what they are, incredulous that such a handsome plant could be a cabbage. The mature heads are dense, but the leaves can spread to a 1m (3ft) span. Edgings of grey-leaved, cream, white or variegated plants show them off to their best, but I love the effect created by planting other blues, reds and purples nearby, clary sage being a favourite for this purpose.

At Villandry they are planted in single file, down long, metre-wide beds like a column of marching soldiers, completely covering the ground between the low box edges.

For maximum impact plant them in groups, but recently I planted them along a narrow bed in a 'W' formation, with triangles of lettuce and beetroot between the arms of the 'W'. After these crops were harvested in early summer, the spaces they left, now reduced by the encroaching cabbage leaves, were filled with red chicory. It worked well.

For top-quality plants, sow in the autumn in modules, keep them in a cold-frame over the winter and plant out in spring at least 45cm (18in) apart. This seems to produce far better plants than the normal spring sowing. Few plants stand in good condition as long as red cabbage, but when the heads are cut, leave the stem in the ground. More leaves, and sometimes secondary heads develop, so the picture remains elegant for several more weeks, even months. It will eventually be destroyed by severe winter weather. Very dry weather sometimes leads to premature bolting, spoiling their impact.
↕ 40cm (16in) ↔ 60cm–1m (2–3ft) **H**
Recommended varieties
'Ruby Ball' Reliable and decorative

SPRING CABBAGE
The typical spring cabbage is small with a neat, pointed, perky head and a fresh green colour. They grow fastest and make most impact in spring, when

a healthy patch is a very pretty sight. To make the best of the space and give the garden a 'busy' look, they can be interplanted between rows of over-wintering leeks, autumn-sown onions, or among red chicories. They will have plenty of room to develop after these crops are cleared. In temperate climates, sow in mid- to late summer, and plant out in early autumn 30cm (12in) or so apart.
↕ 25–30cm (10–12in) ↔ 30–38cm (12–15in) **H**
Recommended varieties
'Avoncrest' and **'Durham Early'** Reliable, pointed-head varieties

SUMMER CABBAGES
Some early varieties of summer cabbage, such as the hybrids 'Hispi' and 'Spitfire' are neatly pointed. They look a picture interplanted with bronze and red loose-headed lettuces: their colour and shape a complete contrast. Quite different is the pointed, puckered-leaved 'Spivoy', a miniature savoy. This can be planted 10cm (4in) apart giving tiny, tender, tennis ball-size 'mini' cabbages. They make a wonderfully dainty patch. Edge them with dark-flowered violas. The later maturing summer cabbages are round-headed. Plant them in groups to get the massed effect of their smooth pates. Choose modern varieties such as the hybrid 'Minicole', which stands for a long time without splitting. Sow in spring, and plant out in late spring to early summer, 35–45cm (14–18in) apart.
↕ 30–40cm (12–16in) ↔ 35–45cm (14–18in) **HH**

WINTER CABBAGES
For truly beautiful texture there is nothing quite like the bubbly-leaved savoy cabbages. Their colours range through light and dusky green to grey-green. So genuinely beautiful are they that, in one famous potager, only the outer leaves are ever picked for the kitchen, leaving the majesty of the plants untouched. Again, they are nearly always most effective grown in groups or planted in the foreground to distract the eye from taller, more gaunt winter greens such as Brussels sprouts and purple sprouting broccoli behind. All varieties are worth growing. The Portuguese 'Tronchuda' or 'Braganza' cabbage is a unique, sturdy type of hardy cabbage, which has beautiful almost cup-shaped leaves distinguished by flaring white midribs and veins. Sow in late spring, and plant in summer about 50cm (20in) apart.
↕ 40cm (16in) ↔ 60cm–1m (2–3ft) **H**

Brussels sprouts

Brussels sprouts 'Rubine'

Kohl rabi (White)

BRUSSELS SPROUTS *Brassica oleracea*
GEMNIFERA GROUP

Brussels sprouts tend to be ungainly plants, and require staking in most situations to keep them upright. I wouldn't normally recommend them for a decorative vegetable garden unless they are inter-cropped with winter salads such as corn salad, land cress and winter purslane.

The one exception is the red-leaved form, which is represented at the time of writing by the variety 'Rubine'. This grows 75cm–1m (2–3ft) high. It has to be said that its performance is erratic: the plants can look mean and straggly, but in good conditions they make impressive tall, purplish spires of colour. They look best in small groups, either in the centre of a bed or towards the back. One year they were used in summer bedding schemes at the Royal Botanic Gardens, Kew, London, their stems hidden behind a silver skirt of *Artemisia* 'Powis Castle'. It would be fun, too, to let canary creeper run through them. For a longer lasting winter disguise, plant the deep green, bushy 'Parcel' celery in the foreground. They also team well with 'Black' kale. The sprouts are small, but any unpicked sprouts run to seed in spring, making a dramatic display of yellow flowers.

Give them a good start by sowing in mid- to late spring, planting them out six weeks later about 70cm (27in) apart. Plant in a slight hollow and earth up the stems as they grow to aid stability.
↕ 1m (3ft) ↔ 60–75cm (24–30in) **H**

KOHL RABI *Brassica oleracea* GONGLODES GROUP

Kohl rabi really is an odd-ball. The edible part is a top-shaped bulb that develops mid-stem, 4cm (1½in) clear of the ground. The smooth-skinned bulbs are deep purple or creamy white (often called green), with slender leaf stalks coming off them in a random picturesque spiral. The leaves are finer than those of most brassicas, a pleasing purple with deeper purple veins in the purple form, and green with purple veins in the green form.

Planted in the foreground or middle ground, a group of kohl rabi seem to skim the surface in a graceful manner. Singly, they make an informal edge to a bed.

They grow fast, being ready to eat within eight to ten weeks of sowing. Sow from early spring to summer, planting out when 5cm (2in) high. Plant them 25cm (10in) apart and the leaves will spread out spaciously, but they grow equally well and look very pretty planted as close as 10cm (4in) apart. This produces delicious bulbs the size of ping-pong balls, rather than the normal tennis ball-size.

Early sowings can be followed by winter leeks or mustards; late sowings will stand into winter. If a few purple plants are left to seed, the purple spires will be 1m (3ft) high. (The young shoots are palatable.) Use modern hybrid varieties where available, as they grow more evenly and stand much longer than old varieties when mature.
↕ 30cm (12in) ↔ 25–40cm (10–16in) **H**

ORIENTAL GREENS *Brassica rapa* spp.

The following oriental greens, all members of the species *Brassica rapa*, differ from traditional western brassicas in ways which have a bearing on their use in a decorative situation.

They are exceptionally fast growing, which makes them ideal wherever there is a need to fill bare ground rapidly and also for intercropping. With their natural vigour, they respond well to cut-and-come-again treatment, not just at the seedling stage, but also as semi-mature and mature plants, provided they are planted in fertile soil and given plenty of moisture.

More versatile than most western brassicas, they can be sown as CCA seedlings and cut very young, or grown together closely and harvested as small plants, or left to develop into large plants. The size is controlled by spacing. They can be planted anything from 10 to 35cm (4 to 14in) apart, depending on the variety and size required. They can even be allowed to run to seed after maturing, the very moment when western greens are consigned to the compost heap. Many then go on to produce

Chinese broccoli

Green-stemmed Pak Choi

Loose-headed Chinese cabbage

delectable (and pretty) flowering shoots. All parts of the plant, leaves, stalks and flowers, are edible, though a few types, such as purple-flowered pak choi, are grown primarily for the flowering shoots.

A potential disadvantage is that most varieties available at the time of writing are naturally adapted to develop during the shortening days of late summer and autumn. When sown in spring or early summer, the odds are they will bolt prematurely and never develop into useable plants. In the main, therefore, they are best sown in mid-summer to early autumn to give late, follow-on crops, the hardy ones being excellent for the winter vegetable garden. A useful exception occurs with CCA seedlings: in most cases, a CCA sowing can be made in spring, with time for one or two cuts before the plants coarsen and run to seed. Several different types of plant are combined in the 'Oriental saladini' mixtures (see p.161).

Another drawback is that the tender leaves of oriental greens are probably more susceptible to brassica pests, particularly caterpillars and flea beetle, than the tougher-leaved western brassicas. Undoubtedly, the best solution for organic gardeners is to grow them under insect-proof netting, posing a dilemma where the aesthetics of a garden are important. These problems are worst in mid-summer; autumn-sown plants and the hardy types pose fewer problems, apart from slug damage. Any troubles with pests are, however, more than offset

by the vivacious green colours of these vegetables, the beautifully shaped leaves and plants, and the wonderful range of flavours.

CHINESE BROCCOLI (CHINESE KALE)

Brassica oleracea var. *alboglabra*

This blue-green, waxy-leaved plant has delicious chunky flowering shoots. It is harvested either as small, young one-shoot plants or allowed to grow into large, multi-stemmed plants. Large plants look handsome but must have good growing conditions. For cultivation see Further Reading, p.201.

↕ 30–45cm (12–18in) ↔ 15–45cm (6–18in) **HH**

PAK CHOI *Brassica rapa* CHINENSIS GROUP

The archetypal pak choi is a loose-headed, upright plant with smooth, fairly stiff leaves, characterized by their white veins and prominent white midribs. These merge into white leaf stalks which widen dramatically at the base where they overlap snugly like Chinese soup spoons. An average mature plant is 30cm (12in) high, but there are many variants. One of these is the smaller, neatly waisted 'Shanghai' type, rarely more than 15cm (6in) high. A pert, appealing plant, its stems and leaf bases are a beautiful light green. In the 'Tai Sai' type the leaves bend outward on delicate, swan-neck stalks.

In spring these pak chois make excellent ground cover: the fast-germinating seedlings start to make an impact within ten days of sowing. Sow them *in situ* in wide drills to in-fill triangular, circular or square patterns, outlined perhaps with leeks or onions. For a more dramatic contrast grow them beside red lettuce, dark-leaved beetroot or purple mustard. They can also be used as short-term intercrops between rows, or larger vegetables. From mid-summer onwards, sow them either as CCA seedlings or set out container-grown plants in groups, to make bold green-and-white patches in the garden. There's a lovely symmetry to a well-grown crop of mature, neatly rounded pak chois.

Recommended varieties

'F₁ Joi Choi' Reliable; white-stemmed
'F₁ Mei Qing Choi' and **'Shanghai'** Small; green-stemmed

↕ and ↔ 10–45cm (4–18in) **HH**

CHINESE CABBAGE *Brassica rapa*
PEKINENSIS GROUP

I am reluctant to recommend the headed Chinese cabbage (or 'Chinese leaves' as it is widely known) for inclusion in a potager as they are among the trickiest of vegetables to grow well. They can develop at a phenomenal rate, but to do so demand the best growing conditions. They are susceptible to a lot of pests. At their best, they are superb, healthy-looking plants.

In the sturdy, compact 'barrel-headed' type, the leaves display a striking network of prominent white veins radiating from a thick, succulent midrib. The taller, looser-headed cylindrical type is an elegant plant. Both look impressive grown in groups.

Easier to grow, and giving a softer, light-coloured impression, are the loose-headed types. There is an enormous range within this group, but among the prettiest are the so-called 'fluffy top' types. Here the plant forms an upright rosette of crinkled leaves, the outer leaves a light green, but the inner leaves a lovely buttery-cream, hence one of the old Chinese names 'Yellow cabbage'.

Generally speaking, grow them in the same way as pak choi. As seedling crops they have a fluffier look than most pak chois, but they come into their own, showing off their creamy centres, as large plants in bold groups. The variety 'Ruffles' is fairly bolt resistant and can be sown in late spring for a mid-summer crop. Otherwise sow in summer for autumn crops, spacing plants about 35cm (14in) apart. The words 'Shantung' and 'Santo' in oriental varieties indicate the loose-headed type.

↕ 30cm (12in) ↔ 35cm (14in) **HH**

MIBUNA GREENS *Brassica rapa* var. *nipposinica*
Probably closely related to mizuna (see opposite), mibuna has been slower to become established in the West. It forms a beautiful spray-like clump of narrow, shiny, deep green leaves, anything from 1 to 4cm (½ to 1½in) wide and well over 38cm (15in) long with neatly rounded tips. It can be grown and used in much the same way as mizuna greens, though it is less tolerant of extremes of heat and cold, less vigorous and is unlikely to re-sprout more than once or twice when cut back. It does not look as striking as mizuna when grown as seedlings, although large individual plants are very handsome, seen at their best in autumn and early winter. Mibuna wouldn't be at all out of place in a flower bed, or growing in a large container.

Plant about 50cm (20in) apart for large plants, but 15cm (6in) for small, neat plants.

↕ 30–45cm (12–18in) ↔ 25–56cm (10–22in) **HH** ⊖

Mibuna 'Green Spray'

MIZUNA GREENS *Brassica rapa* var. *nipposinica*
This exceptionally pretty plant, a gift to lovers of decorative vegetables, only found its way to the West from Japan in the 70s. When grown to maturity it forms a bushy clump of dark green, dissected leaves with thin, glistening white leaf stalks. Both leaves and stems are edible. Although often described as a mustard, there's only the mildest piquancy to its flavour. Some hybrids, such as 'Tokyo Beau' and 'Tokyo Belle', have broader leaves, and are hardier than the original fine-leaved type.

It's a plant with great vitality. The clumps can sometimes be cut back to 5cm (2in) above ground level four or five times over several months, re-sprouting each time. These cut-back plants are far more resistant to frost and the effects of snow than large, leafy plants, and can be useful components of a winter vegetable garden. I have often planted mizuna in early summer between sweet corn: it grows well beneath it, continuing to crop long after the sweet corn has been harvested, sometimes into the following spring. Mizuna looks pretty in groups and as bands between other hardy oriental greens.

Mizuna greens is a typical 'oriental' in growing best during the cool months, but is more adaptable

Mizuna 'Tokyo Beau'

than some. In practice, it can be sown throughout the growing season, though flea beetle is a potentially serious problem in hot weather. As a CCA crop, sow in spring and early summer, using it in any of the ways suggested for pak choi (see p.159). Continue sowing in late summer and early autumn for winter use. It can be sown *in situ* to make an attractive jagged-leaved edge to a winter bed or border, either left unthinned or thinned out to about 15cm (6in) apart for medium-sized plants. Otherwise grow as single plants, sowing any time from spring to late summer, planting them 10–45cm (4–18in) apart, depending on the size of plant required.

↕ 23cm (9in) ↔ 23–38cm (9–15in) **H** ⊖

FLOWERING RAPE HYBRID 'BOUQUET'
Brassica rapa var. *oleifera*
Although the various types of flowering pak choi can be pretty when the shoots are sprinkled with yellow flower buds, their quality is variable. Unless conditions and varieties are well matched, plants can be very straggly, spoiling the effect in a formal potager. A better bet are the hybrid flowering rapes, a group originally grown in China for the lamp oil extracted from their seeds. The modern hybrid 'Bouquet' is far sturdier than its pak choi counterparts, light

Flowering rape 'Bouquet'

Purple-flowered pak choi

Rosette pak choi

green in colour with pretty savoy-like leaves, the shoots densely crowded with yellow flower buds. It is even used for flower arranging.

In temperate climates it grows best as a late summer and early autumn vegetable, but once it has more than a touch of frost, its quality deteriorates. It can make a pretty, light-coloured patch, offset with the blue hues of leeks or cabbage, the dark greens of mizuna or mibuna, or red-toned vegetables.

They can be sown from early summer to mid-autumn. For a neat effect sow *in situ*, thinning plants 15–20cm (6–8in) apart, or set module-raised plants out at that spacing. They mature quickly and can be picked over several weeks. Provided they are well watered, they can be grown in containers.
↕ 25–45cm (10–18in) ↔ 25–38cm (10–15in) **HH**

PURPLE-FLOWERED PAK CHOI (HON TSAI TAI)
Brassica rapa var. *purpurea*
This hardy pak choi is grown for its slender-stemmed flowering shoots. Compared to other pak chois it is an insubstantial, branching plant, with fairly narrow, greenish-blue, purple-veined leaves. Provided you are not over diligent about picking shoots at their most tender, the buds will open into bouquets of pale yellow flowers, a lovely sight against the purple stems in autumn to winter.

Purple pak choi seems to grow best in autumn. Sow in modules or pots in mid- to late summer, setting plants out a few weeks later 35cm (14in) apart if they are to be grown in groups, otherwise

consider dotting them about singly as flippant notes of colour among the autumn and winter greens.
↕ and ↔ 40–45cm (16–18in) **H**

ROSETTE PAK CHOI *Brassica rapa* var. *rosularis*
This, surely, must be one of the most theatrical of the brassicas. The thick puckered leaves are so dark they verge on black ('black cabbage' is one of its Chinese names) but the most striking aspect is the perfect rosette of concentric circles formed by the leaves. In smaller-leaved types the leaves lie flat on the ground, but in larger-leaved varieties the heads are initially erect, looking like giant, green Bourbon roses, gradually assuming a flatter posture as the weather cools in autumn. The rosette pak chois are hardier than other types and slower growing, but highly prized for their flavour.

Their shape, colour and texture contrasts well with other hardy oriental greens such as purple and green mustards, mizuna and mibuna. Planting these in stripes across a bed gives an intriguing effect. Rosette pak choi also makes a neat, original edging to paths and beds, and can easily be worked into the foreground of a flower bed.

For best results, delay sowing until mid-summer to lessen the chance of bolting. They look quite fetching as a CCA seedling crop and can be inter-cropped successfully, for example, between newly planted cauliflowers. However, to make the most of their stylish shape, grow them to their full size, planting them 25–30cm (10–12in) apart.

Recommended varieties
'Sankeiyukima' Large, upright and larger-leaved (at the time of writing, hard to obtain in the West)
'Tah Tsai' Small and round-leaved, horizontal ↕
25–35cm (10–14in) ↔ 25–50cm (10–20in) **H** ⊖

ORIENTAL SALADINI
The seed company *Suffolk Herbs* (see Suppliers, p.201) and I 'invented' this mixture of oriental brassica seeds in 1991 to give westerners a feel of the many types of oriental greens. The original mixture included pak choi, loose-headed Chinese cabbage, purple mustard, mizuna, mibuna and komatsuna, but other, equally good variants can now be found.

It is essentially grown as a CCA seedling crop in the same way as pak choi (see p.159). With its range of leaf colours and textures, it can look very pretty. Cool-weather sowings often stand well over several months. Seedlings can also be thinned 5–7.5cm (2–3in) apart to give larger leaves for stir-frying. To some extent they thin themselves, stronger plants growing at the expense of the weaker. Where winters are mild, patches sown in late summer will overwinter, gaily running to seed and providing edible flowering shoots the following spring.

Chinese amaranth

Ornamental amaranth

Celery 'Parcel'

SALAD AND LEAFY VEGETABLES

Most of the vegetables in this group are eaten raw as salads, though the spinach and chard family are generally cooked. The group includes many of the low-growing vegetables used to create carpeting tapestry effects, such as lettuces, curled endives, red chicories, spinach and the summer purslanes. Here, too, are the fast-growing vegetables suited to quick summer inter-cropping: the 'Salad Bowl' types of lettuce, cresses, salad rape, salad rocket and summer purslanes. In winter, the hardier little salads such as corn salad, land cress, winter purslane, 'Grumolo' chicory and chrysanthemum greens can wend their way between the winter greens, brightening the potager.

AMARANTH *Amaranthus*
The amaranths are a vast group of plants, ranging from humble, all-too-common weeds, through the 'leafy amaranths', which are eaten like spinach, to the giant, theatrical grain amaranths with their huge plumed seedheads (for Grain amaranth, see p.180). Then there are the ornamental garden amaranths such as the red-tasselled 'Love Lies Bleeding'. Typical colours in amaranth leaves and seedheads are greens, bronze, golden-yellow, crimson and pink, all often found in variegated plants.

The leaves of all the amaranths are edible, and all seeds could be harvested for grain. Some are much more suited to one purpose than the other and are divided accordingly. If amaranths grow well in your climate, it is easy to justify their inclusion in the garden. With few exceptions, they are half-hardy plants. They are fast growing, fairly drought tolerant and have few pest or disease problems. Many of the smaller varieties look pretty in containers.

LEAFY AMARANTH *Amaranthus giganticus*
(and other species)
The leafy amaranths are warmth lovers and need a temperature of 20–25°C (68–77°F) to flourish out-doors. Plain, green-leaved forms such as 'Tampala' may be the most productive, but the varieties listed below are more colourful. Best grown in patches, they tolerate light shade and can be intercropped between tall vegetables such as sweet corn.

They can be grown various ways. In cool climates start them off indoors, then plant out once all risk of frost is past (see Grain amaranth, p.180). In warmer climates, sow them *in situ* outdoors when soil temperatures reach about 20°C (68°F). Sow in drills or as CCA patches to cut as large seedlings; plant out or thin to about 10cm (4in) apart in

order to harvest whole as young plants, or to 20cm (8in) apart to harvest over a longer period.

↕ 30–60cm (12–24in) ↔ 20–45cm (8–18in)
HH ⊖ ☽

Recommended varieties
(see also Grain amaranth, p.180)
Chinese amaranth Green with purple markings
'Khulu' Green leaves with violet veins
'Red Stripe' Red markings in the leaf centres

WILD, CUTTING OR LEAF CELERY AND CULTIVATED CELERY
Apium graveolens and *A. g.* var. *dulce*
There are three types of celery. Hardy English trenching celery is grown for its stems, which are earthed-up or blanched by other methods in order to tenderize them. This process requires access and space, making trenching celery an unsuitable crop for a crowded plot. Self-blanching celery, though frost tender and less highly flavoured, is much more manageable. It has dark and light green varieties. There are also pink-stemmed forms, such as the variety 'Pink Ice' in which about 50 per cent of the plants have pink-tinged stems. The colour may vary according to the soil, but they are worth the gamble.

Red orache

Swiss chard 'Feurio'

The wild, cutting, or leaf celery is a much hardier, bushier plant. Leaves and young stems are used in salads and for flavouring. The unique variety 'Parcel' has deeply curled leaves, which remain glossy green even when temperatures fall to -10°C (14°F). Massed densely in a bed, it looks wonderful all winter; it can be a magnificent foil to ornamental kales. Otherwise, use it to edge a spacious bed or to accent the corners. Two or three plants are enough for most households. It self-seeds prolifically, and in spring, still a rich green, looks striking when seeding, easily reaching 1m (3ft).

Celery has tiny seed which germinates erratically. Never sow too early in the season, as it bolts prematurely if temperatures fall below 10°C (50°F) for more than 12 hours. It is best started indoors, sowing on the surface. Sow self-blanching celery in spring, planting in late spring to early summer spacing plants 25cm (10in) apart. Although usually planted in blocks several plants deep (which makes the stems whiter), it looks very striking in rows interplanted with red lettuce or red-leaved beetroots, spacing the celery rows 30cm (12in) apart.

Sow cutting celery throughout the growing season. Treat as a CCA seedling crop, sowing *in situ*

in wide drills, and cutting when very fine and tender. Single, container-grown plants can be spaced 12cm (5in) apart. 'Parcel', however, is best value grown as large plants spaced 30cm (12in) apart.
Self-blanching ↕ 38–45cm (15–18in)
↔ 35cm (14in) **T**
Cutting celery ↕ 30cm (12in)
↔ 30–40cm (12–16in) **H** ⊖
Recommended self-blanching varieties
'F₁ Victoria' One of the hardiest of modern green varieties
'Pink Ice' Pink-tinged stems

RED ORACHE (MOUNTAIN SPINACH)
Atriplex hortensis
There are green, golden and red forms of this ancient vegetable but, for me, the only plant for the potager is the red form, *Atriplex hortensis* 'Rubra'. All of the others seem insipid in comparison. One of the first signs of life in my potager each spring is a flush of purple orache seedlings. In a very short time they have grown to bushy plants anything up to 2.75m (9ft) high, filling every bare cranny with their slender spikes and grey-brushed leaves. The only problem is that they grow so fast they will overwhelm smaller plants, or block the vista of plants beyond. The secret is to keep nipping out the tops to use in salads or as delicious, spinach-like greens. This keeps them under control for weeks, sometimes even months.

Allow a few, in appropriate places, to run to their full height so their beautiful seedheads can develop, imperceptibly changing from scarlet-red to bronze. At this stage orache has an almost tree-like, woody trunk. Allow plants with the purest colours to seed for the following season. Your only task next year will be to thin them out ruthlessly.

Red orache looks lovely when its soft purple harmonizes with the reds of chard, dwarf runner beans, pink poppies, or the blue tints of cabbage, and flowering chicories and borage. If it is being grown to its full height keep it in the background, or use it to disguise unsightly features. Otherwise it is pretty woven into the foreground or middle ground of a vegetable or flower bed.

To establish orache, sow *in situ* outdoors, any time during the growing season. Use either as CCA seedlings, or thin in stages to about 30cm (12in) apart, for larger plants. It bolts fast in dry conditions.

Sea purslane, or sea orache, *Atriplex halimus* is a related maritime shrub with grey-green leaves, which used to be cultivated as an edible hedge in the Mediterranean. Its leaves are eaten raw or pickled in vinegar.
↕ 1.8m (6ft) ↔ 15–50cm (6–20in) **H** ⊖

SWISS CHARD (SEAKALE BEET) AND PERPETUAL SPINACH *Beta vulgaris* ssp. *cicla*
There can be few vegetables that are such good value in a decorative vegetable garden as Swiss chard. The plants are upright and handsome. The thick, glossy, crêped leaves contrast with stout midribs and leaf stalks, which can be pure white, deep red, pink or, more rarely, a brilliant orange-yellow. In the different varieties, leaf colour ranges from light yellowish-green, to dark green, to a rich red, shot through with deep green.

Varieties can be used decoratively in many ways. They have tremendous presence planted densely in a bed, perhaps edged with annual flowers, neat thymes or evergreen marjoram. The variously coloured varieties can be mixed at random, or alternated to make intriguing patterns of dark and light green, or red and green. Single plants can be dotted about to great effect and mix easily with flowers in colourful borders. They can also be inter-cropped: a successful combination is red-leaved 'Feurio' interplanted with blue-green winter leeks,

163

Swiss chard 'Fordhook Giant'

Strawberry spinach

Tree spinach

a lovely contrast of leaf shape and colour. If you have space, allow one or two plants to run to seed. Then they are majestic (especially the red varieties), easily reaching 1.5m (5ft). Another attribute is that seedlings can linger in modules without suffering unduly, so I always keep a few handy to slip into gaps. They fill empty spaces superbly, whether in the foreground or further back in the bed. Chard also looks good in large containers.

Swiss chard stands in good condition for many months, is relatively drought tolerant, moderately hardy and has few natural enemies. The quality of the leaves does, however, deteriorate during wet, cold winters, and the red-leaved varieties have an unfortunate tendency to bolt prematurely, especially from early sowings.

Being highly productive and beautiful, it is worth having chard in the garden all year round. To accomplish this, sow first in mid- to late spring, then again in mid- to late summer, planting five to six weeks later 38cm (15in) apart. The first sowings will stand well into winter, and the second into early summer the following year before running to seed. Swiss chard can be grown as a CCA crop, but sow thinly, as the large 'seeds' are groups of several

seeds, so the seedlings easily become overcrowded. They make bold, strong lines and bands, ideal for intercropping and quick in-filling in much the same way as pak choi (see p.159).

Perpetual spinach, which is a form of chard with more modest dimensions and less prominent midribs and leaf stalks, is also excellent for this purpose. Drills sown in spring can easily remain productive through to early summer the following year, the plants gradually reaching a height of 30–38cm (12–15in). This makes them very suitable for low-maintenance gardens.

↕ and ↔ 45cm (18in) **H** ☉

Recommended varieties

Bieta verde a costa rosa (Pink stem) Green-leaved Italian variety, pink-hued stems; reasonably hardy
'Charlotte' Bright scarlet-coloured leaves
'Feurio' Red-leaved, red-stemmed plant with good bolt-resistance
'Fordhook Giant' Deep green-leaved and white-stemmed; very hardy
'Lucullus' Similar to the above variety but with yellow-green leaves

STRAWBERRY SPINACH AND BEETBERRY
Chenopodium capitatum and C. foliosum
Both species are bushy plants with thin, jagged-edged leaves used like spinach, but they are really grown for the tiny, strawberry-like berries which develop in eye-catching clusters on the flower spikes.

The fruits are edible, though they don't have much flavour but, as a miniature strawberry lookalike it's a lovely plant for children.

Sow in spring, planting about 23–30cm (9–12in) apart. Nip out the growing point early to encourage bushiness. Either grow it in the front of beds in groups or as dot plants in areas where they can be seen. It makes quite a neat edge and sometimes self-seeds. It can be grown in exposed situations.

↕ and ↔ 25–38cm (10–15in) **H** ⬙

TREE SPINACH *Chenopodium giganteum*
'Magentaspreen'
Closely related to the universal edible weed known as fat hen or lamb's quarters, this tall, vigorous plant can be spectacular. The leaves have a dusty, flour-like patina and develop lilac, purple and magenta colours which, coupled with magenta flower spikes and smooth, red-and-green-striped stems, account for its ornamental quality.

Sow in spring, in modules or *in situ* towards the back of a border, spacing plants about 23cm (9in) apart. Tree spinach grows at an astonishing speed. It can self-seed and could become invasive.

↕ 1.8–2.5m (6–8ft) ↔ 25–50cm (10–20in) **H**

Chrysanthemum greens

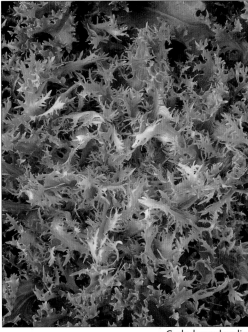

Curly-leaved endive

Broad-leaved endive

CHRYSANTHEMUM GREENS (SHUNGIKU)

Chrysanthemum coronarium

This decorative form of the garden chrysanthemum has very pretty leaves and dainty cream, yellow and orange flowers. The leaves can be skimpy and deeply serrated, or thicker, wider and almost spoon-shaped. Although grown mainly for the well-flavoured leaves, which can be steamed or added to stir fries, the flowers are edible. It is a flexible plant and good value over many months. It can prove a neat edge, if picked often to keep it low. It can be interplanted or sown as a CCA crop beneath sweet corn in summer or brassicas in winter and it always makes a pleasing patch, contrasting nicely with red-leaved lettuce and introducing a colourful note if left to flower. It is worth having plants dotted around a garden for this purpose: it is also perfectly at home in flower borders.

It can be grown throughout the growing season as a CCA crop or as single plants, but remains leafier and is better value in cool weather. Sow in spring for summer use, and in mid-summer for autumn use, spacing plants 10–15cm (4–6in) apart. Pick regularly to delay the plant running to seed and becoming tough. Mature, almost woody plants can sometimes be cut back hard and encouraged to re-sprout. Chrysanthemum greens will self-seed in favourable conditions.

↕ 15cm (6in); 1m (3ft) when flowering
↔ 15–20cm (6–8in) **H** ☉

ENDIVE *Cichorium endivia*

This attractive, fresh green, creamy-centred, low-growing salad has two main types: the deeply curled 'frisée' and the broad-leaved 'Batavia' or 'Scarole'. Being sharp flavoured, endive was traditionally blanched by excluding light for ten days or so to sweeten it. This isn't really necessary with good modern types. On the whole, the curled endive is best for hot weather (it may bolt prematurely after a cold spring spell), while the more rugged 'Batavia' types are hardier. Endive can be grown as single plants or as CCA seedlings: it responds well to CCA treatment at any stage.

Although both types make excellent, healthy patches, I use curly endive most because the frilled leaves are exceptionally decorative, and stay looking good over two to three months. As a CCA seedling crop it is excellent for intercropping, or to fill a section of a pattern. It grows fast and regrows rapidly after cutting. It looks superb interwoven or alternated with the equally curly red 'Lollo' lettuce.

Grown as a single mature plant, it can be planted in late spring for a summer crop, or in late summer for a follow-on autumn crop. It makes a pretty, uniform edge. I often use it as a section boundary within a bed, harvesting alternate plants (sometimes blanching them first by temporarily covering them with a dinner plate), leaving alternate plants to seed. When seeding they make the neatest avenue of pagoda-like spires. Endive is handy in summer to interplant between winter brassicas, a frivolous disguise for their bare stems in the early stages.

It can be sown throughout the growing season, but consult current catalogues for the optimum sowing time for each variety. Space plants 25–38cm (10–15in) apart depending on variety.

↕ 12cm (5in); 30–60cm (12–24in) when seeding
↔ 10–35cm (4–14in) **H–HH** ☉

Recommended varieties

'Ione' and **'Pancaliere'** Curled varieties suited to spring and summer sowing

CHICORY *Cichorium intybus*

This great tribe of vegetables are mostly perennial by nature, but are cultivated as annuals. They are robust, vigorous plants with a slightly sharp flavour, which seems to deter pests. In the red chicories, widely known as 'radicchio', the predominantly red leaf colour embraces all shades from pink to scarlet, often blended with greens and yellows in subtle variegations. In the green chicories, leaves range in shape from the dandelion-like serrations of 'Catalogna' chicory, to the rounded rosette of 'Grumolo' chicory, to the broad-leaved, upright 'Sugar Loaf' type. The leaves are used mainly in salads but can also be cooked.

A common feature of all chicories is that they run to seed in their second season, growing into massive, multi-spiked plants covered with clear blue flowers, which bloom for four to six weeks and generally open early and close by noon. Wherever there is space, leave a couple of plants to run to seed to make a dramatic, colourful backdrop. Occasionally, they produce pink or white flowers.

Sometimes packets of mixed chicory seed are available. Sow them in an out-of-the-way area or in a low-maintenance garden for a wonderfully varied, semi-permanent feature. Alternatively, sow in a vegetable plot in early to mid-summer, for harvesting in their first season. The hardy types remain productive into the following spring. For potager use, it is better to stick to named varieties so you can plan for colour, size and form.

GREEN CHICORY

'Catalogna' or 'Asparagus' chicory is a handsome, tall plant grown mainly for its flowering shoots or 'puntarelle', which are a delicacy when cooked. The leaves are straight edged or jagged like a dandelion; a row makes a striking feature.

Where winters are mild, sow it in summer and plant out in autumn 35cm (14in) apart for the shoots that develop the following spring. In colder areas, sow in summer *in situ*, leave it unthinned and use the leaves in autumn.

↕ 1–1.2m (3–4ft) ↔ 30–60cm (12–24in) **HH**

'Grumolo' is an exceptionally hardy ground-hugging chicory with small, rounded leaves formed into a perfectly shaped rosette, which develops rapidly in spring into a more upright plant with larger, coarser leaves. It is the ideal ground-cover companion to winter brassicas, overwintering onions or garlic, or leeks, filling the spaces between rows. Sow in late summer *in situ*, either in patches or drills, or in modules planting out a few weeks later about 10cm (4in) apart.

↕ 7.5cm (3in) ↔ 7.5–10cm (3–4in) **H**

'Sugar Loaf' chicories form conical heads, with crisp creamy central leaves, which are sweeter than

Red chicory 'Fireball'

those of most chicories. In my experience it is one of the most drought-tolerant salad plants, and best value in the summer to autumn period. It is also grown as a CCA seedling crop, the fast-growing leaves being a useful source of early spring salads. It is naturally productive and responds well to CCA treatment at every stage. Its decorative value lies in its reliability and strong, healthy greenness.

Sow as CCA seedlings in spring, perhaps inter-cropping newly planted onions, leeks or greens, or as an element in creating patterned effects. For large plants, sow in modules in early to mid-summer, planting in mid- to late summer 25cm (10in) apart. They look best grouped together; adjacent patches of red and 'Sugar Loaf' chicory make an excellent, bold combination.

↕ 20cm (8in) ↔ 25–30cm (10–12in) **HH** ☉

Recommended variety

'F₁ Jupiter'

RED CHICORY (Round-headed type)

Many of these varieties start as loose-leaved plants, developing tight, round hearts as night temperatures get cooler, or as they mature. They are naturally at their best in late summer and early autumn when groups can make impressive patches in a decorative vegetable garden. Interplanting Florence fennel and red chicory is a lovely combination and they grow well under tall crops such as sweet corn. They can be cut over a long period, but will not withstand severe frost.

'Sugar loaf' chicory 'F₁ Jupiter'

Sow in seedtrays or modules from late spring to early summer, planting out in summer 25–30cm (10–12in) apart. For maximum impact I plant the seedlings a little closer than recommended, to compensate for any bedraggled outer leaves, and the fact that they 'shrink' at the end of the season.

↕ 10cm (4in) ↔ 23–35cm (9–14in) **HH** ☽

Recommended varieties

'Cesare', 'Fireball', 'Medusa', 'Red Verona'

'TREVISO' TYPE

The 'Treviso' chicory is characterized by its loose cluster of long, narrow-bladed leaves, which never form a compact head. The leaves turn a beautiful clear scarlet in winter. It is very hardy, surviving at least -12°C (10°F), and plays a key role in bringing colour to the winter garden. Plant it in groups (it's very effective across the corners of square beds), or in bands between rows of leeks, winter brassicas, or sweet corn (which it will outlast). 'Treviso' chicory can even be grown as an edging. Its bronze-red spires are impressive in spring when it runs to seed.

Sow broadcast *in situ* in mid-summer or raise individual plants in modules and plant 20–23cm (8–9in) apart.

↕ and ↔ 23–30cm (9–12in) **H**

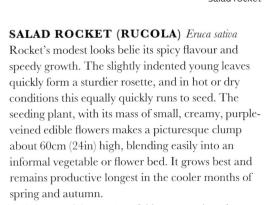

Salad rocket

Semi-cos lettuce 'Little Gem'

Cos lettuce 'Little Leprechaun'

SALAD ROCKET (RUCOLA) *Eruca sativa*

Rocket's modest looks belie its spicy flavour and speedy growth. The slightly indented young leaves quickly form a sturdier rosette, and in hot or dry conditions this equally quickly runs to seed. The seeding plant, with its mass of small, creamy, purple-veined edible flowers makes a picturesque clump about 60cm (24in) high, blending easily into an informal vegetable or flower bed. It grows best and remains productive longest in the cooler months of spring and autumn.

It is one of the most useful intercropping plants. Use it in any of the intercropping ways suggested for pak choi (see p.159). It gives quick results, often germinating in a matter of days, and is sometimes ready to cut within three weeks. In cool weather it can look good planted in a group, but otherwise its susceptibility to flea beetle damage, resulting in ugly holes in the leaves, and the likelihood of running to seed, make it inadvisable to place it prominently except as a short-term filler. It self-seeds with abandon, so a permanent patch is easily established in a low-maintenance garden.

Always sow *in situ*, whether growing it as CCA seedlings, or as individual plants spaced 15cm (6in) apart. Although it can be sown throughout the growing season, it is generally best to avoid very hot, or very dry conditions as it is then likely to bolt.

↕ 7.5–12cm (3–5in) ↔ 12–25cm (5–10in) **H** ⊖

LETTUCE *Lactuca sativa*

There can be few more satisfying sights for a dedicated gardener than a glowingly healthy bed of lettuce. In temperate climates, at least, the wide spectrum of types and varieties available makes it feasible to produce lettuce almost all year round. The key to using it as a decorative feature is to establish which sowing times and varieties are most successful in your conditions, and to concentrate on them. Being low growing, lettuce always needs to be in the foreground.

In good soil conditions, CCA seedling patches remain productive and pretty for a remarkably long time, often over two months. The following are some ways to use drills decoratively: sow single or wide drills between rows of leeks, onions, shallots or garlic; weave circles, figures of eight or zigzags among freshly planted brassicas or large plants such as celery, planting French marigolds at key points; sow on asparagus beds when the cutting season ends. Sow parallel wide drills to fill in dense shapes within a design or pattern. The seedlings quickly spill over to cover the ground completely.

Headed lettuce can look very effective as an intercrop. Here are some ideas: interplant it with spring cabbage, or between rows or plants of either summer or winter brassicas (the lettuce will be harvested long before the greens need to grow into the space); plant between rows of leeks or onions, spacing the rows 30cm (12in) apart; undercrop sweet corn in mid-summer, when the light shade will be beneficial. To make strong patches, plant lettuce with equidistant spacing; alternating red and green varieties creates a patchwork quilt effect.

Use loose-headed 'Salad Bowl' types as a summer edge. One year I alternated green and red varieties as a potager edge. They grew almost 30cm (12in) high and 60cm (24in) across, with frilly indented leaves merging into each other. They were planted out in late spring, and eventually pulled up ten weeks later. For an unusual, undulating edge interplant onion sets with lettuce. Red varieties contrast dramatically with the green of the upright onion leaves.

Lettuces can look very pretty when seeding. The red-leaved varieties are the most spectacular and 'Lollo' the daintiest of all, making neat, red spires 60cm–1m (24in–3ft) high. It looks prettiest in groups: a patch of mixed red and green seeding 'Lollo' spires has a charm of its own.

Cos lettuce 'Winter Density'

Loose-headed lettuce 'Mascara'

Loose-headed lettuce 'Royal Oak Leaf'

Lettuce is a cool-climate plant, growing best at 10–20°C (50–68°F). Being a fast-growing, leafy vegetable it must have very fertile soil and adequate moisture throughout the growing period. It's not always easy to grow: in high temperatures it may fail to germinate, bolt prematurely, taste bitter or suffer from aphid attacks. In damp and cold weather it can be devastated by slugs and fungus diseases.

Providing appropriate varieties are used, it can be sown throughout the growing season, (for sowing details see Further Reading, p.201). For the potager, I always recommend growing individual lettuces in modules. These can be planted out successfully even in hot weather, and give maximum flexibility for intercropping. Very small varieties such as 'Tom Thumb' and 'Little Gem' are spaced 15–20cm (6–8in) apart; larger varieties 25–35cm (10–14in) apart. All other sowings are *in situ* for CCA seedlings. 'Parella' lettuce can also be broadcast (see p.111) for the winter potager.

Each type of lettuce has its own character, and one of the exciting aspects of growing lettuce is that, in virtually every type, there are red or bronze forms, as well as green, offering limitless scope for colourful combinations and contrasts.

BUTTERHEAD TYPE
These have flattish, gently rounded heads and quite buttery, well-flavoured leaves. Although relatively easy to grow, they will not stand long once mature. There is a soft look to a bed of butterheads.

CRISPHEAD TYPE
These crisper-leaved varieties make essentially rounded heads with fairly compact hearts. They are slower maturing than the butterhead lettuces, and stand longer once mature. The group includes the crisp but tasteless 'Iceberg' type, adapted to higher temperatures than other lettuce and trickier to grow well; red-tinted Icebergs such as 'Sioux' and 'Tiger', which seem better flavoured; and the well-flavoured European 'Batavia' crispheads, which often have reddish leaves and are adapted to cool weather.

COS (ROMAINE)
The typical head is conical, upright and fairly loose, but with thick, crunchy, well-flavoured leaves up to 30cm (12in) high. Cos are slow growing, and present a bold outline when grown well, but look feeble when below par. The 'mini' cos 'Little Gem' is a neat, bright-looking lettuce with a sweetly flavoured crisp heart. Several cos varieties are hardy and over-winter outdoors in moderate climates.

LOOSE-HEADED TYPE
This type, typified by the 'Salad Bowl' varieties, forms only rudimentary hearts, but regenerates within days of being cut or picked. Some of the most colourful lettuces available are in this group.

Although the leaves tend to be soft, the group displays good resistance to weather extremes, pests and disease. They can be cut over long periods; moreover, when red or bronze varieties are cut the new leaf, which often develops within a few days, tends to be a darker, striking colour. This intensifies the impact of a patch, quickly compensating for the removed leaves.

They are ideal for CCA seedlings: seed mixtures of green and red varieties are excellent value and produce very pretty effects in the potager. Among the distinct types are the beautiful, deeply-curled 'Lollo' varieties, the tall, jagged-leaved variety 'Catalogna', which has excellent cold resistance, and the smaller European 'cutting' lettuces, used solely for CCA crops. The tiny, flat, exceptionally hardy variety Italian 'Parella' is unique in its size, form and hardiness.

↕ 7.5–30cm (3–12in) ↔ 10–35cm (4–14in)
HH–H ⊖

Recommended varieties
Green arrow-leaved: **'Catalogna'**
Reddish arrow-leaved: **'Cocarde'**
Green butterhead: **'Buttercrunch'**, **'Minetto'**, **'Tom Thumb'**
Red butterhead: **'Juliet'**, **'Marvel of Four Seasons'**, **'Pirat'**, **'Sangria'**
Green cos (romaine): **'Ballon'**, **'Winter Density'**
Red cos (romaine): **'Freckles'** (red splashes), **'Little Leprechaun'** (**'Ruben's Romaine'**),

Garden cress

Iceplant

Winter purslane

'Rosalita', 'Rouge d'Hiver'
Semi-cos: **'Baby Green', 'Bubbles', 'Little Gem'**
Green crisphead: **'Regina dei Ghiacci' ('Queen
of Snows'), 'Summertime'**
Red crisphead: **'Fivia', 'Tiger'**
Green cutting: **'Curled cutting', 'Frisby',
'Smooth cutting'**
Red cutting: **'Biscia Rossa', 'Friulana'**
Red 'Lollo' type: **'Everest', 'Impuls', 'Valeria'**
Green 'Salad Bowl' type: **'Improved Black Seeded
Simpson', 'Oak-Leaved', 'Thai lettuce'**
Red 'Salad Bowl' type: **'Ibis', 'Mascara', 'Red
Fire', 'Redina', 'Red Sails'**

GARDEN CRESS (PEPPERCRESS)

Lepidium sativum
Cress has deeply curled, deep green leaves, giving it
a very pretty, almost moss-like appearance when
growing. Like salad rocket (see p. 167), it has a spicy
flavour, a fast rate of growth and preference for cool
seasons. When seeding, it makes a dainty clump
60cm (24in) high, starred with tiny white flowers.
Unlike rocket, it is *only* grown as a CCA crop, never
as single plants. Grow it for decorative purposes in
any of the ways suggested for pak choi (see p.159).
Cress is often coupled with white mustard, *Sinapsis
alba*. This has pretty, dissected leaves, but it runs to
seed much faster than cress in hot, dry situations,
looks scraggy when seeding and is less suited to
use in a decorative garden.

I have often enjoyed threading single drills of cress
among newly planted brassicas, or tracing a
noughts-and-crosses grid between sweet corn plants.
The lines thicken daily before your eyes, developing
in no time into beautiful, dense bands. In cool,
moist conditions cress can be cut four or five times
before running to seed. Use the more productive
Greek and broad-leaved types where obtainable.

Sow *in situ* in drills or patches. It germinates
within days of sowing.
↕ 7.5–15cm (3–6in) ↔ 5–7.5cm (2–3in) **HH** ⊝

ICEPLANT *Mesembryanthemum crystallinum*

The tiny glands on the thick fleshy leaves and stems
of this sprawling, maritime plant literally sparkle in
the sunshine. It is mainly used in salads, where its
texture and appearance make a more striking
contribution than its fairly bland, sometimes salty
taste. As it is slow bolting, it is used as a spinach
substitute in hot climates.

Provided drainage is good it is undemanding
about soil, and can be a spectacular ground-cover
plant, either in the front of a bed or in a sunny
corner. It is very suitable for containers, catching
the light as it hangs down. Team it with trailing blue

lobelia or brachycome. Once it runs to seed the tiny
flowers are rather insignificant. Stem cuttings taken
early in the season will root in time to take over
when the original plants are exhausted.

Iceplant needs warm weather to flourish, so in
temperate climates sow indoors in mid- to late
spring, planting outside after all risk of frost is past.
Space plants about 30cm (12in) apart, and once they
are growing well, keep picking the young shoots and
leaves to conserve its vigour and freshness.
↕ 10–15cm (4–6in) ↔ 60cm (24in) **HH**

WINTER PURSLANE (MINER'S

LETTUCE) *Montia perfoliata (*syn. *Claytonia perfoliata)*
This is one of the prettiest cool weather salad plants.
The young plants have small, light green, heart-
shaped leaves with tiny flowers nestling in the centre,
and the mature leaves are round and wrap around
the stem, which appears to pierce them. The mild-
flavoured leaves, stems and flowers are all edible.

It can be used as an edge, but uproot it as soon as
its productive life ends: ageing plants make messy
brown clumps. Otherwise plant it at random in the
front of beds. It nestles appealingly between all sorts
of plants. It is reasonably hardy, unless the ground

Chinese violet cress

Buck's horn plantain

Summer purslane

becomes waterlogged, and is pretty grown in winter containers mixed with flowering bulbs. However, the attractive pink-flowered *Montia sibirica* is banned from my garden, on account of its bitter aftertaste.

Winter purslane has an extraordinary ability to self-seed, especially on light, well-drained soil. It is naturalized in North America and will happily take over your garden, disappearing in summer but reappearing in autumn or spring. It is easily pulled up by its roots, or dug in as green manure. It's a perfect plant for low-maintenance gardens.

It can be grown as a CCA seedling crop, but has more impact as single plants spaced 15–20cm (6–8in) apart. Sow in early spring for a summer crop, and in mid-summer to harvest in autumn.
↕ 10–15cm (4–6in) ↔ 10–23cm (4–9in) **H** ⊖

CHINESE VIOLET CRESS
Orychophragmus violaceus
Cultivated in West China for its round, pleasantly flavoured leaves, this modest and moderately hardy plant is occasionally grown as an ornamental in flower borders. Not unlike rocket in habit (see p.167), it has beautiful, clear lilac flowers, formed on lightly branching stems about 45cm (18in) high.

Sow *in situ* in spring or early summer, or in modules, planting out a few weeks later, finally spacing plants about 15cm (6in) apart. Allow a few plants to run to seed to get the benefit of the flowers.
↕ 10–15cm (4–6in) ↔ 15–20cm (6–8in) **H**

BUCK'S HORN PLANTAIN *Plantago coronopus*
This is a decorative little plant, with narrow, toothed leaves spraying out stiffly but neatly from the base, followed by typically chunky plantain seedheads. Although naturally a biennial, it may behave as an annual or a perennial depending on the conditions. Long cultivated in Europe, it is appreciated most from late summer to early spring for its leaves, which remain evergreen much of winter. (Dip them in boiling water to make them palatable in salads.)

It's a profligate self-seeder unfussy about soil or situation, provided there is reasonable drainage, often establishing itself in paths and stony corners. The seedlings are easily transplanted. It can be worked into vegetable or flower beds at random or in small groups, makes a neat edge to a winter potager, and is well suited to a low-maintenance garden and winter containers. The decorative but, barely edible, red-leaved plantain *Plantago*

major 'Rubrifolia' behaves in much the same way and makes a very striking edge.

Sow in spring or late summer in modules or *in situ* planting out a few weeks later, spacing plants 12cm (5in) apart. To prolong its leafy stage, cut off the flowering spikes as they develop.
↕ and ↔ 15–25cm (6–10in) **H**

SUMMER PURSLANE *Portulaca oleracea*
The green form of this succulent salad plant is rather a dull colour with relatively thin leaves, while its gold counterpart has thicker rounder leaves and is usually more vigorous. On decorative grounds I would always opt for the shiny brightness of the yellow form.

Purslane is a tender plant flourishing in warm weather but miserable in cold, wet and windy situations. It does best on light well-drained soil. Both forms respond well to CCA treatment, either as seedlings or as individual plants. The seedlings seem frail initially, but surge once established. To encourage continuous cropping, pick the young leaves and shoots constantly, before the knobbly seedheads develop. It self-seeds in warm climates.

Purslane is excellent for summer intercropping and in-filling: the sturdy leaves maintain an even, dense look over a number of weeks. Try interplanting a zigzag of blue-leaved leeks with triangles of golden purslane for a striking mid- to late summer display. It also looks superb flanked with red 'Salad

Spinach

New Zealand spinach

Corn salad

Bowl' or 'Lollo' lettuce, and the smooth texture contrasts well with the fluffiness of dill or fennel.

In warm climates sow *in situ* in late spring or early summer. Otherwise sow indoors in late spring, planting out 15–20cm (6–8in) apart, after all risk of frost is past.

↕ 18cm (7in) ↔ 10–20cm (4–8in) **HH** ☉

SPINACH *Spinacia oleracea*

Spinach needs no description, but in any decorative situation my personal preference would be to use perpetual spinach (see Swiss chard, p.163) rather than true spinach. The former is more robust, quicker off the mark initially, more flexible over sowing times and much longer lasting. True spinach is notoriously prone to bolting prematurely, especially in hot and dry conditions. It needs fertile soil and plenty of moisture throughout growth.

Provided you are prepared to uproot it when it starts to bolt, spinach *can* be used in a number of different ways. Grow single rows as strong, green boundaries dividing beds into segments; sow CCA patches to fill out patterns; and in summer intercrop it between rows of dwarf peas or climbing beans to benefit from the light shade.

If you yearn for the subtle flavour of real spinach, sow *in situ*, either as a seedling CCA crop or spacing plants about 23cm (9in) apart. The most reliable sowings are in spring for an early summer crop, and mid- to late summer for an autumn crop,

using hardy varieties that will stand over winter into the following spring.

↕ 23–30cm (9–12in) ↔ 25cm (10in) **HH–H** ☉

Recommended varieties

'Bloomsdale', 'F₁ Symphony'

NEW ZEALAND SPINACH

Tetragonia tetragonioides

I used to consider New Zealand spinach a sparse, unattractive plant, but now I know it can have a wondrously vital look to its upright, fleshy leaves, with its long stems generously blanketing the ground. The fault lies in its reputation for tolerating poor, thin soil and dry, shady conditions; it tolerates them, for sure, but only *thrives* in fertile soil with plenty of moisture. Another drawback is that the seed is tricky to germinate, though presoaking for 24 hours before sowing helps break its dormancy. It tolerates light frost at the end of the season.

Where reasonably warm summers are assured, it deserves a place in the flower or vegetable garden as lively ground cover, or as a filler in the foreground. With its semi-trailing habit it looks effective hanging down over an edge. It can be grown in large containers, provided the shoots are picked regularly to keep it in bounds. The triangular leaves are a dark colour and a pleasing foil to nasturtiums or canary creeper rambling over them. It will also grow well undercropping sweet corn or at the feet of Jerusalem artichokes concealing the bare stems.

Sow in late spring, planting out 45cm (18in) apart after all risk of frost is past.

↕ 30–35cm (12–14in) ↔ 1–1.2m (3–4ft) **HH**

CORN SALAD (LAMB'S LETTUCE, MACHE) *Valerianella locusta*

Corn salad may not be a showy plant but, in its quiet way, it is very useful. Its small, mild-flavoured leaves are very hardy and rarely attacked by pests or disease. It germinates and grows best in cool conditions. While it can be sown throughout the growing season, the best sowings are early spring for salads in the late spring to early summer 'vegetable gap', or in mid- to late summer for winter use. Keep these late sowings well watered until they germinate.

It is ideal for intercropping. Sow it between onions and shallots, or rows of winter leeks and brassicas, under sweet corn, or in winter containers as 'ground cover' for flowering bulbs. Always leave some plants to self-seed. When flowering they have a soft, misty look, and the seedlings are always welcome when they suddenly appear. Use this method to grow them in a low-maintenance garden. 'Verte de Cambrai' and other 'Green' ('Verte') varieties are snappier looking and darker coloured than the 'large-leaved' English and Dutch varieties.

Corn salad is almost always sown *in situ*, broadcast or in drills. It is grown both as a CCA seedling crop, or as single plants spaced 10cm (4in) apart.

↕ 10cm (4in) ↔ 10–12cm (4–5in) **H** ☉

Multi-sown bulb onion

Bulb onion 'Stuttgarter Giant'

Oriental bunching onion 'Ishikuro'

ROOTS, BULBS, TUBERS AND SWOLLEN STEMS

Most of the vegetables grown for their storage organs, whether they are swollen bulbs and stems above ground or roots and tubers beneath, are slow maturing. It takes time, and abundant foliage, to manufacture the 'food' that builds up to form their roots and bulbs, so they may be in the ground from spring to autumn. In the decorative vegetable garden the more spreading ones, often with pretty leaves, take on a role as ground cover, while others provide the backbone for intercropping patterns.

ONION, SHALLOT AND ORIENTAL BUNCHING ONION

Allium cepa, A. ascalonicum and *A. fistulosum*
The onion family, which embraces shallots, salad and bulb onions, oriental bunching onions, leeks (see p.173) and several perennial forms (see p.186), has a unique decorative role because the narrow upright leaves are a complete contrast to all other leaf forms. Moreover, they grow steadily and keep fairly compact, which makes them excellent partners in intercropping schemes. The drawback is that bulb onions and shallots die back before they are harvested, and often look unkempt in their later stages, though they can be disguised by intercropping. Use red bulb onions, and reddish-stemmed bunching onions, where available, for an extra touch of colour.

For the many systems of growing onions and the choice of appropriate varieties (influenced by latitude), see Further Reading, page 201.

BULB ONIONS AND SHALLOTS
In northern latitudes, the main crop of bulb onions, which is sown or planted in spring and harvested in summer, lends itself to intercropping. Lettuce is certainly one of the most satisfactory intercrops. Any type can be used, but the red-leaved, loose-headed types seem to have a special quality, filling the ground between the rows and billowing around the onion stems. They can often be cut several times to prolong their season.

Preferably plant the onions and lettuce at the same time in spring, spacing the onions about 15cm (6in) apart in rows at least 30cm (12in) apart. If shallots are used, increase the space between rows to at least 45cm (18in) to allow for their wider spread. Another option is to sow CCA seedlings in wide drills between the onion rows.

Besides lettuce, some possibilities are cress, red mustard, purslane (in late spring), salad rocket, curly kale, pak choi and spinach. Many of these can also be sown between onion rows in late summer and will utilize the ground fully after the onions are lifted. Onions can also be planted, evenly spaced, in beds on their own. Since they are normally cleared by early autumn, a follow-on green manure can then be sown, (see Green Manures, pp.137–8).

For intercropping, plant onion sets (immature bulbs) in spring, rather than sowing seed: sets are much more predictable and grow strongly with no need for thinning. Shallots are mainly raised from sets, planted from mid- to late winter in mild areas, otherwise in late winter or early spring.
↕ 23–30cm (9–12in) ↔ 10cm (4in) **H**

SALAD OR SPRING ONIONS
These quick-maturing onions are grown for their young green leaves and rudimentary bulbs, mainly used in salads. They look bright and neat, and make excellent intercrops between longer-term vegetables such as brassicas or leeks. The variety 'White Lisbon Winter Hardy' can be sown in late summer for use in spring, and is a good subject for a winter potager. Otherwise, sow parallel rows of salad onions wherever a space arises.

Leek 'Giant Winter Wila'

Sow them very thinly, from spring to late summer, in drills as close as 10cm (4in) apart. They can be ready within eight weeks.

↕ 15–23cm (6–9in) ↔ 7.5cm (3in) **H**

Recommended varieties

'White Lisbon Winter Hardy' Exceptionally hardy

ORIENTAL BUNCHING ONION

These strong-looking green onions have been developed from the hardy, perennial Welsh onion. Most varieties are evergreen, except in extreme climates, making them a useful source of fresh onion in winter. There are multi-stemmed types, rather like shallots in habit, which make good edges, and tall single-stemmed types. Planted in a line 20cm (8in) apart, these taller plants make bold boundaries within or between beds, or even a striking edge to a winter bed, holding their own well against tall plants such as kales. They run to seed in spring (although the leaves can still be used) producing decorative, rather fluffy seed-heads. Sow in modules in spring or early summer, planting out when 5–7.5cm (2–3in) high.

↕ 25–56cm (10–22in) ↔ 10–15cm (4–6in) **H**

Recommended varieties

'Ishikuro' Suitable for summer or winter use

Beetroot 'Bull's Blood'

LEEK *Allium porrum*

A good stand of mature leeks looks handsome at any time, while the seedheads of over-wintered plants are spectacular in early summer. Leeks are roughly classified into the early types, which tend to be tall and slender with rather pale leaves and long white shanks, and the stocky, hardier types with more deeply coloured, blue-green leaves, occasionally verging on purple.

There are several ways to emphasize their decorative qualities. The first is to plant them evenly spaced, as is done in long narrow beds at Villandry. This makes a great impact. They are also excellent to use as a boundary or a demarcation within a bed, planted in a single row or, to make a more emphatic division, as a double row.

Intercropping between single rows, or double, paired rows, is another option. Leave at least 30cm (12in) between the double row for small salad intercrops, and more if larger plants such as beetroot are being used.

In summer, intercrop as suggested for onions (see p.172); overwintering leeks can be inter-cropped with hardy red chicories, 'Bull's Blood' beetroot, and winter salads such as land cress, corn salad, winter purslane, 'Grumolo' chicory and 'Parella' lettuce (see Intercropping, pp.108–9). For an autumn show, interplant clumps of leeks with single plants of red chard. Finally, leave a few plants in spring to run to seed, for those striking

globular seedheads on 1.2–1.5m (4–5ft) stems, which can last into early summer. Colours range unpredictably from deep to light purple to creamy-white. They can be dried for winter flower arrangements.

Using appropriate varieties, sow leeks from late winter to late spring, and plant out from spring to early summer. They can be sown *in situ*, planted 'flat' on the surface, but to get more upright plants for a potager, sow in modules and plant them out when about 20cm (8in) tall in 15–20cm (6–8in) deep holes. Leeks can also be 'multi-sown' with up to four seeds per module, planted 'as one' 23cm (9in) apart. They quickly create a dense effect. Otherwise, space leeks 10–23cm (4–9in) apart: the wider the spacing the larger they grow.

Another option is 'mini-leeks'. Sow in drills, from spring to early summer, with seeds spaced 5mm–1cm (¼–½in) apart, for harvesting at their most tender when 15–20cm (6–8in) tall. They stand well, sometimes even over winter, making nice looking lines or patches of delicate, upright leaves. My best results have been with the long-stemmed early varieties such as 'King Richard'.

↕ 30–45cm (12–18in) ↔ 15–30cm (6–12in) **H**

Recommended deeply coloured varieties

'Blue Solaise', 'Giant Winter Wila', 'St. Victor', 'Winter Crop'

BEETROOT *Beta vulgaris* spp. *rubra*

Beetroot is mainly cultivated for its roots, which, in fertile conditions, develop beneath a lush canopy of reddish-green leaves (which are, in fact, edible.) If the plants are struggling in poor soil, that attractive lushness gives way to a browned, chlorotic look. Besides the standard modern beets, there are a handful of older varieties (available from heirloom seed companies) with deep crimson leaves. These are among my favourite potager vegetables. The variety I grow, time and again, is the luridly named 'Bull's Blood'. It produces excellent roots as well as remarkably coloured leaves and, in my experience, is hardier than most beets. The leaf colour deepens in cold weather.

They can be planted in single rows or, for more impact, in staggered double rows. Sometimes I plant them in a complete circle, linking all the segments of my potager, sometimes as straight lines within beds, or as edges, or in a bold backing line behind a soft edge of green lettuce. A good combination, which originally occurred by chance, is 'Bull's Blood' alongside the deep purple-blue and ivory pansy 'Rippling Waters'. Let a few beets run to seed in spring. They make multi-headed reddish spires, 1.2m (4ft) or so high, vivid in the early stages, and striking if blue chicory or borage are flowering alongside – another chance discovery.

Sow from spring to mid-summer *in situ* or in modules. Select varieties and adjust spacing according to whether they are for pulling young, for pickling, or for storage (see Further Reading, p.201). I make two sowings of 'Bull's Blood': the first in early spring for summer, spacing plants 20–23cm (8–9in) apart and the second in early summer for my Winter Potager, spacing them 12cm (5in) apart. The key to success is thinning early to prevent overcrowding.

↕ and ↔ 27–38cm (11–15in) **H**

Recommended dark-leaved varieties

'Chioggia' Relatively dark leaves and beautiful white and pink ringed roots

'Cook's Delight' Dark red leaves and good roots

'MacGregor's Favourite' Originally grown for its narrow, arrow-shaped crimson leaves

CARROT *Daucus carota*

When carrots are growing well, the fern-like tops are a beautiful sight. But they can be stunted and an unhealthy rusty colour if they have to struggle in poorly drained soil, or contend with carrot fly attack. If carrots thrive in your conditions, use them to maximum effect. You can edge beds with them, grow them in sweeping drifts among taller vegetables, or sow patches alongside vegetables with contrasting textures and colours such as chards, leeks or red lettuce.

The only sure remedy against carrot fly for organic gardeners is to grow the carrots under fine nets or within barriers, neither of which are particularly decorative. An alternative is to sow the seed of carrots and annual flowers mingled together. This both creates a pretty plot and seems largely to foil the carrot fly (see Intermingling Annuals, pp.102–3).

Carrot varieties vary in their leafiness, and the varieties with large tops look the best, though they

Carrot 'Early Nantes'

won't necessarily have the biggest roots. Some of the leafiest varieties are the white-rooted, European fodder carrots, which not only have some resistance to root fly but are surprisingly well flavoured.

The standard method of raising carrots is to sow *in situ* from spring to early summer, in drills about 15cm (6in) apart. Thin in stages to 5–10cm (2–4in) apart, depending on the variety and the size required (see Further Reading, p.201).

↕ 23–30cm (9–12in) ↔ 15–20cm (6–8in) **HH**

Recommended varieties with leafy tops

'Autumn King-Vita Longa', 'Bergamo', 'Boston King', 'Chantenay Royal', 'Early Scarlet Horn', 'Long Red Surrey'

FLORENCE FENNEL *Foeniculum vulgare* var. *dulce*

With its gossamer leaves Florence fennel could earn a place in any decorative border. Its natural poise is enhanced by the swollen bulb at its base, the stark whiteness of which is accentuated by the dramatic symmetry of the V-shaped leaf stalks. It is not the easiest plant to grow. It thrives in rich, moist soil, but has a tendency to bolt prematurely if sown too early, or subjected to cold or drought.

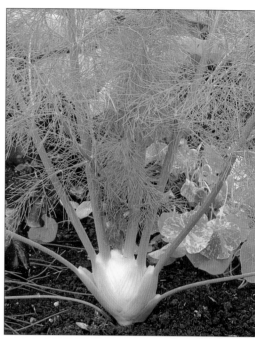
Fennel 'Zefa Tardo'

As with kohl rabi and celeriac, it makes the most striking pattern when planted in groups, bare dark soil perhaps being the best foil for the white bulbs, although the softness of fennel contrasts well with the formality of a low box hedge. A very different, colourful effect can be achieved by interplanting with hardy red chicories, or with either dwarf or trailing nasturtiums.

When harvesting, cut the stems back to 3cm (1in) or so above ground level. Very dainty, fern-like shoots develop from the base, which can be used for flavouring. These trimmed plants, unlike large mature plants, survive light frosts, looking very attractive in early winter.

For the best results sow in modules in early summer, planting out five to six weeks later 30cm (12in) apart.

↕ and ↔ 45cm (18in) **HH**

PARSNIP *Pastinaca sativa*

Although no one considers parsnip a decorative vegetable, its leaves remain a workmanlike green throughout summer into early winter. Parsnips, in the same way as carrots, can be sown mixed with seed of annual flowers to make a colourful patch

Parsnip

Oriental radish in flower

'Black Spanish' radish seedpods

(see Intermingling Annuals, pp.102–3), but their unsung glory is the seeding plant in the second season. The stems then grow over 1.8m (6ft) high with branching seedheads of a radiant golden-yellow – a spectacular picture in mid-summer. It is worth sowing a few at the back of a border or winter potager for this effect alone, or leaving even a solitary root to seed.

Sow *in situ* in spring, and thin to 20–30cm (8–12in) apart, depending on variety. The hardy roots are left in the ground until required for use.
↕ 38cm (15in) ↔ 30cm (12in) **H**

HAMBURG PARSLEY
Petroselinum crispum var. *tuberosum*

This hardy, dual-purpose vegetable has roots that look and taste like parsnip, and vivid green foliage that looks and tastes like broad-leaved parsley (see pp.195–6). Another great asset is that it remains green in winter, down to temperatures of at least -10°C (14°F). It is one of the best winter edging plants for either vegetable or flower beds, though it can equally well be grown in rows or groups. Its dark shiny leaves look good among ornamental kales and alongside red 'Treviso' chicory. It runs

to seed in spring, making quite a pretty plant growing to about 1m (3ft) high.

It is cultivated like parsnip (see pp.174–5), though it requires a shorter growing season, and can be planted closer, about 15cm (6in) apart.
↕ and ↔ 15–25cm (6–10in) **H**

RADISH AND ORIENTAL RADISH
Raphanus sativus
LONGIFERUM GROUP

Radishes are grown mainly for their hotly flavoured roots. They are wonderfully diverse, ranging from the small, neat European varieties to the Asiatic giants. Roots can be anything from 2–60cm (¾–24in) long, commonly with white-, pink- or red-coloured skin, but more rarely yellow, violet or black skin. In the decorative vegetable garden their main asset is their fast growth. They can also be sown for leafy CCA seedlings; while any radishes can be used for this purpose, fast-germinating, large-leaved varieties are most suitable.

The less appreciated aspects of radishes are that seeding radishes produce masses of dainty, usually pink, flowers and the seedpods are edible (and very crunchy if picked while plump and

green). So let a few plants run to seed, when they will grow 60cm–1.2m (24in–4ft) high. Generally, the larger the radish, the more spectacular the seeding plant will be.

SMALL-ROOTED RADISH

The small radishes are among the fastest growing vegetables, often sown and cleared within three or four weeks. The young leaves have an endearing freshness but older leaves quickly become coarse. Their exceptionally speedy growth makes them ideal for intercropping. Sow them in single drills to sketch fine green lines wherever there are gaps.

Appropriate varieties can be sown throughout the growing season. Sow thinly in drills leaving about 13cm (5in) between rows, thinning promptly to at least 2cm (¾in) apart.
↕ and ↔ 10–12cm (4–5in) **HH** ⊖
Recommended varieties
'Munchen Bier' Large seedpods
ORIENTAL RADISH

Popularly known as daiku or mooli, these are big radishes, often growing into large plants that form beautiful rosettes of elegantly sculpted leaves. They also produce an abundance of edible seedpods.

Sow in modules or *in situ* mainly in summer, spacing the plants 23–40cm (9–16in) apart.
↕ 20–45cm (8–18in) ↔ 35–45cm (14–18in)
HH–H ⊖
Recommended varieties
'Bisai', '40 Days', 'Raba'

Salsify in flower

Scorzonera

Potato in flower

SCORZONERA *Scorzonera hispanica*
Scorzonera is very closely related to salsify (see below), but it is a true perennial, only treated as a biennial. It is an attractive plant with long, relatively broad leaves. The yellow flowers are less eye-catching than those of salsify. Grow it in the same way as salsify.
↕ 30–45cm (12–18in) ↔ 25–38cm (10–15in) **H**

POTATO *Solanum tuberosum*
Potatoes are not the easiest of vegetables to have in a potager. They may radiate verdant vitality when growing, but they look an awful mess when the haulm dies down in late summer. They sprawl and engulf nearby plants, and need space around them for earthing-up operations. This leaves little scope for intercropping, other than sowing quick-maturing seedlings, such as cress, above them when first planted, and maybe allowing trailing marrows to find a way through them.
　The flowers, however, can be subtle shades of mauve, purple-blue and pink, or else creamy white, contrasted in a delightful way with bright yellow centres. The effect depends on the variety: some are a mass of colour, others shy flowering.

Seed catalogues rarely mention the flowers, so it is a question of keeping your eyes open. A few acknowledged 'good flowerers' are listed below. These all look wonderful worked into flower or vegetable beds, singly or in groups. Tuck them behind flowers that are 30cm (12in) or so high, or grow Florence fennel, dill or any similar plant in front to hide them at the end of the season. They blend well with blue, grey and reddish plants, such as red cabbage, rue or flowering chicory.
　Treating the potato as an ornamental is not a new idea. In 1658 Olaus Rudbeck of Upsala stated it was 'equally suitable for the flower border and the table', while in an 18th-century effort to promote it, Louis XIV accepted a bouquet of potato flowers from the apothecary Parmentier.
　For practical purposes varieties are divided into fast-maturing but generally lower-yielding 'earlies', and slower-maturing, heavier-yielding 'maincrop'.
↕ 30–75cm (12–30in) ↔ 60cm–1m (24in–3ft) **HH**
Recommended varieties
Coloured flowers, earlies: **'Charlotte'**, **'Maris Bard'**, **'Maris Peer'**, **'Ratte'**, **'Rocket'**; maincrop: **'Desiree'**, **'Golden Wonder'**, **'Maris Piper'**, **'Nadine'**

Cream flowers, earlies: **'Carlingford'**, **'Estima'**, **'Foremost'**, **'Marfona'**, **'Nicola'**, **'Wilja'**; maincrop: **'Cara'**, **'Pink Fir Apple'**

SALSIFY (OYSTER PLANT)
Tragopogon porrifolius
Salsify is a hardy biennial in the daisy family, grown for its delicately flavoured, pale-skinned roots. Equally delicious, in my opinion, are its flowering shoots and buds which develop on 1–1.2m (3–4ft) stems. The flowers are a clear lilac, evolving into exquisite powder-puff seedheads.
　Salsify only does well on light, well-drained soil, so unless you have the ideal conditions (the sort of soil where carrots thrive), my advice would be to abandon the idea of growing it for its roots. Let the plants overwinter, enjoy the shoots in the following year, and leave a few plants to flower.
　Sow *in situ* in spring, in well-prepared and well-drained soil. Salsify looks best in random groups dotted around vegetable or flower beds. Germination can be erratic and slow, so it is best to sow several seeds 'per station', initially, in circles or small drifts, thinning germinated seedlings to 7.5cm (3in) apart. No further work is needed, other than keeping them weed-free. In their second season they flower throughout summer, and may well self-seed. They add unexpected, delicate touches of colour wherever they appear.
↕ 30–45cm (12–18in) ↔ 25–30cm (10–12in) **H**

Lablab bean

Runner bean 'Painted Lady'

PODDED VEGETABLES

The podded vegetables include delicacies like peas and beans, which taste superb when freshly picked. Many are natural climbers with colourful flowers, which give an extra motive for including them in a vegetable garden. They may scramble over existing structures but, on the whole, their twining stems require special supports (see Supports, pp.71–3). The bushier types may need to be propped up subtly with twigs and criss-crossed canes. Remember that peas and beans grown for drying will occupy ground much longer than fresh picked legumes, and may look bedraggled in the later stages. Most beans originate in warm regions, so have limitations in cooler climates.

LABLAB BEAN (HYACINTH BEAN)
Dolichos lablab
This oriental bean is one of the most beautiful climbing vegetables. The purple form has prolific clusters of purple and lilac flowers, which develop into short, flat, deep purple pods. Its decorative virtues have been so extolled by gardeners that its culinary qualities are sometimes overlooked.

Grow it like climbing French beans (see p.178), but it needs high summer temperatures, ideally between 28–30°C (82–86°F), to flourish.
↕ 2.5m (8ft) ↔ 45–60cm (18–24in) **T**

RUNNER BEAN *Phaseolus coccineus*
The runner bean originated in Central America and was introduced into Europe for its ornamental qualities, so it's ironic that it has become the quintessential British bean, dominating countless gardens and making exemplary use of vertical space.

A prolific, vigorous bean, it needs very fertile soil, shelter from strong winds to encourage pollination by bees, and a season of about 100 frost-free days. The seed won't germinate at soil temperatures below about 12°C (54°F), so in cold areas start them in seedtrays in late spring, planting out when 7.5cm (3in) high, after all risk of frost is past. Like all beans, they can stand quite a lot of competition. Plant them 15cm (6in) apart, or plant two plants together sharing the same support, spacing each pair 30cm (12in) apart. Keep plants well watered, especially once flowering starts.

They can be trained on poles or trelliswork as background screens; grown over pergolas and archways; or used as an eye-catching centrepiece trained up cane or string wigwams, or metal obelisks. Whatever the support, it must be very strong, as a mature crop amounts to a great weight and is liable to catch the wind. The stems need relatively thin canes, strings, wire or net to twine around, and may need tying-in during the early stages. The leading shoots can be pinched out when they reach the top of their supports, or left to dangle down in a rather charming, desultory way.

To some extent, they can also be trained on metal, wood or heavy plastic hoops, but make them as high in the centre as possible. They can also climb up strong-stemmed plants such as sunflowers. Wait until the sunflower is well-established and at least 30cm (12in) high, then plant the runner bean at its base. On reaching the top, the bean may well grab onto a neighbouring sunflower, eventually making a colourful, aerial fringe to the garden.

They are good mixers. I have planted various climbing gourds, cucumbers and sweet peas among them using the same supports, resulting in a lovely blend of leaf textures and colours. Morning glory and *Cobaea scandens* would also fit in well.

Much of the glory of the runner bean resides in its range of flower colours: they can be white, orange-red, pink or bicoloured, depending on variety. I have grown all four colours along with purple-flowered French beans, in a semicircle radiating from the arch above the seat in my Little Potager.
↕ 3m (10ft) or more ↔ 25cm (10in) **HH**
Recommended varieties
Bicoloured orange and white: **'Painted Lady'**
Pink-flowered: **'Sunset'**
Red-flowered: **'Liberty', 'Polestar', 'Red Knight', 'Scarlet Emperor'**
White-flowered: **'Czar', 'Desirée', 'Mergoles', 'White Emergo'**
DWARF RUNNER BEAN
Dwarf forms of runners grow very evenly and all bear prominent red flowers. Plant them 23cm (9in) apart to get a solid effect; even if the bushes are eventually overshadowed by neighbouring plants, they still produce beans. I love to see them merging with the shades of red chard, orache and bold red cabbage. It is possible to convert ordinary climbing

Climbing French bean 'Purple Podded'

Dwarf French bean 'Royalty'

Mangetout pea 'Dwarf de Grace'

varieties into dwarf forms: pinch out the leading shoot when the plant is 20cm (8in) high, then nip out secondary shoots that develop beyond the second leaf. Dwarf forms crop about two weeks earlier than climbers, but have much lower yields. ↕ 45cm (18in) ↔ 38–45cm (15–18in) **HH**
Recommended varieties
'Dwarf Bees', 'Gulliver', 'Hammond's Dwarf', 'Pickwick'

FRENCH BEAN (SNAP BEAN) *Phaseolus vulgaris*
French bean plants look much like runner beans, and also have climbing and dwarf forms. The dwarf forms are more popular, being heavy croppers, easily managed and earlier maturing than the climbing or pole varieties. French beans are that little bit more tender than runner beans, and less likely to do well in cool summers; conversely, they are more successful in very hot weather. (They are self-pollinating and not dependent on insect pollination.) Grow them like runner beans. The native Americans traditionally interplanted them with maize, letting them climb up the stems.

Most French bean flowers are creamy coloured and fairly inconspicuous. The notable exceptions

are the purple-podded varieties, which have pretty purple flowers and often dark, nearly purple foliage to match. They stand out wherever they are grown and have great flavour. Otherwise, the pods are the most ornamental feature in French beans: the buttery-looking, golden-yellow 'wax pod' varieties, the red-and-purple-flecked forms, and the thin 'filet' types all look wonderful when cropping abundantly. Happily, their good looks are allied to good flavour. Bush forms ↕ and ↔ 30–45cm (12–18in) **HH** Climbing forms ↕ 1.5–3m (5–10ft) ↔ 30–38cm (12–15in) **HH**
Recommended varieties
Flecked: (bush) **'Deuil Fin Precoce', 'Triomphe de Farcy'**; (climbing) **'Borlotto', 'Oregon Giant Snap', 'Robsplash', 'Tongue of Fire'**
Purple-podded: (bush) **'Purple Tepee', 'Royalty'**; (climbing) **'Blue Coco', 'Purple Podded'**
Yellow-podded: (bush) **'Kinghorn Wax', 'Mont d'Or', 'Rocquencourt', 'Wachs Goldperle'**; (climbing) **'Burro d'Ignegnoli', 'Corono d'Oro', 'Marvel of Venice'**

PEA *Pisum sativum*
There's a lightness of texture to the leaves and tendrils of peas, and the small white (occasionally purple or pink) flowers have the charm of sweet peas. The pods have character too, both in the sturdy solidity of shelling peas and edible-podded snap peas, and the delicate transparency of the

mangetouts. They are cool-season plants, growing best at 13–18°C (55–64°F); although the plants are normally hardy, flowers can be damaged by frost.

Support is the key to using peas decoratively, and the more elegant it is, the better. Even very dwarf varieties crop better with some kind of twiggy support, though they can look pretty scrambling on the ground. Medium and tall types can be grown against nets or wire fencing, on old-fashioned pea-sticks, or be kept in place with canes and string.

Tall varieties are best grown at the back of borders, or to separate different areas of a garden. Alternatively, give them prominence by making a circular feature with pea-sticks or a wire-netting. Low- to medium-height peas can be sown across beds in 10–20cm (4–8in) bands to create neat divisions: cross two bands in the centre, either on the square or diagonally, and grow lettuce, spinach, radish or beet in the gaps for contrast.

There are two lesser known types of peas that can be used to great effect in the potager. The first of these is the semi-leafless pea, a 20th-century development in which many leaves are modified into tendrils, enabling plants to twine together in virtually self-supporting groups. The airy mass of

Pea 'Purple Podded'

Asparagus pea

Broad bean 'The Sutton'

stems, which resemble green barbed wire, have an intriguing architectural quality. The well-ventilated plants are healthy and bear well. Place clumps prominently in the foreground. A very different effect is achieved by using old varieties of peas (available from heirloom seed companies), which often have deep purple flowers; the same colour is found in most drying peas, in the purple-podded pea and some mangetout varieties. The central keel petals of the tall mangetout 'Carouby de Maussane's' flowers are the deepest burgundy. Grow these lovely types whenever you find them.

Sow *in situ*, and make several successive sowings using appropriate varieties. How peas are spaced depends largely on how they will be supported. Single drills, circles or spacing the seeds evenly across a bed about 5cm (2in) apart, are some options.
↕ 45cm–1.8m (18in–6ft) ↔ 10–30cm (4–12in) **H**
Recommended varieties
Coloured flowers: (drying) **'Capucijner Blue Pod', 'Dun'**; (mangetout) **'Bambi', 'Carouby de Maussane', 'Dwarf de Grace', 'Roi de Carouby'**; (shelling) **'Purple podded'**
Semi-leafless: **'Bikini', 'Markana', 'Novella', 'Twiggy'**

ASPARAGUS PEA *Tetragonolobus purpureus*
With its delicate leaflets and striking scarlet-brown flowers, asparagus pea probably has more to offer as a decorative plant than as an edible. Its strange-looking, winged, four-angled pods, which are borne fairly sparsely, are only tasty if picked young. It makes a neat bush and looks pretty planted in groups or used as an edging, perhaps seen best alongside a path, or in front of standard fruit trees. It grows quite well in containers. Confusingly, the perennial tropical climbing bean *Psophocarpus tetragonolobus* has similar pods and is also called 'asparagus pea'.

Sow *in situ* or in modules in mid- to late spring. Plant when 5cm (2in) high; spacing plants 30cm (12in) apart. Support the branches with twigs to keep the bushes upright.
↕ 30–45cm (12–18in) ↔ 45–60cm (18–24in) **H**

BROAD BEAN (FAVA BEAN) *Vicia faba*
It is not until you look into the cream-with-a-hint-of-purple, chocolate-coloured centred flower of a broad bean, and smell its sweet fragrance that you appreciate the aesthetic qualities of this rugged European bean. With its somewhat pointed, grey-green leaves it can be quite handsome, but most varieties grow large and weighty, with a tendency to flop over unless firmly supported or penned in as a group with canes and string. This restricts their use in a decorative situation. The exception is the dwarf 'fan' type. These sturdy plants are very compact and produce a mass of flowers and pods. They make an impact in groups and look very handsome when grown in large containers.

In temperate climates, broad beans are mainly sown *in situ* in mid- to late autumn, spaced 25–30cm (10–12in) apart, for harvesting in late spring the following year. This makes them a useful follow-on crop, as they occupy ground in winter. Alternatively, treat them as an early crop in a winter potager to be cleared in time to plant winter leeks or brassicas.

Unusual-flowered varieties are available from heirloom seed companies, one such being the 'Crimson-flowered' bean, which makes a brilliant splash of colour in spring. Consider, also, sowing the 'field bean' green manure, which grows over 1.2m (4ft) high (see pp.137–8). It looks superb in spring before it is dug in as fertilizer. The young leaves, flowers and beans are edible and bees love it. The variety 'Red Epicure' has pretty white flowers, though they are sometimes wrongly described as red.
Dwarf varieties ↕ 30cm (12in) ↔ 30–35cm (12–14in) **H**
Recommended varieties
Dwarf types: **'Bonny Lad', 'The Sutton'**

Grain amaranth

Chili pepper

FRUITING AND SEEDING VEGETABLES

Most vegetables that are grown for their fruit and seed require a long season and fairly high temperatures: in cool climates considerable skill may be needed to bring them to fruition. In almost all cases the maturing fruits are colourful, but the species and varieties listed here have other decorative qualities that earn them a place in the potager throughout the growing season.

GRAIN AMARANTH *Amaranthus hypochondriacus* (and other species)
These are mostly tall plants with green, crimson or yellow plumes and colourful foliage. They need a warm growing season of 80 to 125 days for the grain to mature. They look flamboyant at the back of beds, or on a boundary, but avoid exposed sites. Some varieties are more wind resistant than others.

In warm climates sow *in situ* in spring; in cool areas sow indoors in late spring, planting out after all risk of frost is past, 45–60cm (18–24in) apart.
↕ 1.2–2.7m (4–9ft) ↔ 38–75cm (15–30in) **T**
Recommended varieties
Purple and red colouring: **'Burgundy'**, **'Hopi Red Dye'**, **'Intense Purple'**
Gold and orange colouring: **'Golden Giant'**, **'Greek'**, **'Manna'**

CHILI PEPPER *Capsicum annuum* LONGUM GROUP and *C. frutescens*
The chili peppers are much more ornamental than the widely grown sweet peppers. The plants are bushier and the dainty leaves are often attractive purple colours or variegated. The chilies themselves can be all colours, turning as they mature (and depending on variety) from green or purple to red, brown, orange or yellow. Some varieties display the whole multicoloured spectrum simultaneously, and over many weeks. But it is the sheer profusion of chilies that makes the plants so spectacular. A single plant may have well over 100 fruit, held clear of the leaves or drooping down. The peppers can be tiny and round, long and thin, squat, bullet-shaped, mushroom-shaped or long and broad.

The dwarfer varieties are excellent as ground cover or in containers. With small varieties, such as 'Apache', two or three can be planted in a shallow pot 13cm (5in) high and with a diameter of 38cm (15in). Taller, more branched plants, are best sited in the middle of flower or vegetable beds, lightly staked and tied if necessary. For connoisseurs, there is the downy-leaved 'tree chili', *C. pubescens*, growing up to 3m (10ft) high and probably even tolerating a touch of frost.

While some varieties really require subtropical temperatures, most need much the same conditions as sweet peppers or tomatoes, and are grown the same way (see Tomato, p.181). Space dwarf plants 25–30cm (10–12in) apart, and taller varieties about 45cm (18in) apart. Don't pamper them: flowers may drop off without setting when grown too lushly.

With the surge of interest in chilies, seed firms are offering more decorative varieties. Some of the most interesting, however, can only be found in heirloom seed catalogues.
↕ 20–45cm (8–18in) ↔ 30–60cm (12–24in) **HH**
Recommended varieties
Colourful varieties for containers or ground cover: **'Apache'**, ***'Chinese Five Colour'**, ***'Korean Hot Pepper'**, ***'Park's Giant Thai Hot'**, **'Peruvian Purple'**, **'Super Chili'**, ***'Thai Hot Pepper'**
Purple-leaved: **'Aurora'** (purple tint), ***'Bolivian Rainbow'**, **'Ecuador Hot'**, ***'Firecracker'**, **'Peruvian Purple'**, ***'Pretty in Purple'**, **'Purple Brazilian Serrano'**, **'Purple Prince'**, ***'Purple Tiger'**
Varieties with forms with variegated leaves (not all plants will be variegated): **'Aurora'**, ***'Pretty in Purple'**, **'Purple Prince'**, **'Variegata'**
Varieties with attractive habit at least 45cm (18in) high: **'Black Prince'**, **'Cayenne'**, ***'Charleston Hot Cayenne'**, ***'Fiesta'**, ***'Mirasol'**, **'Serrano'**, **'Yellow Cayenne'**
*Multicoloured effects

QUINOA *Chenopodium quinoa*
This popular grain plant (pronounced 'Keen-wa'), has great panicles of green, brown, ochre or yellow-red seedheads, making it a marvellous landscaping plant for screening or for the back of a border. (When I first grew 'Andean Hybrid', I had been told it was a demure 1m- (3ft-) high plant, so I put it in the middle of a bed. To my surprise, its stems, which were an amazing, luminous orange-pink, grew over 2.1m (7ft) tall.) Quinoa grows best where daytime temperatures are below 32°C (90°F) and nights are cool. It suits high altitudes, is drought-tolerant and frost-tolerant to -5°C (23°F).

Sow *in situ* in light soil in spring; germination is fastest at soil temperatures of 12–15°C (54–59°F). Thin in stages to 10–30cm (4–12in) apart for small plants that will remain stable and to 50–60cm (20–24in) apart for large, but less stable plants. Thinnings can be eaten as greens. They take from 90 to over 200 days to mature, depending on the variety. Harvest the seed after frost.
↕ 1–2.1m (3–7ft) ↔ 30cm–1m (1–3ft) **H**

Quinoa

Tomato 'F₁ Tumbler'

Tomatillo

Recommended varieties

'Andean Hybrid' Fast-maturing with orange-pink stems and golden seedheads; **'Dave'** (syn. **'Four-O-Seven'**) Short-season, adaptable variety with yellow-brown seedheads; **'Faro Traditional'** Adaptable, with creamy-yellow seedheads; **'Isluga Traditional'** Early maturing, with golden-yellow or pink seedheads; **'Temuco'** Suited to maritime climates, with yellow-green or brilliant red seedheads

TOMATO AND CURRANT TOMATO

Lycopersicon esculentum and *L. pimpinellifolium*
Tomatoes grow best at temperatures of 21–24°C (70–75°F). Unless they flourish in your area, they are likely to be disappointing in a decorative setting. It is not easy to fit the tall, 'indeterminate' types into a potager, as the stakes and support systems they require inevitably have a severity about them. Among tall tomatoes, the cherry type are naturally robust and colourful when fruiting, and so are among the best for potagers.

In contrast to the tall varieties, the bushy types develop masses of side branches instead of a main shoot, and so don't need to have the sideshoots removed. They can be left to sprawl as ground cover and look good in flower borders. The less vigorous varieties will trail down from containers or over the edges of raised beds. The American variety 'Whippersnapper' makes the neatest of edges, with the bonus of very early and tasty fruits. (Flavour is often lacking in the bush and dwarf varieties.)

The upright, very compact 'dwarf' type, rarely reaches a height of more than 25cm (10in) high, and is excellent for pots, for tidy edges or in groups in the foreground of beds.

In temperate climates, sow seed indoors seven weeks before the last frost, at a temperature of 20°C (68°F). Unless grown in large modules, pot the seedlings into 5–7.5cm (2–3in) pots at the three-leaf stage. Harden them off well, and plant them out in late spring or early summer when about 18cm (7in) high and with the first flowers showing. Choose a warm, sheltered position. According to variety, space upright types 38–45cm (15–18in) apart, bush types 60cm (24in) apart and dwarf types 25–30cm (10–12in) apart.
Tall types ↕ 1–1.8m (3–6ft) ↔ 38–45cm (15–18in)
Bush types ↕ 45–60cm (18–24in) ↔ 45–75cm (18–30in); Dwarf types ↕ 30–45cm (12–18in) ↔ 25–30cm (10–12in) all **HH**

Recommended varieties
Bush and semi-bush varieties for ground-cover use: **'Brasero', 'Chello', 'F₁ Pixie', 'F₁ Small Fry', 'F₁ Taxi', 'F₁ Tornado', 'F₁ Toy Boy', 'F₁ Tumbler', 'Golden Sunrise', 'Red Alert', 'Roma VF', 'The Amateur', 'Tigerette Cherry'**
Varieties for containers or beds: **'Aurega', 'Brasero', 'F₁ Patio', 'F₁ Phyra', 'F₁ Prisca', *'F₁ Red Robin', 'F₁ Superb Super Bush', *'F₁ Totem', *'Gold Nugget', *'Minibel', *'Tiny Tim', 'Washington Cherry', 'Whippersnapper'**
*Very compact dwarfs
Suitable for hanging baskets: **'Basket King', 'F₁ Pixie', 'F₁ Toy Boy', 'F₁ Tumbler', 'Red Pear', 'Yellow Pear', 'Whippersnapper'**
Tall cherry types: **'Camp Joy Cherry', 'F₁ Sungold', 'F₁ Sweet Million', 'Gardener's Delight'**

TOMATILLO AND GROUND CHERRY

Physalis ixocarpa and *P. pruinosa* (syn. *P. pubescens*)
With their bright yellow flowers and the 'paper lantern' husks of the mature fruits, the members of the *Physalis* family are tempting to grow. However, their straggly nature makes them awkward to fit in beds. (Be warned: there is much confusion over naming, and seed can prove very variable.)

Tomatillo fruits are up to 5cm (2in) diameter, and are used green for 'salsa' and eaten raw when ripe. A good support system is essential. Keep them in the middle ground of a bed, spaced 1m (3ft) apart.

181

Ground cherry has cherry-sized fruits on a downy-leaved, sprawly plant that is pretty as ground cover, or tumbling down from a container. Both types grow wherever outdoor tomatoes succeed, and are cultivated the same way (see p.181). They don't need very fertile soil and, although drought-tolerant, perform better if watered regularly.

Tomatillo ↕ 1–1.2m (3–4ft) ↔ 1–1.5m (3–5ft) **T**

Ground cherry ↕ 30–60cm (12–24in) ↔ 1–1.8m (3–6ft) **T**

Recommended variety

Tomatillo 'Purple de Milpa' Purplish colouring, with fruits turning to deep purple when ripe

AUBERGINE (EGGPLANT) *Solanum melongena*

Most aubergines are handsome upright plants, with pretty purple-tinted stems and velvety, purplish leaves. The potato-like flowers can be a beautiful lavender-blue. Grouped together, they do look impressive, but they are subtropical plants and need high humidity and summer temperatures of 25–30°C (77–86°F) to flourish.

Besides the familiar glossy, dark-skinned aubergines there are white, pink, striped, yellow, orange and green forms, in every shape including 30cm (12in) long cylinders, egg-shaped and round. The 30cm (12in) high 'Bambino', with its prolific round fruits, is ideal for small containers or low edges. Most varieties can be grown in large pots.

Raise them like tomatoes (see p.181) planting 30–75cm (12–30in) apart according to variety.

↕ 30–75cm (12–30in) ↔ 25–60cm (10–24in) **T**

Recommended varieties

White egg-shaped: **'Caspar', 'Easter Egg', 'Italian White', 'Osterei', 'Ova', 'White Egg'**

Very long: **'Chinese', 'Orient Express'**

Lavender, pink, pinkish and striped: **'Asian Bride', 'Italian Pink', 'Neon', 'Rosa Bianca', 'Violette di Firenze'**

Rounded orange and yellow: **'Thai', 'Turkish Orange'**

SWEET CORN (CORN) *Zea mays*

Sweet corn is a plant with style. The long, plain leaves with their white midribs stand proud of the downy stems, the branching male spikes dominate the skyline, while the soft silks glint with silver, gold, bronze and red. There are a number of spectacular

Aubergine 'Easter Egg'

Sweet corn

varieties with red-coloured foliage and husks. These are mainly traditional field or 'starch' corns used for flour or dried for their decorative black, blue, red or multicoloured cobs. They are all edible when very young, and are mostly tall and late maturing. 'Super Sweet' varieties are superbly flavoured but less robust than standard types. Do not grow them in the same garden as standard varieties as their sweetness is lost by cross-pollination. Popcorn is easy to grow and the plants are neat looking.

Corn looks impressive planted in groups, or in a circle. Tall types make excellent screens if they are planted three to four deep, which also helps to ensure pollination. Because the foliage is not dense, it is ideal for intercropping with everything from celery to nasturtiums. Squashes and climbing beans can clamber up the stems. For more intercropping ideas see below, and p.109.

Depending on variety, sweet corn needs four frost-free months to mature, and soil temperatures of 15°C (59°F) to germinate rapidly. In cool climates, sow in modules, planting out after all risk of frost is past. To ensure maximum pollination, always plant in groups, spacing plants 38cm–1m (15in–3ft) apart. Spacing closer than this allows for

intercropping with salad plants; wider for trailing marrows or dwarf beans. Earth up the stems to 15cm (6in) high to make the plants more stable, although they may also need staking in very exposed situations. In dry conditions, watering is beneficial once the cobs start to develop.

↕ 1.35–2.75m (4½–9ft) ↔ 45cm–1m (18in–3ft) **HH**

Recommended varieties

Edible sweet corn with colourful features:

'F₁ Champ Super Sweet' Reddish-tinged leaves

'F₁ Kandy Corn' Faint red striping on the husks

'Sugar Dots' A reddish hue throughout; red tassels

'True Platinum' Purple-leaved; purple-burgundy coloured husks

Traditional ornamental varieties with strikingly colourful features:

'Burgundy Delight' Mahogany-red leaf colouring, which develops as the plants mature

'Little Jewels' Medium height; very early developing; over half the ears have purple husks

'Red Stalker' Striking red and purple stalks

'Striped Quadricolor' Dark green leaves with contrasting pink and white stripes

'Wampum' A 'mini-ornamental' with tiny ears, purple and white husks and multicoloured tassels

Watermelon

GOURDS AND SQUASHES

Gourds and squashes are all members of the Cucurbit *family, which embraces a huge range of plants from the commonplace cucumber through to marrows, pumpkins and exotic bottle gourds. In many cases the young shoots and flowers are also edible. None are frost hardy. While the hardiest will tolerate cool, temperate climates but need warm temperate conditions of at least 18°C (64°F) to thrive, others need subtropical conditions, with average summer temperatures of at least 21°C (70°F), or tropical conditions, with average summer temperatures over 24°C (75°F). As a rule, the warmer it is the more willingly they will grow.*

THE CURCUBIT FAMILY

The curcubits are mostly large leaved with a climbing or trailing habit. Not only is there an enormous variation in their natural vigour, but plants that seem feeble in cool regions can become unstoppable in favourable conditions. The strongest, more rampant types are best treated as ground cover on a grand scale, unless exceptionally strong supports are erected. Those with a more genteel habit can be trained over strong fences or trellises, or up strings or canes attached to well-anchored supports (see Supports, pp.71–3).

Cucumber 'Burpee Hybrid'

Trailing types can also be coiled into neat, dome-like circles, using steel pins or wooden pegs to guide the leading shoots (see p.94). Some cucurbits (most courgettes, for example) naturally form compact or relatively compact bushes, suitable for small gardens. Depending on the species, the gourds and squashes can have lovely leaves, large bold flowers, corkscrew-like tendrils, downy stems, and often very beautiful fruits: there is nothing more spectacular than large orange pumpkins.

There is considerable confusion over naming squashes. Here, I will use the term 'summer squash' for (a) European marrows, (b) their immature form 'courgettes', and (c) the American squashes such as 'crookneck', which are eaten immature. 'Winter squash' includes the types that develop harder skins and can be stored for anything from two to six months, such as butternut squashes and the classic orange pumpkins.

The cardinal rule of cultivation is to grow only those cucurbits that are suitable for your climate. In cool climates, start them indoors, sowing seeds singly, on their sides, in small pots. Plant them out after all risk of frost is past, spacing them 45cm (18in) apart for climbing lightweights such as cucum-

Cucumber 'Crystal Apple'

bers, 1m (3ft) apart for bush types and at least 1.8m (6ft) apart for large trailing plants. In warm climates, sow *in situ*. They all require good drainage, so are often planted on slight mounds. They also need deep, fertile soil into which plenty of well-rotted organic matter has been dug, and a steady supply of moisture to sustain them.

WATERMELON *Citrullus lanatus*
Watermelons have dainty, deeply-lobed leaves that look pretty while the plant is growing. They require subtropical temperatures and the larger, more rampant types also require a long growing season. Several early-maturing hybrids have shorter vines or a semi-bush habit and can be trained up supports.
↕ 45cm (18in) ↔ 1–3.8m (3–12ft)
Recommended varieties
Compact early maturing hybrids: **'Sin'**, **'Sugar Baby'**, **'Yellow Baby'**
SWEET MELON *Cucumis melo* ssp. *melo*
The cantaloupe, musk and honeydew melons look much like cucumbers when growing and need warm temperatures to flourish. Let them romp over the ground or over low fences. In cooler climates, train them up reasonably strong supports.
↕ 1.8–2.1m (6–7ft) ↔ 30–45cm (12–18in)
CUCUMBER *Cucumis sativus*
Cucumbers have fairly small leaves and flowers, and while they have a pleasing appearance in their prime, they are less decorative at the season's end or in unfavourable conditions. Most need moderately

183

Malabar gourd

Pumpkin 'Turk's Turban'

Winter squash 'Sweet Dumpling'

high temperatures but the modern Japanese types are adapted to growing outdoors in cool, temperate climates. Cucumbers always grow best trained up supports, the exception being the neat, compact, bush varieties. The round-fruited 'lemon' and 'apple' types look pretty when growing well.

Climbing forms ↕ 1.5–1.8m (5–6ft) ↔ 45cm (18in)

Bush forms ↕ 45–56cm (18–22in) ↔ 60–75cm (24–30in)

Recommended varieties

Bush: **'F₁ Bush Champion', 'F₁ Bush Crop'**

Cold-tolerant: **'Burpee Hybrid', 'F₁ Burpless Tasty Green', 'F₁ Tokyo Slicer', 'Yamato'**

Round-fruited: **'Crystal Apple', 'Lemon Cucumber'**

MALABAR GOURD (CHILACAYOTE) *Cucurbita ficifolia*

This rampant gourd tolerates a temperate climate, producing large, roundish, dark green gourds with regular white mottling. It has deeply lobed, rather prickly leaves and eye-catching yellow to orange flowers. I grew it one year to disguise the framework of a dismantled greenhouse and it did the job superbly. Its stems coiled themselves around a developing gourd, embracing and supporting it. It is a voracious ground-cover plant, or climber, in which case it needs very strong supports.

↕ trails up to 24m (80ft)

WINTER SQUASH AND PUMPKINS

Cucurbita maxima, C. moschata, C. pepo

The winter squashes and pumpkins must be the most diverse group of beautiful vegetables. They range from miniature pumpkins such as 'Baby Bear' and 'Jack Be Little', about 10–18cm (4–7in) diameter, to 'Atlantic Giant', which clocked in for the world weight record at over 300kg (660lb). As for shape, they can be round, cylindrical, flat, boxy, spinning-top or teardrop-shaped, clubbed, ridged or crowned with a top-knot like the 'Turk's Turban'. Cream, red, yellow, orange, green and blue are some of the colours, often displayed in striped, patterned or glorious multicoloured combinations. Skin texture can vary from smooth to the alligator-skin wartiness of the French 'Galeuse d'Eysine'.

Then there are the picturesque ornamental gourds, perhaps the prettiest being the variegated, pear-shaped 'Coloquinte' types. These are all edible when very young, but are mainly grown for dried ornaments. In temperate climates, they are ideal for covering trellises and arbours.

The fruits are highly decorative, but the leaves can be lovely too. The larger-leaved varieties wilt in midday heat, but early in the day the magnificent, almost bowl-shaped leaves are held crisply erect, a gorgeous sight glistening with morning dew.

They can be used as ground cover, as climbers on trellises, low fences or strong supports, or simply positioned as dot plants. The appropriate choice for each variety depends on their vigour, habit and the weather, which influences the vigour in any season.

The few varieties that grow as compact bushes can be dot plants or focal points, as can any trailing varieties when trained into a circle. Another handful have fairly small or dainty leaves and are moderately vigorous: choose these to trail up or over supports. The majority, however, have large leaves on strong, all-engulfing vines and, especially if their fruits are large, must be grown as ground cover. There is no better way to utilize a large piece of ground.

Massed pumpkin plants have a lovely, almost velvet quality and as the leaves are lost, the beauty of the maturing gourds more than compensates.

Unless seed catalogues state clearly otherwise, assume any winter squashes will be vigorous plants. They are well adapted to temperate climates, but to reach full maturity some varieties require a longer, frost-free season than others. For details consult seed catalogues.

Recommended varieties

Compact bush: **'Cream of the Crop', 'Jackpot'**

Moderately vigorous climbers: **'Delicata', 'Little Gem', 'Rolet', 'Sweet Dumpling'**

Moderately vigorous in cool climates: **'Jack Be Little', 'Mini Red Turban', Spaghetti marrows/ squash and most ornamental gourds**

Bush ↕ 60cm (24in) ↔ 1–1.2m (3–4ft)

Trailing ↕ 60cm (24in) ↔ 1.8–6m (6–20ft)

MARROWS (SUMMER SQUASH, COURGETTES)

Cucurbita pepo

Marrows come in many shapes, such as the chunky cylindrical British 'vegetable marrow', the flat, fluted custard or 'Patty Pan' types, round marrows

Courgette 'Clarella'

Custard marrow 'F₁ Sunburst'

Bottle gourd

and the curved and bulbous crooknecks. Courgettes are merely juvenile marrows, but modern courgettes are varieties especially selected for their tender skins when young. Courgettes, crooknecks and custard marrows are bush plants, but the 'vegetable'-type marrows are trailing. All have large, showy flowers and are temperate-climate plants. The prettier bush forms and climbing marrows have the most decorative potential.

The trailing marrows are vigorous and willing climbers, clinging with their tendrils to any support from trellises to willow fencing. The white or green-skinned marrows hang down with varying degrees of gracefulness. Courgettes look their best planted singly in vegetable beds or borders; to my mind, the most effective are those with silver-grey and blotched leaves, though the variety 'Burpee Golden Zucchini' has pretty, yellow leaves. The grey-leaved varieties blend into any colour combinations, but the yellow-fruited varieties have a special, bright quality. Courgettes grow well in large containers provided the soil is rich and moisture retentive.

The custard marrows are larger bushes with plain green but handsome leaves. Some have a fine, upright, statuesque habit. The prettily shaped white,

pale green or golden fruits are borne profusely and are particularly appealing when tiny. Plant them singly in a small, round bed to get the most impact.

Recommended varieties
Bush plants with an 'architectural' quality: (custard marrows) **'F₁ Sunburst', 'Patty Green Tint', 'Scallopini';** (round fruited) **'Triple Five'**
Courgettes with silvery foliage: (yellow fruited) **'F₁ Blondy', 'F₁ Goldfinger', 'F₁ Goldrush';** (green fruited) **'Clarella', 'F₁ Ambassador', 'F₁ Greyzini';** (round fruited): **'Rond de Nice' ('Rondo di Nizza')**
Bush courgettes ↕ 45cm (18in) ↔ 60cm (24in)
Custard marrows ↕ 60cm (24in) ↔ 1m (3ft)
Trailing marrows ↕ 60cm (24in) ↔ up to 3m (10ft)

BOTTLE GOURD, CALABASH GOURD
Lagenaria siceraria
Although associated with the tropics, the bottle gourds are surprisingly adaptable to temperate climates. There are many types. In most, the young fruits are edible, while the mature fruits harden like wood and are carved decoratively, or made into utensils. They have gorgeous, soft textured, downy leaves with a strange musky scent, and white, sweetly scented flowers borne on long stalks. The branched tendrils grip strings, wires, fences or any strong supports with impressive tenacity, making them great plants for covering an arbour. The related 'Tromboncino' or 'Zucca Rampicante' has very long, narrow, light-coloured gourds with a swollen end. The fruits stand out with dramatic

starkness against the darker leaves, and grow well on tall bamboo structures. Use them as you would a summer squash.
Trailing or climbing ↕ 3–10m (10–33ft)
BITTER GOURD (BITTER MELON), KARELLA *Momordica charantia*
This is one of the daintier subtropical vines, with prettily indented light-coloured leaves, small, fragrant flowers and stunning, pendulous fruits with warty, alligator skins. They can be silver or green at first, turning to brilliant red. It's a lovely trellis plant, but needs subtropical temperatures to perform well.
↔ trails to over 3.8m (12ft)
Other recommended gourds and squashes
The following are some of those decorative and edible gourds worth growing in warm climates.
Korila *Cylanthera pedata*
A sprawling or climbing plant with branching tendrils, scented flowers and exceptionally pretty finely-cut leaves, shaped like maple leaves. The small fruits are eaten raw like cucumbers, or cooked.
Angled luffa *Luffa acutangula*
This vigorous vine has deeply cut, silvery-blotched leaves and yellow flowers which are wonderfully scented at night.
Chayote (Christophine) *Sechium edule*
Another vigorous climber or trailer with pretty, lobed leaves, corkscrew tendrils and ridged, pear-shaped fruits. It can be grown in sheltered situations in warm, temperate climates.

Nodding onion

Welsh onion

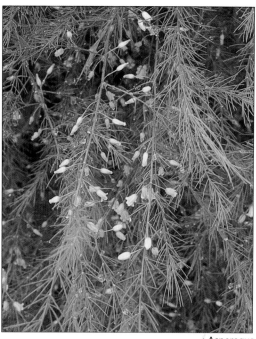

Asparagus

PERENNIALS

The most obvious feature of perennial vegetables is that they require little attention. Many are deep rooted and relatively drought tolerant. With the exception of tender perennials, which may require cossetting under cover in winter, they just reappear every year, and are often productive early in the season when fresh vegetables are scarce. Perennials have to be carefully sited, but give a reassuring air of permanence to the vegetable garden.

ONION *Allium* spp.

The perennial onions are mostly very hardy and evergreen, providing fresh green leaf for flavouring all year, and often edible flowers in summer. Grow them in the open on well-drained soil; the clumps can serve as permanent edging. The following are the main culinary forms, although others, and ornamental onions, are edible.

Propagate by lifting and dividing old plants in autumn or spring, spacing them 23–30cm (9–12in) apart to accommodate their spread.

EVERLASTING ONION *A. cepa* 'Perutile'

The fine leaves of everlasting onion make a delicate clump. It has no flowers so it can only be propagated by division.

↕ and ↔ 15–20cm (6–8in) **H**

TREE ONION (EGYPTIAN ONION)

A. cepa PROLIFERUM GROUP

This type of onion forms picturesque clusters of tiny aerial bulbils on long stems, sometimes developing several tiers. They eventually bend over to 'plant' the bulbils. Allow plants a 45–60cm (18–24in) area in which to develop.

↕ 45cm–1.2m (18in–4ft) ↔ 45–60cm (18–24in) **H**

NODDING ONION *A. cernuum*

This is a pretty, flat-leaved onion available in white- and pink-flowered forms.

↕ 30–45cm (12–18in) ↔ 25cm (10in) **H**

WELSH ONION (CIBOULE) *A. fistulosum*

This forms bold clumps of strong, round, hollow leaves and is easily raised from seed. Sow in modules or *in situ* in spring or early summer, eventually spacing plants 23cm (9in) apart.

↕ 30cm (12in) ↔ 23–35cm (9–14in) **H**

ASPARAGUS *Asparagus officinalis*

Although everyone loves the light texture of asparagus fern and the bright red berries of the female plants, it occupies a lot of space for many years. Traditionally, an asparagus bed (invariably square or rectangular in shape) was made in well-drained soil to one side of the garden. But there is no reason why single plants shouldn't be worked into herbaceous borders and flower beds, or set in the corner or at the back of vegetable beds. Another option is to break with tradition and

make a small, circular asparagus bed as a centrepiece. An edging of box, herbs or grey-leaved plants shows off the fern to perfection. The most productive modern varieties are 'all-male', so if you want the cheeriness of berries, choose traditional varieties.

One-year-old crowns, which can be obtained from nurseries, should be planted 10cm (4in) deep and 30–45cm (12–18in) apart in spring.

↕ 1m (3ft) ↔ 30–45cm (12–18in) **H**

DAUBENTON PERENNIAL KALE

Brassica oleracea ACEPHALA GROUP

This rugged plant is one for the low-maintenance garden. It grows into a huge, branching plant with long broad leaves marked by contrasting white veins. Each year the branches produce a mass of delicious shoots in spring. Use it to screen off unsightly areas.

Raise it in the same way as ordinary kale (see p.155), giving plants at least 1m (3ft) elbow room in each direction. It is advisable to replace plants every four or five years as they start to deteriorate, becoming straggly and unsightly.

↕ 45–75cm (18–30in) ↔ 60cm–1.2m (2–4ft) **H**

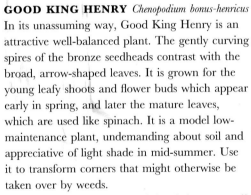

'Daubenton' perennial kale

Good King Henry

Seakale

GOOD KING HENRY *Chenopodium bonus-henricus*
In its unassuming way, Good King Henry is an attractive well-balanced plant. The gently curving spires of the bronze seedheads contrast with the broad, arrow-shaped leaves. It is grown for the young leafy shoots and flower buds which appear early in spring, and later the mature leaves, which are used like spinach. It is a model low-maintenance plant, undemanding about soil and appreciative of light shade in mid-summer. Use it to transform corners that might otherwise be taken over by weeds.

It can be raised from seed, but it is more easily started by dividing an established plant.
↕ and ↔ 30–45cm (12–18in) **H** 🌢◗

TARO (DASHEEN) *Colocasia esculenta*
This stately perennial plant, with its large shapely leaves arising elegantly from the base and growing 1m (3ft) high, belongs in the tropics. I saw a pot-grown specimen commanding the landscape in a Vermont garden, where it was overwintered in a conservatory. It is grown mainly for its tubers, but the leaves are edible, too. Never strip a plant; leave one leaf so it continues growing. Taro lines

the irrigation canals in Chinese fields, growing and looking best alongside water.

It is raised from small corms planted 15cm (6in) deep and about 38cm (15in) apart in spring.
↕ 1m (3ft) ↔ 60cm–1m (2–3ft) **T**

SEAKALE *Crambe maritima*
This magnificent plant has undulating, glaucous blue-grey leaves, easily marred with a thumb print. Treat it as a large-scale ground-cover plant, growing single specimens or groups in a well-drained spot where they can remain undisturbed for four or five years. After the crowns die back in autumn they can be covered with seakale pots or buckets, at least 38cm (15in) high, to blanch the young shoots. Cut the shoots in spring, then let the leaves develop. Flowering shoots should be cut off to conserve the plant's energy, but the tall inflorescence is beautiful and could arguably be left on aesthetic grounds.

Raise seakale from seed sown in modules or *in situ*, or from thongs (sprouting root cuttings) planted in spring 38–75cm (15–30in) apart, the wider spacing for more dramatic effects.
↕ 45–60cm (18–24in) ↔ 1–1.2m (3–4ft) **H**

CARDOON *Cynara cardunculus*
Cardoons are statuesque plants with multi-branched thistle heads towering up to 2.5m (8ft) high. The prickly buds develop into purple flowers then fluffy seedheads, offset by handsome grey-blue leaves. They may remain evergreen through mild winters.

There is a conflict between culinary use and beauty. Cardoons for eating are sown annually in spring. In autumn the young stems are wrapped with sacking or cardboard to blanch them, prior to being lifted. Truly spectacular plants only result from leaving them to grow from year to year. The leaves often deteriorate in summer, but cutting off the stems after flowering rejuvenates the foliage dramatically. Use cardoons as a backdrop, a screen, or a centrepiece, but remember the stems can be snapped off by high winds.

For ornamental purposes, sow in modules in spring, and plant out in summer, either singly or spaced 1.8m (6ft) apart.
↕ 1–2.5m (3–8ft) ↔ 1.2–1.8m (4–6ft) **H**

GLOBE ARTICHOKE *Cynara scolymus*
Globe artichokes have the blue-grey, thistle-like leaves and stately habit of cardoons, but are more compact. The beautifully shaped, edible flower buds form on the tips of thick, succulent stems. Depending on the variety, their scaly bracts can be dramatically sharp or overlapping, with the

Globe artichoke

Jerusalem artichoke

Sweet potato

smoothness of porcelain. Sometimes they are pink and purple hued rather than green.

If space allows, treat them to a bed of their own: the massed silhouettes of the stiff leaves and tall stems are strangely effective whatever the shape or size of the bed. Otherwise plant them individually in flower borders, where the blue-grey softens the garishness of bright flowers, but harmonizes with subtle shades. Single plants and small groups can be used as a focal point.

In autumn cover the crowns with 10cm (4in) of dried leaves if there is any risk of frost. They will produce heads towards the end of their first season, but will flower earlier in subsequent years. Plants can be replaced every three years, but this is unnecessary if they are still vigorous.

As globe artichokes raised from seed are very variable, plant rooted offsets, taken from good-quality plants, in spring. Space them 75cm–1m (30in–3ft) apart.

↕ 60cm–1m (2–3ft), up to 1.5m (5ft) when flowering ↔ 1–1.2m (3–4ft) **HH**

JERUSALEM ARTICHOKE (SUNCHOKE)
Helianthus tuberosus
This hardy perennial in the sunflower family has knobbly, sweetly flavoured tubers. It is easily grown, tolerating a wide range of conditions and soil. The obvious way to use these giants is at the back of a border or as a screen; they grow fast,

and soon block out ugly features. A less conventional approach is to make a feature of their height by confining them within a formal box-edged bed (see p.81). They will also serve as a windbreak if planted in a band, three to four plants deep around a garden.

Plant small tubers in spring 13cm (5in) deep and 30cm (12in) apart. When the stems are 30cm (12in) high, earth them up to make them more stable, and when they flower, shorten the stems to 1.5–1.8m (5–6ft) to concentrate energy in the tubers. Cut them back in autumn to 8cm (3½in) above ground. To prevent them from becoming invasive, carefully dig up every tuber in winter. Except in very severe climates, where they can be stored in straw-covered clamps, dig them as required for use during winter. Keep a few to plant out the following spring.

↕ 2.1–2.5m (7–8ft) ↔ 38–60cm (15–24in) **H**

SWEET POTATO *Ipomoea batatas*
This tropical plant requires very long hot summers if it is to produce tubers, though the leaf tips can also be eaten. A member of the morning glory family, it has pretty leaves, occasional large pink

flowers and a trailing habit. It spreads up to 3m (10ft), unless kept in check, making it an excellent ground-cover vegetable. Although a perennial it is cultivated as an annual. Varieties bred for cooler climates are grown in southern Europe and warm regions of the USA. Plant tubers 8cm (3in) deep and 30cm (12in) apart in spring or early summer.

↕ 45cm (18in) ↔ up to 1.5m (5ft) **T**

MALLOW *Malva* spp.
There is a worldwide tradition of cooking the young shoots, stems and leaves of wild mallows, and using the young leaves and flowers raw in salads. Many are tall, branching plants with leaves shaped like vine leaves and prolific flowers, which can be white, tinged with pink or deep crimson. Most are hardy perennials remaining green even after the first frosts, but even the annuals (*M. crispa* and *M. verticillata*) perpetuate themselves by self-seeding. Use them as hedges along the back of borders, or work single plants into herbaceous borders or low-maintenance gardens.

Sow seed in modules in spring, planting them in their permanent position in autumn. Space them 45–60cm (18–24in) apart, using the closer spacing for annual forms.

M. crispa has highly ornamental and deeply puckered leaves, and grows up to 1.2m (4ft) high. It has small, pinkish-white flowers. *M. moschata* (Musk mallow) grows up to 1m (3ft) high, has

Mallow mauritiana

Alfalfa

Oca

fern-like leaves, and large rose-pink flowers. The leaves can be harvested in spring until the plant flowers, and then it should be cut back for a fresh crop of leaves in autumn. *M. sylvestris* (Common mallow) is pink-flowered and grows 60cm–1m (2–3ft) high. *M. mauritiana* has brilliant crimson flowers nearly 7cm (2½in) in diameter.

↕ see above ↔ 1m (3ft) **H**

ALFALFA (LUCERNE) *Medicago sativa*
Alfalfa is a pretty, evergreen plant: its clover-like leaves and sweet, bluish-purple flowers are used in salads. Grow it as an informal hedge in a low-maintenance garden, or use it to divide beds or sections within a garden.

Alfalfa is deep rooting and can survive in very shallow soil. (Self-sown plants flourish between paving slabs in my garden.) It can also thrive in a wide range of climatic conditions, from the temperate to the tropical.

Sow it in a single row *in situ* in spring, thinning to 25cm (10in) apart. It will grow to 60cm (24in) when flowering in summer, but afterwards cut it back to 10cm (4in) or so for neat winter greenery. Renew plants every three or four years. It can also

be sown as a CCA seedling crop in spring or late summer, or grown as a green manure crop.

↕ 30–45cm (12–18in) ↔ 25–60cm (10–24in) **H** ⊕

OCA *Oxalis tuberosa*
This pretty perennial produces small, variously coloured tubers. It has a neat bushy habit and dainty clover-like leaves, which droop demurely in extreme temperatures, making an odd chequered pattern of light and shade. Some varieties have attractive, reddish leaves. Tubers do not start forming until the shorter days of late summer, but the plants need a very long growing season.

It is an excellent ground-cover plant, remaining green into early winter. Use it to edge paths or large beds, or grow it as single specimens worked into flower or vegetable beds, or containers. It is fairly shade tolerant, and can be grown under climbing bean structures or between sweet corn plants. The shoots can be eaten raw or cooked, but the tubers should be left in the sun for several days before eating, or boiled for 15 minutes to destroy the harmful oxalates in them.

Plant tubers in mid- to late spring about 5cm (2in) deep, and up to 60cm (24in) apart. The more

space they have, the larger they grow. Earth-up the stems to about 7.5cm (3in) high in the same way as potatoes (see p.176).

↕ 30–45cm (12–18in) ↔ 35–75cm (14–30in) **H** ⋮)

YACON *Polymnia sonchifolia*
Yacon is an easily grown vegetable from South America, producing sweet, crunchy tubers that weigh about 1kg (2lb) each. It has small, yellow, daisy-like flowers and soft luxuriant foliage, the light green, spear-shaped leaves being 40cm (16in) long and 30cm (12in) wide. It tolerates shade and can be grown in a flower border.

Buy tubers or divide the old rootstock, planting sections with at least one vegetative bud, after all risk of frost is past. Space them 80cm–1m (2½–3ft) apart. Ideally they need a five to six month season. Lift them in the autumn, carefully remove the fleshiest tubers to use, cut back the foliage and store the rootstock and small attached tubers in a box of sand in a frost-free shed over the winter.

↕ 1.2–1.5cm (4–5ft) ↔ 50–70cm (20–28in) **HH** ⋮)

RHUBARB *Rheum × cultorum*
Rhubarb is the most majestic of ground-cover plants. Shadows play across the crêped surface of the large, palm-shaped leaves, while the sun catches the red leaf stalks beneath. In early summer the spikes of crumbly flowers tower upwards, turning to overlapping, oval, papery bracts, beige

189

Rhubarb

Buckler-leaved sorrel

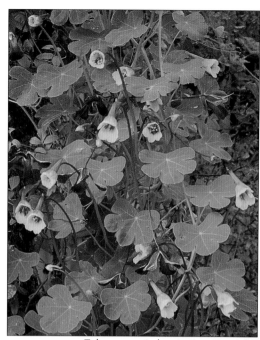
Tuberous-rooted nasturtium 'Ken Aslet'

with dark centres, then darkening to deep bronze. In autumn the plants collapse in unsightly piles, only to herald spring in the kitchen garden with the brilliant freshness of the uncoiling leaves.

Grow them behind vegetable beds, in a bed of their own, or backed by the contrasting foliage of sweet cicely or angelica. They look good, too, on the corners of flower borders, linking a lawn with taller plants behind.

Rhubarb must have fertile soil, but it tolerates light shade and, once established, the deep roots make it remarkably drought tolerant. It will last many years. The flowering shoots should be cut off young to prevent the plant being weakened.

Start with sets (pieces of root with a terminal bud) planted when dormant, 75cm–1m (30in–3ft) apart. Only pull the stems sparingly in the first two seasons. After that crowns can be covered with rhubarb pots in early winter to get very early, tender, pale pink stems.
↕ 1m (3ft); 1.8m (6ft) when seeding ↔ 1.2–1.5m (4–5ft) **H** ⋮**◗**

COMMON SORREL (BROAD-LEAVED) AND BUCKLER-LEAVED SORREL
Rumex acetosa and *R. scutatus*
Sorrel is a most useful ground-cover plant as it tolerates moderate shade and poor acid soils, and provides sharply flavoured leaves for salads, soups and sauces from early in the year. Common sorrel

has light green, arrow-shaped leaves up to 10cm (4in) wide, and sometimes beautifully striped stems. Although very adaptable, it thrives in damp situations. There is a striking red-leaved form, *Rumex montanum*. Buckler-leaved sorrel is much more delicate, with small, pointed, shield-shaped leaves on thin stalks. It has a floppy, bushy habit, self-seeds profusely unless curtailed, tolerates dry situations and has an excellent lemon flavour. (There's a lovely variegated form 'Silver Shield'.) Confusingly, both are called 'French' sorrel.

Both types remain green in winter until knocked back by moderate frosts. Use them as edges, as patches in a low-maintenance garden, or to fill corners that might otherwise be neglected.

Either sow seed in modules in spring, planting about 30cm (12in) apart, or divide existing clumps every few years when their vigour seems to be declining. The red sorrel rarely sets seed, so must be propagated by division. Cut back seedheads to encourage a second flush of leaves.
Common sorrel ↕ 30–60cm (12–24in); up to 1.2m (4ft) when seeding ↔ 30cm (12in) **H** ⋮**◗** Buckler-leaved sorrel ↕ 30cm (12in) ↔ 60cm (24in) **H** ⋮**◗**

TUBEROUS-ROOTED NASTURTIUM (MASHUA, ANU) *Tropaeolum tuberosum*
A climbing plant related to nasturtium, mashua has dainty orange flowers and equally dainty, wavy-edged, nasturtium-like leaves. Leaf tips and

flowers are edible, but it is mainly grown for its large tubers, which can be creamy-white with picturesque red flecking. The foliage is damaged by frost but the tubers, provided they are 5cm (2in) deep in the soil, survive light frosts and taste best if lifted just after the first frost.

It tolerates poor soil and light shade, and grows best in coolish summers. It scrambles happily over fences, up any kind of support and it trails over the ground, so it can be used as a screen, a back-drop, or for ground cover. It can romp through sweet corn plants or mingle attractively with climbing beans and gourds.

Where winters are mild it regenerates each spring, quickly creating a hedge if it has something to climb on. It can equally be grown on an arch-way or tunnel leading to the vegetable garden. Its colourful, edible flowers form a natural link between the culinary and the decorative.

Plant the tubers about 5cm (2in) deep in spring, after all risk of frost is past, spaced about 1m (3ft) apart. Most varieties only start forming tubers late in the year, but the variety 'Ken Aslet' is adapted to a short season and matures early.
↕ and ↔ (trailing) 1.8m (6ft) **HH** ⋮**◗**

Common chives

HERBS

Herbs are the great 'softeners' in the kitchen garden. Ground-cover herbs such as creeping thymes and mints, and the low-growing marjorams round off harsh edges and hide ugly joins in brick and concrete slab paths. When in flower, herbs such as lavender, hyssop and coriander create a fragrant and colourful mistiness. Seeding herbs, such as dill and parsley, create special effects, flowing into spaces between plants, or rising above them. The light on the flat, angled heads of the umbelliferous herbs – dill, fennel, lovage, sweet cicely – is just one of those unexpected delights of the garden.

Herbs are generally undemanding, and many are good subjects for containers. This section looks briefly at some of the most decorative culinary herbs, but don't overlook the ornamental qualities of the many medicinal herbs, bee and dye plants, and herbs grown primarily for their scent.

COMMON CHIVES AND GIANT CHIVES
Allium schoenoprasum and *A. s.* var. *sibiricum*
Chives are the most dependable of herbs, being among the first to poke through the ground in early spring. In summer their neat, round, slender-stalked flowerheads invariably bring bright splashes of

Chinese chives

mauve, occasionally pink, to the vegetable beds. The leaves and flowers are edible, both having a distinctive onion flavour. Once the flowers start to fade, cut them off to conserve vigour.

In addition to being used as edges, chives make excellent demarcation lines between sections in a bed: for several years I had a bold circle of giant chives in my potager separating the outer squares and the inner triangles. Chives can also be worked, singly or in groups, into flower beds. There are several decorative, but still edible, pink-and-white-flowered varieties such as 'Forescate', 'Blush' and 'Roseum' (see Suppliers, p.201).

Sow in seedtrays or modules in spring, planting groups of three to four seedlings in clumps spaced 23–30cm (9–12in) apart, using the wider spacing for giant chives. Clumps should be divided every four years, in spring or summer, and replanted in a fresh site. This is the easiest way to raise new plants.

Chives must have plenty of moisture and fertile soil if they are to flourish. Mulching them with manure every spring is recommended.
Ordinary chives ↕ 20–25cm (8–10in) ↔ 23cm (9in) **H** Giant chives ↕ 30–45cm (12–18in) ↔ 30cm (12in) **H**

CHINESE CHIVES (GARLIC CHIVES)
Allium tuberosum
This exceptionally adaptable perennial tolerates extreme temperatures and most soils. It makes a neat clump of narrow, flat, light green leaves, from which burst long stems of white, starry flowers in mid- to late summer. The fading blooms turn to balled, net-like seedheads that hang on the bare stems well into winter.

In my garden the clumps steadily enlarge year by year with little sign of deterioration: in gardens in the east and west of the USA I have seen great drifts of self-sown Chinese chives. The leaves, young stems and flowers are all edible.

Chinese chives make a trouble-free permanent edge, are attractive dot plants in flower or vegetable borders, and are ideal for planting at the foot of an arch or gatepost, or around the trunks of small fruit trees to conceal their bareness at ground level. They also grow well and look effective in large containers.

They are slower growing than ordinary chives, but cultivated in the same way. Sow in modules from spring to early summer; they can be multi-sown with up to ten seeds in a module. Plant out when 5cm (2in) high, with at least six seedlings in a clump. In fertile soil, plants can live up to 30 years. Only divide them and replant if they are declining.
↕ 30–45cm (12–18in) ↔ 30cm (12in) **H**

LEMON VERBENA *Aloysia triphylla*
(syn. *Lippia citriodora*)
In cool climates lemon verbena is a timid plant, and is usually grown against a sunny wall or in a large pot as a specimen shrub, so it can be moved into frost-free premises to overwinter. In warm climates it can grow into a superb bushy tree 3m (10ft) high. It's a pretty plant, with bright, narrow leaves and, in late summer, tiny lavender-and-purple flowers on the shoot tips. The leaves have an exhilarating, pure lemon fragrance, and are used fresh or dried in cooking or to make a tea.

In warm climates, grow lemon verbena as a background plant in the vegetable garden, or grow it in a container as a bush or trained as a standard. Use it either as a centrepiece, grouping smaller pots around it, or place pots on either side of a gateway – wherever its fragrance can be appreciated. At Villandry lemon verbena has been grown as ground

Dill

Chervil

cover, planted 30cm (12in) apart and trimmed neatly to 45cm (18in) high (see Special Effects with Ground Cover, p.95).

It needs well-drained, but not over-rich soil. Propagate by early summer softwood cuttings. In cool climates, protect the roots of outdoor plants in winter by covering them with straw: they survive to -5°C (23°F). Bring potted plants indoors; they usually lose their leaves, and may not show life until late the following spring. Prune the branches back lightly in spring to shape the plant. It will benefit from being planted out in the ground in summer.

↕ (in cool climates) 1–1.2m (3–4ft) ↔ 60cm–1m (2–3ft) **HH–H**

DILL *Anethum graveolens*
Young dill is a low-growing feathery plant, but it shoots up into dainty umbelliferous seedheads (see Drama from Seedheads and Flowering Vegetables, p.83). It is beautiful at every stage, from young plants to seedheads. All parts have a culinary use. In a decorative garden use it for quick growing, textured CCA seedling patches on its own or worked into patterns with, for example, the contrasting colour and texture of red lettuce (see Seedling Patches, pp.110–3). Remember, it may bolt fairly quickly. It is a self-seeder producing delightful, unexpected seedlings everywhere.

Sow *in situ* from spring to mid-summer in weed-free soil: weeds would soon swamp the delicate seedlings. If grown as a leafy crop, leave unthinned; but plants can be thinned (though it is not essential) to 13cm (5in) apart if the main requirement is for larger seeding plants.

Leafy stage ↕ 13cm (5in) ↔ 10cm (4in) **HH–H**
Seeding stage ↕ 1.2m (4ft) ↔ 60cm (24in) **HH–H** ☉

ANGELICA *Angelica archangelica*
Angelica has lustrous, attractive leaves, and its magnificent, light-coloured, globular seedheads make towering candelabras up to 2m (6½ft) high. Because of its size, it is only a practical proposition as a background plant in a spacious garden. It may flower in its second season, or not until its third or fourth season; it normally dies after flowering, but its useful life can be prolonged for another year if the seedheads are cut off before the seed sets. It does best in slightly moist, rich soil.

If allowed to set seed, it will self-seed freely so, in practice, it regenerates itself. It can be raised from fresh seed sown in autumn, either in modules for planting the following spring, or *in situ*, and thinned in stages to 1.5m (5ft) apart.

↕ 1.5m (5ft) ↔ 1.2m (4ft) **H**

CHERVIL *Anthriscus cerefolium*
Chervil's soft, lacy leaves billow in the borders before the plant runs to seed in a messy haze of elongated leafy spikes and tiny white flowers. By nature a cool-season crop, it withstands some frost and remains green in winter. Its refreshing aniseed flavour is invaluable in salads, sauces and chervil soup. It tolerates any well-drained soil and makes an unusual, graceful edge. Chervil can be intercropped between tall plants or rows of peas or beans, and I've seen it growing successfully under large trees. Left to its own devices, it self-seeds year after year. Don't hesitate to pull it out if it threatens to take over, but a permanent patch will make good use of a shaded corner. Plants can be cut frequently over a period of several months.

For a spring to summer edge in cool climates or slightly shaded situations, sow in modules in late winter and plant out in spring, or sow *in situ* as soon as the soil is workable. Space plants 23cm (9in) apart. For a winter edge, which should be in full sun, sow similarly in late summer.

(Watch out for the reintroduction of the closely related turnip-rooted chervil, a delicious 'lost' root vegetable, rediscovered in France. I experimented with a variety that grew into handsome plants about 45cm (18in) high with beautiful, moss-like foliage.)

↕ 30–35cm (12–14in) ↔ 20–25cm (8–10in) **H**

COMMON FENNEL AND BRONZE FENNEL
Foeniculum vulgare and *F. v.* 'Purpureum'
The garden form of wild fennel is a hardy perennial, cultivated for its aniseed-flavoured leaves. It is a tall, feathery plant. The common form has blue-green leaves, and bronze fennel has delightful, rusty-bronze leaves. Bronze fennel seems particularly robust, self-seeding prolifically and it is among the first plants to appear in spring. In summer fennel produces a mass of elegant seedheads. Unless kept compact by constant picking, fennel is best planted towards the back of borders, though it can fend for itself in the middle ground of informal cottage garden plantings or flower beds.

Hyssop

Lovage

Pineapple mint

Sow *in situ* in spring, or in modules, planting out when about 7.5cm (3in) high. Although plants can be grouped about 75cm (30in) apart, I feel they are better value as single specimens.
↕ 1.2m (4ft) ↔ 60cm (24in) **H**

COMMON HYSSOP AND ROCK HYSSOP

Hyssopus officinalis and *H. o.* ssp. *aristatus*

Hyssop is a lovely plant. I use its small, hard, dark green leaves in much the same way as thyme or savory, but grow it mainly for the flowers, which bloom throughout summer attracting masses of bees. Ordinary hyssop has blue-, pink- and white-flowered forms, while the more compact rock hyssop has bright, deep blue flowers. Hyssop likes a sunny position and well-drained soil but is hardy, often remaining green well into winter.

Use hyssop for a colourful low hedge or an, admittedly, space-consuming edge for large beds. Rock hyssop is an excellent plant for defining the corners of beds.

Plants can be raised from softwood cuttings taken in spring, or from seed, sown in modules in spring and planted out when 7.5cm (3in) high. Space plants 45–60cm (18–24in) apart. Never be afraid to prune

hyssop hard. Cut off the flowers when they fade, prune straggly tips in autumn to reshape the bush, and prune back hard in spring when it is starting into growth.
Common hyssop ↕ 80cm (2½ft) ↔ 1m (3ft) **H**
Rock hyssop ↕ 30cm (12in) ↔ 60cm (24in) **H**

LOVAGE *Levisticum officinale*

Lovage is another of the giant, hardy *Umbelliferae* perennials, too large for modest-sized gardens, but a superb background or screening plant. Its shiny leaves radiate vitality, and have a strong, celery-like flavour. They appear in early spring, followed in summer by seedheads that turn from gold to khaki to brown, with a nut-like solidity; I use them in fresh and dried flower arrangements. Lovage grows best in slightly damp, fertile soil.

Sow fresh seed in autumn in modules, planting out in spring or the following autumn. Propagate by dividing the rootstocks of established plants in the dormant season, each piece having a bud, which is planted 5cm (2in) below soil level. For a lovage 'hedge', space plants 1.2m (4ft) apart.
↕ 1.8m (6ft) ↔ 1.2–1.5m (4–5ft) **H** ⬧◗

MINT *Mentha* sp.

Most members of the mint family, because of their tendency to spread uncontrollably, should only be introduced into the vegetable garden with caution. Exceptions are the creeping mints, which have a

role as ground cover and even as paths in lightly trodden areas (see Soft Paths, p.57 and Special Effects with Ground Cover, p.94). I would also make an exception for two variegated culinary mints: the pert, gold-and-green-leaved ginger or Scottish mint, *Mentha* x *gracilis* (syn. *M.* x *gentilis*), and the downy-leaved, white-and-green pineapple mint, *M. suaveolens* 'Variegata', which is the variegated form of apple mint. Both are much less rampant than other mints, and add a subtlety to vegetable or flower beds. They can be grown in large containers, and, though I haven't tried it, pineapple mint is said to grow well in hanging baskets.

Mint is a perennial, and needs fertile, reasonably moist soil. Where space allows, permanent beds of culinary mints make excellent use of ground. Most have beautiful flower spikes.

Buy plants initially, or lift established plants in spring or autumn, cut off pieces of root 5cm (2in) long, and plant them horizontally 5cm (2in) deep and 23cm (9in) apart.
Ginger and pineapple mint ↕ 30cm (12in)
↔ 10–20cm (4–8in) **H**

SWEET CICELY *Myrrhis odorata*

The perennial sweet cicely is an airy, pretty plant with soft, fern-like leaves. From early summer it is covered in white flowers, which fade into strikingly dark, erect seedheads. The leaves and seeds both have a strong, sweet aniseed flavour, and are used in

Sweet cicely

Myrtle

Purple-leaved basil

salads and as a sugar substitute. It grows well in a large container. Plant it in an under-utilized corner or on the outside or towards the back of a bed. Sweet cicely looks best grown as a single plant, but can be planted in groups or as an informal, summer hedge, spacing plants at least 60cm (24in) apart.

The quickest way to obtain new plants is to lift and divide a mature plant in the dormant season. Otherwise, sow fresh seed in late summer, in modules, leave them outside in a cold-frame in winter, planting them out in spring 1m (3ft) apart.
↕ and ↔ 1–1.2m (3–4ft) **H** ⛅ ◗

COMMON MYRTLE AND TARENTINA MYRTLE *Myrtus communis* and *M. c.* ssp. *tarentina*
Myrtle is a handsome evergreen shrub, with small, shiny, spicy-flavoured leaves. The fragrant creamy flowers can be used in salads once the bitter, outer green sepals have been removed. In warm climates, myrtle grows into a large shrub, but where winter temperatures are liable to fall to between -5 and -10°C (23 and 14°F) it must be grown in well-drained soil in a warm, sheltered position, or in pots that can be taken indoors to overwinter. The smaller-leaved Tarentina myrtle is more compact and hardier. Both have pretty variegated forms.

Myrtle stands trimming well and can be grown in pots trained as a standard or shaped into a pyramid (see Topiary, p.70). It can also be trained against a wall as an espalier or fan, or grown as a hedge,

spacing plants 60cm (24in) apart. Prune plants lightly in spring to maintain their shape.

Buy plants initially, or propagate from softwood cuttings in spring, or semi-ripe cuttings in summer.
Common myrtle ↕ and ↔ (in cool climates)
2m (6½ft) **H**
Tarentina myrtle ↕ and ↔ (in cool climates)
1.5m (5ft) **H**

BASIL *Ocimum basilicum*
Most cooks would kill for the flavour of fresh basil leaves and flowers, but in climates with unreliable, cool summers or chilly nights, growing basil outdoors is a gamble. It must have warm conditions. Given the right climate and a sunny, sheltered garden, several different types of basil stand out for their decorative potential.

The lush, giant basils, typified by 'Lettuce-leaved' basil, grow into bushy plants that fill space and make strong patches of foliage. The miniature basils form compact, ground-hugging mounds, and make an endearing and neat edge to vegetable or flower beds. They are also easily intercropped between tall vegetables, such as staked tomatoes, or plants of contrasting colours, like red lettuce, or colourful

annuals such as lobelia or ageratum. Their tiny leaves are exquisitely flavoured and can be picked over many weeks without affecting the rounded mound-shape of the plant. Identify miniature basils by their names (see below), but be prepared to discover a few lanky plants in any packet of seed. The 'bush' basils, though fairly small, are taller and much less compact.

There are several basils with pretty flower spikes, often pink or purple with purple hues to the stem. The purple-leaved basils, which generally have purple flowers, are a striking colour but poorly flavoured. This is also true of the eye-catching 'Ruffles' type, which has ruffled, fringed leaves in red and green varieties. These decorative basils all look their best grouped in the foreground, among flowers or vegetables. They are also, along with the compact basils, suitable for containers.

Sow basil in seedtrays or modules in spring, planting out after all risk of frost is past, 10–20cm (4–8in) apart depending on variety. Most will branch freely after the leaves are cut.
Large ↕ 45cm (18in) ↔ 30–35cm (12–14in) **T**
Compact ↕ 10–15cm (4–6in) ↔ 10–25cm (4–10in) **T**
Ornamental and purple ↕ 30–38cm (12–15in) ↔ 20–30cm (8–12in) **T**
Recommended varieties
Large: **'Genovese', 'Lettuce-leaved', 'Neapolitanum'**

Golden marjoram

Green perilla

Broad-leaved parsley

Compact: **'Compact'**, **'Dwarf'**, **'Greek'**,
'Miniature', **'Piccolo'**, *O. b.* var. *minimum*
Ornamental-flowered: **'Anise'**, **'Cinnamon'**,
'Holy' (syn. **'Sacred'**), **'Horapha'**, **'Thai'**
Purple-leaved: **'Dark Opal'**, **'Red Rubin'**,
O. b. var. *purpurascens*

MARJORAM *Origanum* spp.

Almost all of the many species and varieties of
marjoram are decorative, and the majority have
culinary value, so there's infinite scope for using
them creatively in the kitchen garden. Below are
details of the three groups I have found most useful.

First are the compact, evergreen types that make
excellent edges and ground cover, and are especially
valuable in the winter potager. Several have tall,
flowering shoots in summer, but die back into neat
mats or low plants in winter. Second are the various
golden and variegated marjorams, valued for their
ability to illuminate the garden. Use them as ground
cover or edging, avoiding positions in the full glare
of summer sun, which may scorch the leaves. Third
are marjorams with exceptionally pretty flowers and
habit. Grow these in flower or vegetable beds for
permanent summer colour.

All are hardy perennials, easily propagated from
softwood cuttings taken in spring, or by dividing
mature plants in spring or autumn. Space plants
23–30cm (9–12in) apart in well-drained soil and
trim them back after flowering. All are suitable for
growing in containers.
Compact varieties ↕ 15–23cm (6–9in)
↔ 30cm (12in) **H** Others ↕ 20–38cm (8–15in)
↔ 30–45cm (12–18in) **H**
Recommended varieties
Compact in winter: **Origanum x applei** (syn. **O.**
heracleoticum), **O. laevigatum**, **O. vulgare**
'Compactum'
Golden-leaved and variegated: **O. rotundifolium**
'Aureum', **O. vulgare 'Aureum'**, **O. v. 'Aureum**
crispum', **O. v. 'Country Cream'**, **O. v. 'Gold Tip'**
Decorative: **O. 'Kent Beauty'**, **O. laevigatum**,
O. l. 'Herrenhausen', **O. l. 'Hopleys'**

PERILLA (SHISO) *Perilla frutescens*

This oriental herb has soft, nettle-like leaves. There
are distinct red- and green-leaved forms. The green
is a subdued colour with creamy flower spikes: its
strongly flavoured leaves are used in Japanese
cooking. The more vigorous, purple-flowered, red
perilla is often mistaken for purple-leaved basil. It
has little flavour, but is used to dye pickles a delicate
rose colour.

Perilla requires much the same conditions as
basil (see earlier entry), but is a little tougher.

Having worked hard to coax plants into growth in
the UK, I was amazed to see a flaming 1m (3ft) high
'hedge' of red perilla in New York. It mixes well
with flowers: green perilla mingled with nasturtiums
and pinks looks marvellous. Red perilla is best
contrasting with greys, blues or white, and teams
well with lavender.

Sow seed in modules in spring, planting out after
all risk of frost is past 25–30cm (10–12in) apart. If
germination is erratic, try putting seeds into a fridge
at 5°C (41°F) for three days before sowing.
↕ 45cm (18in) ↔ 30cm (12in) **T**

PARSLEY *Petroselinum crispum*

Curled parsley, with its deeply crinkled leaves, is a
beautiful plant, but the taller, broad- or flat-leaved
Italian and French type has a better flavour. All
have dark green leaves which make a great impact
when growing well. This is no easy matter: parsley
only thrives in fertile, well-drained soil with plenty of
moisture throughout growth. In poor soils and dry
conditions the leaves die back and it is prey to
aphid-borne virus diseases with no practical remedy.
Where parsley does well, use it liberally for edging,
in broad bands to divide beds, or in patches at

Rosemary

Purple sage

equidistant spacing. For an even look, keep to one or other type but for an interesting, textured effect the broad and curly types can be mixed. Leave a plant here and there to seed (see Drama from Seedheads and Flowering Vegetables, p.83); the branched seedheads blend well with pot marigolds and seeding dill.

For a summer supply of plants, sow in spring; for an autumn supply, sow in early summer. Either sow in modules, planting when 5cm (2in) high, or sow *in situ*, making sure the seedlings stay moist and weed-free. Space plants 20–25cm (8–10in) apart. Unprotected parsley is killed by heavy frost.
Curly ↕ and ↔ 23cm (9in) **H**
Broad-leaved ↕ and ↔ 30cm (12in) **H**

COMMON ROSEMARY *Rosmarinus officinalis*

One of the loveliest shrubby herbs for the kitchen garden, rosemary flourishes in warm climates and sunny, sheltered sites, but when temperatures are below -10°C (14°F) it is at risk, especially on heavy, poorly drained soil. For this reason, it is frequently grown in pots as a bush or trained as a topiary (see Topiary, p.70), then brought under cover in winter. In suitable climates, grow it as a low hedge (see Dwarf Hedges, p.64), as ground cover, as a bush in the background, or trimmed into a pyramid in a key position; there are varieties to suit all these sites. It looks good planted on the corners of beds. Prostrate and semi-prostrate forms can trail on banks, over low walls or the edges of pots. Do not cut rosemary until the second season, and prune established bushes lightly after flowering to keep them shapely. Common rosemary and its white-flowered form, *R. o.* var. *albiflorus* are usually considered the hardiest. For propagation see page 64.

Sow *R. officinalis* in spring in modules at 21°C (70°F), planting out when 7.5cm (3in) high.
↕ and ↔ 1m (3ft) **H**

COMMON SAGE (GARDEN SAGE)
Salvia officinalis

The culinary sages are the most *sympathique* kitchen garden plants, their soft, velvety leaves melding with all kinds of foliage. They need well-drained soil, a sunny situation and space to bush out. Common sage has blue-grey leaves, lilac-blue flowers and spikes of crisp, papery seedheads. It is the hardiest culinary sage; the decorative, coloured-leaved forms are more tender. Take cuttings in summer in case the plants are ruined by frost.

The dusky leaves of *S. o.* 'Purpurascens', purple sage, look wonderful growing with red-leaved 'Bull's Blood' beetroot, purple mustard, red cabbage or ornamental kales, or with black or purple pansies at its feet. For different effects use the multi-variegated *S. o.* 'Tricolor', otherwise one of the gold-and-green variegated sages, *S. o.* 'Icterina' and 'Kew Gold'. This was once used in Kew Gardens' bedding scheme: a striking golden carpet punctuated by spires of 'Miss Jessop's Upright' rosemary.

On the whole, sages are best grown on the outskirts of a potager. Use them as ground cover or to block out ugly features at low level. I have seen buxom bushes of purple and variegated sage blanketing the ground beneath standard quinces.

Common sage can be raised from seed sown in modules in spring and planted in summer. For other varieties, buy plants initially, and renew them about every four years or so by taking cuttings in spring or summer, or by layering in spring or autumn. Space them 45–60cm (18–24in) apart.
↕ 60cm (24in) ↔ 60cm–1m (2–3ft) **H**

WINTER SAVORY *Satureja montana*

Although it can be rather straggly, winter savory is evergreen and relatively hardy if grown on light, well-drained soil, so it is a useful winter herb. It has small, pretty, usually pale purple flowers in summer. I grow it on the edge of the bed, but at Villandry I spotted it trained in a neat, ground-cover 'patch' (see Special Effects with Ground Cover, p.95).

Sow seed in late summer, planting out in spring 25–30cm (10–12in) apart, or raise it from softwood cuttings taken in spring. Prune it back each spring to 8cm (3in) high. It is an easy plant for containers, and a nice, winter, indoor pot plant.
↕ 23–30cm (9–12in) ↔ 25cm (10in) **H**

THYME *Thymus* sp.

The thymes are charming, colourful plants, which flourish in sunny situations in light, well-drained soil. Their main use in the kitchen garden is ground cover and as edging plants (see Special Effects with Ground Cover p.94 and Living Edges, p.92). They are also excellent plants for growing in containers.

Only common thyme, *T. vulgaris*, and creeping thyme, *T. serpyllum*, can be raised from seed. Sow in spring, planting out in summer 20cm (8in) apart. All thymes are easily raised from softwood cuttings taken in spring. After flowering, trim plants back lightly to keep them in shape.
↕ (in flower) 18–30cm (7–12in) ↔ 30cm (12in) **H**

Daisy 'Clutch of Pearls'

Daisy 'Goliath'

White-flowered borage

EDIBLE FLOWERS

The easiest way to turn a kitchen garden into a colourful paradise is to grow flowers along with the vegetables. For the pragmatic gardener-cook, the lure of edible flowers is irresistible. As it happens, many vegetables have edible flowers, for example beans, peas, members of the genus Allium *(onions, chives and leeks), brassicas, squashes, chicories, salsify, scorzonera, corn salad, and many more. Culinary herbs, too, are a rich source of intriguingly flavoured edible flowers, from thyme and fennel to lavender and rosemary. Add to these a list of decorative but edible flowering plants, stretching from the commonplace nasturtium to the exotic yucca, and the choice is huge.*

Flowers have been eaten, both cooked and raw, since time immemorial. I have included here only the few that have won a permanent place in my own potagers. See page 199 for suggestions for others, and Further Reading, page 201 for detailed information on their culture and use.

ANISE HYSSOP *Agastache foeniculum*
(syn. *A. anaethiodora*)
Anise hyssop is an erect, branching plant with lovely, dense spikes of lavender flowers (occasionally pink or white) in summer, up to 15cm (6in) long.

Bees love it, and the gentle aniseed flavour pervades the leaves and flowers, hence its use in cooking, salads, and for flavouring drinks. It blends into crowded, informal planting, can play a prominent role in formal beds, and looks good in containers. It is a great self-seeder, looking 'just right' wherever it chooses to appear.

A hardy perennial, dying down in autumn, it won't survive much below -5°C (-23°F), unless it is protected. In mild climates, sow *in situ* in autumn, but, in cool climates, sow the tiny seed indoors in spring, planting in a sunny place in early summer 45cm (18in) apart. It will flower in its first season. Cut the flower spikes as they fade to encourage a second flush.
↕ 60cm (24in) ↔ 45cm (18in) **H**

DAISY (ENGLISH DAISY) *Bellis perennis*
This unassuming, brightly coloured daisy, a sophisticated form of the little white lawn daisy, has been used in salads for centuries. The leaves form a compact rosette, making it an excellent edging plant. Its main flowering season is from late spring to mid-summer. The flowers come in shades of pink, red, crimson or white, ranging in size from small

double flowers to large pompon types. These plants, typified by the giant varieties 'Goliath', 'Spring Star' and 'Super Enorma' make more of a splash, but I prefer the daintier, smaller ones like 'Clutch of Pearls', 'Kito' and the Carpet and Pomponette 'Buttons' series. Although perennial, the daisy is best grown as a biennial, but if the plants seem to be deteriorating towards the end of the season, pull them up in summer and replant the edge with lettuce or winter pansies.

Sow in summer *in situ* (in warm climates) or in a seedtray, planting out when large enough to handle, 15–23cm (6–9in) apart. It grows anywhere except in very dry situations. Keep plants deadheaded to encourage continuous flowering and a second flush in late summer.
↕ 10–15cm (4–6in) ↔ 13–18cm (5–7in) **H**

BORAGE *Borago officinalis*
Borage is a robust annual plant, though its bristly stems and leaves and the downy hairs on the sepals, give it a dreamy, misty quality. It grows tall and, from spring to autumn, is a mass of tiny, star-shaped, blue flowers, haunted by bees. There is a rarer, white-flowered variety: the two make a lovely

Pot marigold 'Orange King'

Sunflower

Nasturtium

planting together. Confine borage to informal or perennial beds, rather than growing it among vegetables. The brittle stems collapse in heavy rain or wind and can crush surrounding plants.

In temperate climates you need to sow borage only once in a lifetime. Sow in summer *in situ* or in seedtrays, planting 5–8cm (2–3in) high seedlings about 45cm (18in) apart. From then on borage self-seeds: unwanted seedlings must be uprooted to prevent them from swamping the garden.
↕ 1m (3ft) ↔ 60cm–1m (2–3ft) **H**

POT MARIGOLD (CALENDULA)
Calendula officinalis
Gloriously colourful and easily grown, pot marigold has a long history of culinary and medicinal use. Traditional varieties were orange and yellow, but the modern colour range extends from pink-tinged, creamy-apricot to mahogany. My favourites are the old-fashioned, large orange-flowered 'Orange King' and 'Indian Prince', with its mysterious, dark brown centre. I also love the iridescent quality of the newer 'Neon' (sadly, hard to come by), which I have planted in striking diagonals across the potager beds. It never failed to attract attention.

Let calendula grow casually among vegetables as it attracts beneficial insects, or among flowers or herbs in informal beds. It looks superb mingling with the burnished gold of dill and fennel seedheads.

Sow in spring, either in seedtrays, planting out when 5cm (2in) high, or *in situ* thinning early to 25cm (10in) apart. Keep plants deadheaded to prolong flowering into late summer. It's a prolific self-seeder: uproot unwanted seedlings mercilessly.
↕ 30cm (12in) ↔ 23–30cm (9–12in) **H**

SUNFLOWER *Helianthus annuus*
Not only do sunflowers have edible buds, petals and seeds, but they make great cut flowers, superb background, hedging or screening plants, and can serve as supports for climbing beans (see Culinary Climbers, p.87). Everyone knows the traditional, huge, dark-centred, golden-petalled sunflower but there are now many, smaller-flowered, subtly coloured and multi-headed varieties. Try the mahogany 'Velvet Queen', the pale lemon 'Moonwalker' and 'Valentine', the creamy 'Italian White' and 'Vanilla Ice' and the multi-headed, almost pollen-free 'Prado Red' and 'Prado Yellow'.

Sow *in situ* in spring, thinning to 20–30cm (8–12in) apart, using the closer spacing for more upright and stable plants. For a dense screen grow sunflowers several rows deep, mixing varieties, with the tallest at the back.
↕ 60cm–2.5m (2–8ft) ↔ 30–60cm (12–24in) **H**

NASTURTIUM *Tropaeolum majus*
There are climbing or trailing, semi-trailing and dwarf forms of nasturtiums, all brightly coloured with edible flowers, leaves and seedheads. I always grow the non-rampant, semi-trailing 'Alaska' among vegetables: its daintily variegated, white-and-light-green leaves convey a feel of dappled sunshine. 'Jewel of Africa' is similar but more vigorous, and both are lovely hanging over the edges of raised beds or tubs. Dwarf varieties, such as the reddish-leaved 'Empress of India', can be used for edging, and the vigorous, slightly less showy climbers will scramble over fences.

Sow *in situ* in spring spacing seeds 15cm (6in) apart. Nasturtiums self-seed prolifically, thrive in poor soil (leaves become gross in rich soil), and can transform dry sunny corners with a blaze of colour.
↕ Dwarf 15–23cm (6–9in) Climbers 1.2–1.5m (4–5ft) ↔ 15–30cm (6–12in) **HH–T**

VIOLAS *Viola* spp.
Garden pansies (*V.* x *wittrockiana*) make the perfect edge: low-growing but not invasive, pretty and flowering over many weeks. Any violas can be found a niche in the vegetable garden, and all are suitable

Viola 'Joker Light Blue'

Begonia 'Pin-up'

Carnation 'Constance Finnis'

for containers. With careful planning they can provide colour all year round. Sow indoors and plant out at the four-leaf stage, about 20cm (8in) apart. Using appropriate varieties, sow in spring for summer flowering, late spring to summer for autumn, in summer for winter, and in autumn for an early spring display. The tiny heartease (Johnny Jump-ups), *Viola tricolor*, flower intermittently over many months, self-seeding delightfully among established plants, between paving stones and in paths. Sow from spring to late summer.
↕ 10–15cm (4–6in) ↔ 15–23cm (6–9in) **H**

OTHER COLOURFUL EDIBLE FLOWERS

Pineapple guava *Acca sellowiana* (syn. *Feijoa*) Large shrub producing crimson-and-white flowers.
↕ 1.8m (6ft) **H–HH**

Hollyhock *Althaea rosea* Available in a wide spectrum of soft colours.
↕ up to 2m (6½ft) **H**

Alkanet *Anchusa azurea* Clear blue flowers.
↕ up to 1.3m (4½ft) **H**

Tuberous-rooted begonias *Begonia* x *tuberhydrida* Broad spectrum of colours.
↕ 30–60cm (12–24in) **HH**

Chrysanthemum greens *Chrysanthemum coranarium* (see p.165).

Florist's chrysanthemum *Dendranthema* x *grandiflorum* (syn. *D* x *morifolium*) Wonderful range of flower types and colours mainly blooming in late summer and autumn.
↕ up to 1m (3ft) **HH**

Carnations *Dianthus* spp. All with colours in the white, pink and crimson range, often with wonderful fragrance.
↕ up to 60cm (24in) **H–HH**

Garden or clove pinks
↕ 15cm (6in) **H**

Sweet william
↕ up to 60cm (24in) **H**

Sweet woodruff *Galium odoratum* A useful ground-cover plant with star-shaped leaves and bright white flowers.
↕ 15cm (6in) **H**

Daylilies *Hemerocallis* spp. Wide range of shades in yellow to red spectrum.
↕ 30–60cm (12–24in) **H**

Houttuynia *Houttuynia cordata* Ground cover plant with white flowers and heart-shaped leaves.
↕ up to 60cm (24in) **H**

Lavender *Lavandula* spp. Bushes with blue, pink and white flowers.
↕ up to 1m (3ft) **H–HH**

Bergamot (Bee Balm) *Monarda didyma* Scarlet, pink or near-white flowers.
↕ 45cm–1m (1½–3ft) **H**

Scented-leaved geraniums *Pelargonium* spp. Delicate flowers and wide range of fragrant-leaved varieties.
↕ up to 1.2m (4ft) **T**

Roses *Rosa* spp. Bushes and climbers. All fragrant rose petals are useable. Recommended varieties *Rosa rugosa*, *R. r.* 'Alba' and 'Graham Thomas'.
↕ varies according to type **H**

Clary sage *Salvia sclarea* Pastel lilac, pink and cream flower spikes.
↕ up to 1m (3ft) **H**

Elderflower *Sambucus nigra* Hedgerow shrub with masses of creamy flowers.
↕ up to 6m (20ft) **H**

Signet marigold (Gem series) *Tagetes tenuifolia* (*signata*) Small orange and yellow flowers.
↕ 20cm (8in) **T**

Society garlic *Tulbaghia violacea* Lilac flowers with mild garlic flavour; there are also forms with variegated leaves.
↕ 60cm (24in) **HH**

Yucca *Yucca* spp. Spikes of white flowers.
↕ 60cm (24in) **HH–H**

GLOSSARY

Annual Plant that germinates, flowers and dies within a year.

Basal leaf/leaves Leaf/leaves arising near the base of a stem or shoot.

Biennial Plant whose life cycle normally spans two years.

Biologique The term used in France for gardening without the use of chemicals.

Blanch To exclude light from plants to make them paler and sweeter.

Bolt To flower prematurely, often due to unsuitable weather conditions.

Brassicas Plants in the *Cruciferae* family within the genus *Brassica*. Includes cabbages and related plants.

Broadcast To sow seed by scattering it over the surface.

Catch crop A fast-growing crop, sown to utilize ground that has been cleared and is shortly intended for another crop.

Check Growth being halted through adverse conditions such as drought or cold.

Cultivar The correct term for a variety raised in cultivation (see variety).

Cuttings Pieces of stem used for propagation, and put into a light sandy compost to root. **Softwood cuttings** young growths taken in spring. **Semi-hardwood cuttings** more mature growths taken in summer. **Hardwood cuttings** mature current year's growth taken at the end of the season, and often rooted in the ground outdoors. **Heel cutting** sideshoot cutting with a small piece of stem or bark from the main shoot, at the base when it is pulled away from the stem.

Dormancy A period when a plant ceases to grow and seeds will not germinate.

Earthing up Drawing soil up around the base and stems of the plant, usually for additional support or to exclude light.

Established plants The stage when the roots of transplanted plants start to function again and the plant continues to grow.

Festoon The art of bending branches, sometimes with the use of weights and strings, to encourage fruiting, restrict growth, and develop a weeping form.

F₁ hybrid Cultivar bred by crossing two inbred lines, to get plants of exceptional vigour and uniformity.

Forcing Bringing a plant into earlier growth by giving it warmer conditions.

Grafting The technique of joining a shoot or 'scion' of one plant onto the 'rootstock' of another so they fuse and grow together. The scion would have good fruiting or ornamental qualities, while the rootstock influences the growth and often disease resistance of the scion (see Rootstocks below).

Growing point The tip of the plant's stem or shoot, which is often nipped off to encourage the development of sideshoots.

Half-hardy Plants which survive only limited cold or very light frost unless in a protected site or situation.

Harden-off Gradually acclimatize plants raised indoors to lower temperatures so they are not checked when planted out.

Hardy Plant surviving outdoors in a given climate zone. Generally implies that it has some frost resistance.

Haulm The top growth of plants. Commonly used for potatoes and peas.

Heirloom Name given to old, traditional varieties that are no longer in general or commercial cultivation.

***in situ* sowing** Sowing a plant directly in the ground in the position where it will grow to maturity.

Intercrop To grow rows of two or more crops alongside or between each other, or within the same row. Fast-growing crops are often combined with slower-growing ones to maximize the use of space.

Lateral A sideshoot or branch on a stem. Sub-laterals are shoots arising on laterals.

Layering Bending down a stem and pinning or burying it in the soil to encourage rooting for propagation purposes.

Legumes Plants in the *Leguminosae* family, which are usually podded, often having nitrogen fixing nodules on their roots.

Long day plants Plants that only flower and seed when day length is *longer* than a certain critical minimum (generally 12 hours). In **Short day plants** day length must be *shorter* than this period.

Maiden A one year old tree or shrub, or a grafted tree in its first year.

Offset Young plant that arises at the base of a plant and is easily separated.

Organic The term used for gardening without the use of chemical products.

Parterres Beds at ground level, usually laid out in formal designs.

Perennial Plant that lives for several years.

Permaculture An approach to growing with a strong emphasis on perennial crops, sustainability, and harnessing the natural inter-relationships between plants, animals and the environment.

Pinch out To remove young shoots or shoot tips by nipping them off by hand.

Potting compost A light, well-draining mixture of soil, peat (or peat substitute), sand and nutrients, used for plant raising indoors and for growing in containers.

Pot on To move a seedling or young plant into a larger pot or container.

Prick out To move a seedling from where it germinated into a seedtray or pot.

Rod and spur system Pruning system used for the main stems (rods) of grapes. In summer nip shoots back to two leaves beyond the first cluster of grapes; prune sub-laterals that develop to one leaf. In winter prune shoots on the rods to one bud.

Rootstock (fruit) Plant used as the root system for a grafted tree (see above). Fruit rootstocks are used primarily to control the eventual size and vigour of the tree, for example with apples: M9 is very dwarfing; M26 dwarfing; MM106 semi-dwarfing. Several factors must be considered when choosing rootstocks. Seek specialist advice.

Seed leaves (Cotyledons) The first tiny leaves (or leaf) to emerge from the seed after germination. The 'true leaves' that develop next are much larger and often differently shaped.

Short day plants (see Long day plants.)

Sideshoot (see Lateral.)

Species (sp.) Groups of closely related plants, differing only in minor details and crossing freely with each other. They are grouped into a *Genus*, for example *Lactuca sativa* (Lettuce) – *Lactuca* is the genus, *sativa* the species. Sub-species (ssp.); plural of species (spp.).

Spit The depth of a spade, ie 23cm (9in).

Spurs Short stubby branches on stems that bear fruit buds. **Spur system** a mass of spurs. **Spur fruiting** trees in which fruit is mainly borne on spurs rather than on the tips of branches.

Station sowing Sowing small groups of seeds at regular intervals along a drill.

Stopping Removing the growing point of a plant or shoot, usually to encourage the growth of more branches (laterals), or develop a bushier shape.

Successional sowing Making continuous sowings to get a continual cropping. As a rough guide, make the next sowing as soon as the seedlings from the previous sowing are visible.

Tap-root A large, single, usually deep root, as opposed to a mass of fibrous roots.

Tender Used both to describe plants that a) are injured by cold weather or frost, and b) can only be grown in greenhouses in a given climate.

Tilth A crumbly structure on the surface of the soil.

Tip bearers Fruit trees that only bear fruit on the tips of branches.

Undercrop Type of intercropping in which a low-growing crop is grown beneath a tall one.

Underplant To plant one crop beneath, or very close, to another.

Variety (var.) Distinct form of species (see above) that occurs in the wild. In popular use the term is applied to 'cultivar'.

Viability The ability of seed to germinate, which diminishes with age.

Wattle A frame of rods or stakes interwoven with twigs to make a fence.

SEASONS

To enable this book to be used in different regions, 'seasons' are used throughout instead of months. The dividing line between one season and the next is not rigid because weather varies from one year to the next, and according to the area of the country in which the garden is located, as well as the prevailing conditions in the individual gardens.

Season	Northern Hemisphere	Southern Hemisphere
mid-winter	January	July
late winter	February	August
early spring	March	September
mid-spring	April	October
late spring	May	November
early summer	June	December
mid-summer	July	January
late summer	August	February
early autumn	September	March
mid-autumn	October	April
late autumn	November	May
early winter	December	June

FURTHER READING

Some of these books are out of print but can be obtained through lending libraries

Other books by Joy Larkcom
Oriental Vegetables (John Murray, 1991)
The Salad Garden (Frances Lincoln, 1984)
The Vegetable Garden Displayed (The Royal Horticultural Society, 1992)
Salads for Small Gardens (Hamlyn, 1995)
Vegetables for Small Gardens (Hamlyn, 1995)

Vegetables
The Complete Book of Edible Landscaping, Rosalind Creasy (Sierra Club, 1982)
The Beautiful Food Garden, Kate Gessert (Garden Way Publishing, 1987)
The Complete Manual of Organic Gardening (Headline Book Publishing, 1992)
The Vegetable Garden, Vilmorin Andrieux (John Murray, 1985)
Vegetables, Roger Phillips and Martyn Rix (Pan Books Ltd, 1993)
Vegetables in the Tropics, H D Tindall (Macmillan Education Ltd, 1983)
Your Edible Landscape Naturally, Robert Kourik (Metamorphic Press, 1986)

Fruit Growing
Grapes Indoors and Out, Harry Baker and Roy Waite (Cassell/The Royal Horticultural Society, 1992)
Growing Tree Fruits, Bonham Bazeley (Collins, 1990)
Pruning, The Royal Horticultural Society
The Complete Book of Fruit Growing in Australia, Louis Glowinski (Lothian Publishing Company, 1991)
The Fruit Garden Displayed, Harry Baker (Cassell, 1996)

Herbs and Edible Flowers
Edible Flowers, Cathy Wilkinson Barash (Fulcrum Publishing, 1993)
Edible Wild Plants, Roger Phillips (Pan Books Ltd, 1983)
Gardening with Herbs, John Stevens (Collins & Brown, 1996)
Herb Garden Design, Ethne Clarke (Frances Lincoln, 1995)
Jekka's Complete Book of Herbs, Jekka McVicar (Kyle Cathie Ltd, 1994)

Trees, Shrubs, Edible Wild Plants, Ornamentals
Hardy Perennials, Graham Rice (Viking, 1995)
The Hillier Manual of Trees and Shrubs (David & Charles, 1996)
Topiary: The Art of Clipping Trees and Ornamental Hedges, A M Clevely (Salem House, 1988)

General Interest
Forest Gardening, Robert Hart (Green Earth Books, revised 1996)
Planting in Patterns, Patrick Taylor (The National Trust Gardening Guides, Pavilion Books, 1989)
The Garden Sourcebook, ed Caroline Boisset (Mitchell Beazley, 1993)
Yates Gardening Guide, (HarperCollins, Australia, 40th edition)

SUPPLIERS

Frequently updated resource directories:
The Australian Plant Finder, Frances Hutchinson (Simon and Schuster)
The Fruit & Veg Finder Henry Doubleday Research Association, UK (nurseries, seed suppliers)
The RHS Plant Finder, ed Tony Lord, Moorland Publishing Company, UK (perennial plants, nurseries, seed suppliers)

Seed companies with an exceptionally wide range of vegetable seed and/or Heirloom varieties
(see Fruit & Veg Finder for addresses of other UK seed firms)
Arch Noah A-3553 Schloss Schiltern, Austria
Chiltern Seeds, Bortree Stile, Ulverston, Cumbria, LA12 7PB, UK
Ferme de Saint Marthe, SARL, BP10, 41700 Cour-Cheverny, France
Future Foods, PO Box 1564, Wedmore, Somerset BS28 4DP, UK
Graines Baumaux, BP590, 54009 Nancy Cedex, France
Heritage Seed Library (members only) Henry Doubleday Research Association, Ryton on Dunsmore, Coventry CV8 3LG, UK
Jardin Bio, des Fraternités Ouvrières, 58 Rue Charles-Quint, 7700 Mouscron, Belgium
Plants for a Future, The Field, Higher Penpol, St Veep, Lostwithiel, Bodmin, Cornwall PL22 0NG, UK
Suffolk Herbs, Coggeshall Road, Kelvedon, Essex CO5 9PG, UK
Terre de Semences, BP2 03210 Saint-Menoux, France

Australian and New Zealand seed sources:
Diggers Garden Company, P O Box 300, Dromana, Vic 3936, Australia
Eden Seeds, MS 316, Gympie, Queens Land 4570, Australia
Kings Herb Seeds, P O Box 19–084, Avondale, Auckland, New Zealand
New Gippsland Seed Farm, P O Box 1, Silvan, Vic 3975, Australia
Phoenix Seeds, P O Box 207, Sug, Tas 7054, Australia

For current suppliers of garden equipment, see advertisements in gardening magazines.

I would like to thank the following for supplying plants and products used in my potagers:
Agralan, The Old Brickyard, Ashton Keyes, Swindon, Wiltshire SN6 6QR (mulches, fleece, netting)
Anglian Alpines, Needingworth Rd, Bluntisham, Huntingdon, Cambridgeshire PE17 3RJ (commercial edible plant and herb raisers)
Ballerina Trees Ltd, Maris Lane, Trumpington, Cambridgeshire CB2 2LQ (Ballerina apple trees)
Bressingham Gardens Plant Centre, Bressingham, Diss, Norfolk IP22 2AB (strawberry plants)
Highfield Nurseries, School Lane, Whitminster, Gloucestershire GL2 7PB (fruit trees)
Samuel Dobie & Son, Broomhill Way, Torquay, Devon TQ2 7QW (strawberry plants)
Jekka Herb Farm, Rose Cottage, Shellard's Lane, Alveston, Bristol BS12 2SY (herbs)
S E Marshall & Co, Wisbech, Cambridgeshire PE13 2RF (vegetable plants)
Melcourt Industries Ltd, Eight Bells House, Tetbury, Gloucestershire GL8 8JG (ornamental bark and forest biomulch)
Muir, Ken Honeypot Farm, Rectory Road, Weeley Heath, Essex CO16 9BJ (strawberry plants)
Read Nurseries, Hales Hall, Loddon, Norfolk NR14 6QW (vines, fruit, shrubs)
Van Tubergen UK Ltd, Bressingham, Diss, Norfolk IP22 2AB (bulbs)
The Willow Bank, Steve Pickup, Y Fron, Llawr-y-Glyn, Caersws, Powys, SY17 5RJ (willow rods, consultancy)

INDEX

Page numbers in *italic* refer to the illustrations. **Bold** page numbers refer to the A–Z Directory.

INDEX

ACKNOWLEDGEMENTS

First, my thanks to everyone who helped with the potagers at Montrose Farm: as gardeners, path layers and on construction – Malcolm Burrows, Richard Lovick, Robin Moody, Kirsten Pollard, Pete Simmonds, Dominic St. John Clarke, Rufus Wilson, and, many moons ago, Brendan Pollard, Jacqui Hurst and David Robinson; and for creating the willow fence, a special thank you to Martin Nunn.

For enabling me to visit so many other gardens, special thanks to my tolerant companions/chauffeurs: Sylvia Landsberg, Sheila Lewis, Sue Stickland and Rosemary Wilkinson. Thanks for all sorts of help to Peter Bazeley, Christopher Bailes, Peter Dudney, Marion Dunlop, Beverly Geist, Dominique Guy, Noreen Jackson, Anne Jennings, Bill Masser, John Matthissen, Anya Medlin, Eileen O'Donovan, Ulrike Paradine, Frances Pemberton, Jenny Plucknett, Diana Protz, David Searle, Ake Truedsson, John Walker, Maurice Ward, and Sally Williams of *Garden Literature Press*.

For technical advice, many thanks to the following, who were enormously patient with my queries: Thomas Arres (Arres & Son, dry stone dykers), David Beaumont (Hatfield House), Elizabeth Braimbridge (Langley Boxwood Nursery), Ruth Gooch (Thorncroft Clematis Nursery), Joan Greenway and Trevor Wellington (Highfield Nurseries), Marion Grierson, David Jeffery (Unwins Seeds), Jan Michalak (Ickworth House), Richard Massey (Marshgill's Seeds), Chris Nye (CN Seeds), Steve Pickup (The Willow Bank), Colin Randel (Mr Fothergill's Seeds), Terry Read (Read's Nurseries), Duncan Ross (Poyntzfield Herb Nursery), Clive Simms (specialist fruit supplier).

My heartfelt thanks for their hospitality and help to the owners of the gardens Stephen Robson photographed (see the picture credit list below), and to Elsoms Seeds, Mr. Fothergill's Seeds and Tozer's Seeds for allowing John Fielding to photograph on their trial grounds. Very special thanks to Susan Brooke of Overstroud Cottage, Ann Huntington of The Old Rectory, and Gail and Jon Barnard, Portland, USA for letting us use their gardens as the basis for Garden Plans, and to Rosemary Verey, who has always been so generous with her encouragement and advice.

My warm thanks too, to the many people who let me visit their gardens: Janet Allen, Mme de Bagneux, Mme de Curel (Saint-Jean de Beauregard), Marilyn Godden, Peter Harper and Roger McLennan at the *Centre for Alternative Technology*, Robert Hart, Helen Hardy, Hugh and Judy Johnson, Diana Leech, Ann and Michael Mumford, Tessa and Benedict Rubra, Denny Swete, Sylvia Norton, Michael O'Connor, Steve Pickup of *The Willow Bank*, Anne Marie Owens at *Le Manoir aux Quat' Saisons* and Susan Stancombe.

My thanks to the owners and gardeners of the following gardens, who took so much trouble to send us information: Burton Agnes Hall (Susan Cunliffe-Lister), Chatsworth House (Jim Link), Dale House (Jane and Jonathan Newdick), Daylesford House (Andrew Ayre), Helmingham Hall (Lady Tollemache), Michael O'Conner, Prinknash Abbey (Brother Anthony), Diana Protz, Saltmarshe Hall (Mr and Mrs Philip Bean), The Croft (Peter Carver), The Old Rectory (Helen Hardy) and Weaver's Cottage (Sylvia Norton).

In the USA very special thanks for organizing, networking, hospitality, driving and companionship to Caitlin and Patrick Evans, Bob and Eleanor Grant, Twink Hinds, Robert Kourik, Jill Lapper, Dianna MacLeod, Bob and Sue Moss, Mark Musick, Vern Nelson, Shep and Ellen Ogden of *Cook's Garden*, Paul Schell, Renee Shepherd of *Shepherd's Garden Seeds*, Carolyn Schieber, Pat Simpson, Howard Stenn and the masterminder Jil Stenn.

For welcoming us to your gardens, guiding, informing, and helping in various ways, very warm thanks to Barbara Anderson, Kip Anderson of *The Victory Garden*, Brooklyn Botanic Garden, David Baylon, Beth Benjamin, Scott Bowler, Betsy Clebsch, Shirley Collins, Byron Cook, Robert Cuthill, Jeff Dawson, Sally Ditzler, Malinda Futrelle, Sandy Goldman, Doug Gosling, Bob Grunnet, Allen Haskell and Gene Bertrand of *Allen C Haskell & Son's Nursery*, Anne Heimlich, Freda Hennessy, Arthur Lee Jacobson, Sally Jacobsen of *Sassafras Herbs*, Wendy Johnson of *Green Gulch*, Ellen Kirby, Carolyn Montie, Guest Perry, Ralph Reed, Ron and Carolann Rule, Jack Ruttle, Toby Sanchez, Gil Schieber, Lisa Schreibman, Dan and Ann Streissguth, Phil Tietz of *The Green Guerilas*, VanDausen Botanical Gardens Association, Paul Vossen, Wayne Winterrowd and Jo Eck

of North Hill, and Joyce Weston. And a very special thank you to the owners of the gardens photographed by Stephen Robson, (see below).

My very warm thanks to our photographer Stephen Robson, for rising at dawn to capture gardens at their most beautiful, and to John Fielding, for his energy in tracking down unusual vegetables.

Another special thank you to Graham Rice, who somehow found time to read the manuscript, and made many constructive comments, always softened with gentle humour.

A big thank you to the team at Mitchell Beazley: Jane Aspden, Kirsty Brackenridge, Guy Croton, Jenny Faithfull, Terry Hirst, Ruth Hope, Dave McCourt, Glen Wilkins, but above all to the editor Selina Higgins, without whose unflagging support, energy, efficiency (and shoulder to cry on) this book would never have been completed.

Finally, the biggest thank you to my husband Don Pollard, for all the fun we've had in the garden, and for your help in every sphere in the many years this book has been gestating.

My apologies to anyone I have forgotten.

Joy Larkcom

JOY LARKCOM

GARDENS PHOTOGRAPHED

BRITAIN
For full addresses of gardens open to the public in England and Wales see Gardens of England and Wales *(The National Gardens Scheme Charitable Trust, updated annually).*

Ballymaloe Cookery School Gardens (Darina Allen), Shanagarry, County Cork, Eire (Ireland)

Barnsley House (Rosemary Verey), Gloucestershire

Bryan's Ground (David Wheeler and Simon Dorrell), Herefordshire

Burns' Cottage, Alloway, Ayr

Cannings Court (Rose and David Dennison), Dorset

Cranborne Manor Gardens (Viscount and Viscountess Cranborne), Dorset

Hadspen Garden (Nori and Sandra Pope), Somerset

Hatfield House (Lady Salisbury), Hertfordshire

Heligan Gardens (Tim Smit and John Nelson), Cornwall

Littlecote Gardens, Berkshire

Llanllowell House (Miskey and Hamish Sandison), Monmouthshire

Melplash Court (Mr and Mrs Timothy Lewis), Dorset

Montrose Farm (Joy Larkcom and Don Pollard), Suffolk

Oswalds (Pat Davidson), Kent

Overstroud Cottage (Susan Brooke), Bucks

Penpergwm Lodge (Catriona Boyle), Garden School, Gwent

Preen Manor (Mr and Mrs P. Trevor-Jones), Shropshire

The Old Rectory (Ann and Antony Huntington,) Northamptonshire

The RHS Garden Rosemoor, Devon

6 Fanner's Green (Gunilla Pickard), Essex

Snape Cottage (Angela and Ian Whinfield), Dorset

Sticky Wicket (Peter and Pam Lewis), Dorset

Trostrey Lodge (Frances Pemberton), Gwent

West Dean Gardens (Sarah Wain and Jim Buckland), West Sussex

Wildfield House (Evelyn Macdonald), Norfolk

Wretham Lodge (Anne Hoellering), Norfolk

US AND CANADA
Gail and Jon Barnard, Portland, Oregon

Susan Campbell, Portland, Oregon

Fetzer Winery, Hopland, California

Karen Jensen, Seattle, Washington

Cynthia Lute, Seattle, Washington

Dianna MacLeod, Seattle, Washington

Joe McDonnald and Virginia Wyman, Seattle, Washington

Vern and Maggie Nelson, Portland, Oregon

New York Community Gardens, New York

Occidental Arts and Ecology Center, Occidental, California

Dean Riddle, Phoenicia, New York

Seattle Tilth Garden, Seattle, Washington

Paul Schell, Whidbey Island, Washington

Sooke Harbour House, (Fredrica and Sinclair Philip), Vancouver Island

PHOTOGRAPHIC ACKNOWLEDGEMENTS

Front cover: **Andrew Lawson**
Back cover: **REED INTERNATIONAL BOOKS LTD**/Stephen Robson
Back flap:**BBC GARDENER'S WORLD**/**Tim Sandall**

COLLECTION OF THE CHATEAU DE VILLANDRY 38 bottom

John Fielding 16 bottom left, 34 top, 35, 48, 57 top right, 84 bottom left, 85 centre, 90, 97 top right, 97 top left, 97 bottom, 101 left, 102 top left, 103 right, 107 left, 139 bottom, 152 left, 152 right, 154 left, 154 centre, 154 right, 155 left, 155 right, 156 left, 156 centre, 156 right, 157 left, 157 right, 158 left, 158 centre, 158 right, 159 left, 159 centre, 159 right, 160 left, 160 right, 161 left, 161 centre, 161 right, 162 centre, 162 right, 163 left, 165 left, 165 centre, 165 right, 166 left, 166 right, 167 left, 168 left, 168 centre, 168 right, 169 left, 169 centre, 170 right, 171 left, 171 centre, 171 right, 172 left, 172 right, 173 left, 173 right, 174 right, 176 left, 176 right, 178 left, 179 centre, 179 right, 182 left, 184 left, 184 centre, 184 right, 185 left, 185 centre, 186 right, 187 centre, 187 right, 188 left, 190 left, 190 right, 191 left, 191 right, 192 right, 193 left, 193 right, 194 centre, 194 right, 195 left, 195 centre, 195 right, 197 right, 198 left, 198 right, 199 left, 199 centre, 199 right

GARDEN PICTURE LIBRARY
Brian Carter 16 top
John Glover 117 bottom left, 148
Michael Howes 174 left
Lamontagne 183 left
Marianne Majerus 185 right
Zara McCalmont 123, 125 bottom
Howard Rice 128
Ron Sutherland 46 top
Brigitte Thomas 188 centre

John Glover 136 top left, 143;
Jerry Harpur 141
JILL HEDGES GARDEN ARCHIVE 11
Jacqui Hurst 162 left
Joy Larkcom 54 left, 55, 95 bottom, 108 right, 120 bottom left, 163 right, 164 centre, 170 centre, 176 centre, 177 left, 180 left, 180 right, 181 left, 189 left,193 centre, 194 left

Andrew Lawson 65 top, 65 bottom
Ulrike Paradine 189 right

REED INTERNATIONAL BOOKS LTD/
Jerry Harpur 50, 57 bottom right, 197 centre
Neil Holmes 82 top left, 187 left
Andrew Lawson 59 bottom left
Steven Wooster 117 top right
George Wright 139 top right, 164 left
Vivian Russell 10 bottom left, 12, 41

SKYSCAN BALLOON PHOTOGRAPHY 12/13
HARRY SMITH COLLECTION 34 bottom, 136 top right, 136 bottom, 139 top left, 151, 164 right, 167 centre, 167 right, 169 right, 172 centre, 175 left, 175 centre, 177 right, 178 centre, 181 centre, 182 right, 183 centre, 183 right, 186 left, 186 centre, 188 right, 189 centre, 192 left, 196 left, 197 left, 198 centre.

Pictures taken by Stephen Robson (Reed International Books Ltd)
150/151, 170 left, 175 right, 178 right, 179 left, 181 right, 190 centre, 196 right

UK
BALLYMALOE COOKERY SCHOOL back jacket middle, 27, 38 top, 53 right, 75 right, 86, 93 bottom left, 95 top, 134, 144
BARNSLEY HOUSE 13 right, 14, 63, 70 top, 70 top, 70 bottom, 71 left, 105 bottom, 107 bottom, 112 left
BRYAN'S GROUND 24, 39 right
CANNINGS COURT 15 top
CRANBORNE MANOR GARDENS title page, 49 top, 59 top right, 88 right, 98 bottom, 114, 121, 125 top, 131 top, 131 bottom
HADSPEN GARDEN 6, 15 bottom, 16 bottom right, 48, 81 top, 82 bottom right, 85 left, 102 bottom right
HATFIELD HOUSE 53 left, 68 right, 69 top, 69 bottom, 122 top
LITTLECOTE GARDENS 42 right, 64 right
MELPLASH COURT title page, 83, 92 top, 99 right
MONTROSE FARM back jacket top, 8, 9 top, 9 bottom, 36 left, 36 right, 47 right, 49 bottom, 62 right, 84 bottom right, 87 top, 92 bottom, 96 top, 99 left, 100 bottom, 107 top, 111 left, 111 right, 112 right, 137, 138 top;
OSWALDS 130
OVERSTROUD COTTAGE 30, 59 top left, 61 top, 76, 77 bottom, 120 top
PENPERGWM 100
PREEN MANOR 42 left, 45 top, 52 bottom left, 115, 117 bottom right, 147 top
6 FANNER'S GREEN back jacket middle, 22, 52 bottom right, 89, 146
SNAPE COTTAGE 60 top, 102 bottom left
STICKY WICKET 87 bottom
THE OLD RECTORY half title page, 20, 28 left, 28 right, 39 centre, 64 left, 71 right, 81 bottom left, 81 bottom right, 88 left, 91 left, 98 top, 118, 126/7, 132
THE RHS GARDEN, ROSEMOOR 108 left
TROSTREY LODGE 21, 62 left, 73 top right, 96 bottom
WEST DEAN GARDENS 10 top, 78 bottom right
WILDFIELD HOUSE 147 bottom
WRETHAM LODGE 47 bottom

US and Canada
GAIL AND JON BARNARD 32 left, 32 right, 75 left, 119 top
SUSAN CAMPBELL 74
FETZER WINERY 42/3, 140 right
KAREN JENSEN 43 bottom right, 59 bottom right, 129 bottom right
CYNTHIA LUTE 133 top
DIANNA MACLEOD 47 left, 75 top, 80 bottom, 119 bottom, 142
JOE MCDONNALD AND VIRGINIA WYMAN 45 bottom, 67
VERN AND MAGGIE NELSON 19 top, 93 bottom right, 100 top, 122 bottom right, 122 bottom left
NEW YORK COMMUNITY GARDENS 17, 18 bottom, 40, 58 left, 58 centre, 58 right, 60 bottom, 66 bottom, 68 left, 78, 80 top, 109, 116, 129 top, 145 top, 145 bottom
OCCIDENTAL ARTS AND ECOLOGY CENTER 10 bottom right, 19 bottom, 66 top, 72, 73 top left, 73 bottom left, 82 top right, 93 top, 113, 140 left
DEAN RIDDLE 7, 23, 44, 57 top left, 61 bottom, 77 top, 103 bottom
PAUL SCHELL 25, 46 bottom, 51, 52 top
SEATTLE TILTH GARDEN 54 right, 56 left, 56 right, 79, 91 right, 129 bottom left, 138 bottom
SOOKE HARBOUR HOUSE endpapers, 18 top, 39 left, 43 top, 82 bottom left, 84 top, 85 right, 101 right, 104, 105 top, 106, 120 bottom right, 133 bottom, 135